Springer

Berlin
Heidelberg
New York
Barcelona
Budapest
Hong Kong
London
Milan
Paris
Santa Clara
Singapore
Tokyo

Prolog: The Standard

P. Deransart   A. Ed-Dbali   L. Cervoni

Prolog: The Standard

Reference Manual

Foreword by C. Biro
Preface by R.S. Scowen

Springer

Dr. Pierre Deransart
INRIA Rocquencourt
BP 105
F-78153 Le Chesnay Cedex

Dr. Laurent Cervoni
EDS International
60 Avenue du Président Wilson
Immeuble le Guillaumet
F-92046 Paris la Défense

Dr. AbdelAli Ed-Dbali
Université d'Orléans
Centre Universitaire de Bourges, UFR Sciences
BP 4043, Rue Gaston Berger
F-18028 Bourges Cedex

Cataloging-in-Publication Data applied for
Die Deutsche Bibliothek – CIP-Einheitsaufnahme

Deransart, Pierre:
Prolog : the standard ; reference manual / Pierre Deransart ;
AbdelAli Ed-Dbali ; Laurent Cervoni. Foreword by Ch. Biro.
Pref. by R. S. Scowen. - Berlin ; Heidelberg ; New York ;
Barcelona ; Budapest ; Hong Kong ; London ; Milan ; Paris ;
Santa Clara ; Singapore ; Tokyo : Springer, 1996
  ISBN 3-540-59304-7
NE: Ed-Dbali, AbdelAli:; Cervoni, Laurent:

With 8 Figures and 6 Tables

CR Subject Classification (1991): D.1.6, D.3.0-3, A.2, K.1, F.4.2,
I.3.6, I.2.3, I.2.5

ISBN 3-540-59304-7 Springer-Verlag Berlin Heidelberg New York

© Springer-Verlag Berlin Heidelberg 1996
Printed in Germany

Cover Design: Künkel + Lopka Werbeagentur, Ilvesheim
Typesetting: Camera ready by authors
Printed on acid-free paper   SPIN 10501650   45/3142 – 5 4 3 2 1 0

Foreword

From the viewpoint of an "industrial" this book is most welcome, as one of the most significant demonstrations of the maturity of Prolog.

Logic programming is a fascinating area in computer science, which held for years – and still does – the promise of freeing ourselves from programming based on the "Von Neumann" machine. In addition computer programming has long been for solid theoretical foundations. While conventional engineering, dealing mainly with "analogical complexity", developed over some hundred years a complete body of mathematical tools, no such toolset was available for "digital complexity". The only mathematical discipline which deals with digital complexity is logic and Prolog is certainly the operational tool which comes closest to the logical programming ideal.

So, why does Prolog, despite nearly twenty years of development, still appear to many today to be more of a research or academic tool, rather than an industrial programming language?

A few reasons may explain this:

- First, I think Prolog suffers from having been largely assimilated into – and thus followed the fate of – Artificial Intelligence. Much hype in the late 1980 created overexpectations and failed to deliver, and the counterreaction threw both AI and Prolog into relative obscurity. In a way, maybe this is a new chance for the Prolog community: the ability to carry out real work and progress without the disturbance of limelights and the unrealistic claims of various gurus.
- Second, programming in Prolog is a new experience for computer professionals. To quote Kowalski, "algorithm = logic + control", the beauty of logic programming is of course the ability for a developer to focus on the problem, describing in a coherent, unified and declarative formalism the knowledge about the problem-domain and the problem itself. But all programmers who learned from the very beginning to think primarily about control and about the "machine", making a u-turn is a cultural shock and may take a whole generation to change.
- Third, from an industrial developer's point of view, Prolog appeared as a "mixed blessing" in its early years. For the average DP manager, burdened by the maintenance of thousands of line of Cobol (spaghetti) code, eating up to 70% of his resources, the declarative nature of Prolog and some of its features like referential transparency appeared attractive as a promising tool for alleviating his biggest burden: maintenance. On the other hand, Prolog had a number of shortcomings, namely: difficulty in interoperating with other languages, the lack of explicit control directives, of modularity, and of development environments. This latter point was especially serious as the unconventional programming paradigm of Prolog requires completely new guides for design, programming, and debugging.

And finally, the dozens of dialects, from various universities and small companies (usually university spin-offs) left an impression of immaturity.

Pierre Deransart, AbdelAli Ed-Dbali and Laurent Cervoni's book appears as a major advance in giving credibility to Prolog through the first clear and readable account of the new standard, with many practical examples and comments. The authors – who were involved in the task–force for the definition of the standard Prolog – are a perfectly representative team of the academic and industrial world, thus bringing together the theoretical rigour and pedagogical clarity of the former and the pragmatism of the latter. The result is a book which should be on the bookshelf of students and of all those who are interested in the real-world applications of Prolog.

A standard is a significant step in improving the industrial strength of Prolog: I am convinced that this book is a major contribution to the transformation of programming from an art to an industrial, engineering discipline.

Nanterre, January 1996

Charles Biro
Manager of Managing Consulting Services – Technology Advisory
Services, EDS-France

Preface

As I breast the tape on completing a 10-year marathon as convener and project editor for the Prolog standardization working group, Pierre Deransart rings me up, "Can you write a preface for our book?"

The late 1970s were a bleak period for Artificial Intelligence (AI) in Britain. A report by Professor Lighthill had suggested that the whole subject was flawed and had no promise. Such reports are always eagerly accepted by politicians, and AI research funding became almost impossible to obtain.

Then, in 1982, Japan announced its Fifth Generation Computer Project, based on Prolog, and British politicians discovered UK had a world expertise. They woke up: microprocessors and IT were important – Britain has to do something. The Alvey Project encouraging collaborative research was quickly set up. I worked at the National Physical Laboratory (NPL) which, being publicly funded, was ineligible to take part and receive yet more public money. Its current remit was neither to compete with industry producing products, nor to compete with universities in pure research. However, standardization was a public good, worthwhile, and therefore approved. NPL had experience in the standardization of programming languages, and I had been editor of the British Standard BS 6154 (a standard variant of Backus Naur Form). So British Standards Institution (BSI) agreed to set up a programme to define an international standard for Prolog with NPL providing the convener and secretariat. Prolog had spread all over the world, and a British standard would be a waste of time and unlikely to influence the progress of Prolog. France, in particular, had pioneered and had a strong interest in Prolog.

Work therefore started in Britain in late 1984 with membership open to anyone in any country, and a firm intention that work would continue internationally as soon as a New Work Item Proposal was approved. AFNOR (Association Française de Normalisation) formed a Prolog group in 1985, and cooperation proceeded smoothly. For reasons outside the control of BSI and AFNOR, an international working group, ISO/IEC JTC1/SC22 WG17, was not formed until the end of 1987. Delays then resulted because many decisions taken by the standards groups in BSI and AFNOR were re-opened and re-discussed.

The standardization of most programming languages is usually initiated by experts in the language, but novices at standardization. At first, therefore, there was great optimism and enthusiasm – Prolog was a simple and logical language: several people had produced formal definitions of the language, and a standard could be prepared in two years. We would concentrate on standardizing existing practice. In fact, existing systems were found to have unsuspected but important differences, the formal definitions were incomplete, and some changes were necessary for general international acceptance.

One key issue was how to define the semantics of Prolog in the standard: in English (or French) it would be difficult to avoid ambiguity, unintentional incompleteness, and to check for consistency and accuracy. Pierre Deransart claimed that he could define all the semantics in "stratified logic" which would be both formal and yet the basis of an executable interpreter. Further, the method was sufficiently powerful to cope with any feature that the standardizers might decide should be included in the standard language.

I remember my anxious 1986 query, "Are you sure this is so? The standardizers will not be constrained by difficulties of definition. And can you see the definition through to completion and publication?" (I was aware of the difficulties and delay that can arise when a project editor has to abandon work).

I also remember his reply, "Yes, I'm sure". And indeed he did see the work through to completion, and coped with all the changes.

The BSI/AFNOR decision to rely on a formal semantics became a contentious issue when the standardization became fully international. Some countries claimed such a definition was difficult to understand, others believed it was unnecessary. In the end, it was decided to make the formal definition an "informative" annex of the standard, and to rely on an "informal" semantics in the body of the standard. However, any programming language standard has to be precise, and it is arguable whether the precise informal semantics is any simpler and easier to understand than the formal semantics.

I think many members of the standardization working group have failed to appreciate the beneficial side effects of the formal definition. Pierre Deransart and AbdelAli Ed-Dbali have needed to read each draft extremely carefully in order to keep the formal specification consistent with the changes. This meant they discovered many errors and inconsistencies in the drafts. And their tools, which permit them to obtain an executable version, have allowed them to check almost all the examples in the standard.

Standard Prolog is a version of Prolog which makes plain what experts had known but never expressed, for example, when unification is undefined. The standard also makes it plain that the semantics is based on the abstract (not the concrete) syntax. Standard Prolog programs are also simpler to debug because misprints in programs can be found simply, and invalid arguments are more likely to raise an exception than result in silent failure. A final benefit is that safe powerful optimization is possible.

All Prolog users and implementers will benefit from standard Prolog, and I am pleased Pierre and his colleagues have written the first book about it. Their executable specification of **Standard Prolog** (available by anonymous ftp) will enable readers to discover what **Standard Prolog** requires, without needing to read the standard itself.

January 1996

Roger Scowen
ISO/IEC JTC1 SC22 WG17 (Prolog) convener and project editor

Acknowledgments

The authors are very grateful to the many people who contributed to this book in different ways:

- Colleagues and students who participated in the design of the formal specification and its runnable counterpart. J.-L. BOUQUART, B. DUMANT, G. FERRAND, M. N'GOMO, S. RENAULT, G. RICHARD, M. TÉGUIA.

- Colleagues in the standardisation group, and particularly M. VAN CANEGHEM, P. CHAN, E. FERMAUT, G. NARBONI, J.-F. PIQUE in the French AFNOR panel and C. BIERLE, E. BOERGER, D. BOWEN, M. CARLSSON, B. DEMOEN, K. DÄSSLER, A. DODD, J. HODGSON, L. JENSEN, C.D.S. MOSS, K. NAKAMURA, T. MANSFIELD, U. NEUMERKEL, N. NORTH, C. PICHLER, S. SZPAKOWICZ, G. THWAITES, A. VELLINO in the ISO working group and R. SCOWEN, its convener, by whom the editoral work was carried out up to the last day (27th February 1995). Some parts of this book (sources, sinks, flags and directives) are just adaptations of the text of the standard, excellently edited by R. SCOWEN.

- The publisher (Springer Verlag) and particularly H. WÖSSNER who was from the beginning very enthusiatic in publishing this book.

- INRIA who supported participation in this work and part of the editing of the standard, EDS who helped in improving the proofs of this book, the University of Orléans who supported the development of the standard and the executable formal specification, and finally the PMG members (the Prolog Management group), its President at that time A.-F. DOUIX and its dynamic manager A. ROTH, who were very encouraging.

Table of Contents

List of Figures and Tables

Figures

Tables

1. Introduction

"Prolog, the Standard", is the first reference manual on the ISO international standard [2] on the programming language Prolog called in this book **Standard Prolog**.

The standardisation of Prolog is the result of ten years of international discussions which began in 1985, which ended in February 1995. In a paper entitled *The birth of Prolog* [4], Alain COLMERAUER and Philippe ROUSSEL suggest 1972 as the birth date of the language. Therefore it took more than ten years to feel the need for a standard: the explosion of many dialects based on the seminal ideas of the inventors imposed this idea progressively. It took another ten years to achieve the project.

This book is its result presented in a fully comprehensive form.

Prolog is used in industry, in many areas such as computer aided manufacturing (operations research, CAD, robotics, circuit design and realisation, planning), software engineering (test generation, prototyping and system programming, specification, windowing, multimedia and documentation), AI systems (expert systems, knowledge bases, man-machine interfaces, natural languages analysis), data bases, and application fields like transportation, telecommunications, and banking. There are certainly many other potential domains of use. The current trends seem to be use of Prolog mixed with procedural languages as C or C++.

Prolog is also the kernel language of many emerging logic programming languages which support constraints, functions, and concurrency.

Existing practice has shown that the use of Prolog increases software reliability, reduces production costs, and facilitates product maintenance.

This book contains a full description of **Standard Prolog** together with an executable specification. The latter is the updated version of the one which has been maintained by the authors during the whole process of standardisation. With this book, any application programmer or Prolog user will be able to get acquainted and start working with any standard conforming processor.

The book is organised as follows:

The first three chapters present an introduction to basic concepts of the language and some auxiliary concepts which are needed to understand its semantics. The main features are: term structures, the unification, and the execution model which explains what nondeterminism (viewed as the multiplicity of solutions), backtracking, and control are.

The fourth chapter is devoted to the description of the primitives of the language, consisting of 112 built-in predicates in alphabetical order. Each built-in predicate is described in such a way that it is, as far as possible, self-explanatory by reading a single page. This has been obtained at the cost of some redundancy, but facilitates understanding.

The remaining chapters are devoted to particular aspects of **Standard Prolog**: arithmetic functors, environment with the file system (sources and sinks), flags and directives, syntax, and finally some explanations aimed at helping to write portable programs.

The printed part of the book is completed by a short bibliography and an annex, which contains a glossary with the definitions of additional concepts used in the book, elements on the lexical analysis, an introduction to the non-printed part (the `ftp` package), compliance rules, and finally a thematic index of the built-in predicates and a full index of the main words referring to their definition in the text.

The non-printed part is a package available on the `ftp` server of Springer-Verlag. The package contains among different files a runnable specification which may be used for two different purposes. One is to try the standard, the other is to test a standard conforming processor.

The runnable specification is a complete description of the syntax of **Standard Prolog** and all the built-in predicates; it is a simulation of the execution model and can be run on most existing processors and allows many more examples to be tested than one could imagine. However, it is not at all optimised and only very small pieces of code can be tested.

The package also contains the file of all the examples which have been discussed by the standardisers and more. So it is possible to use this file to verify whether the processor you are using conforms to the standard, using these examples as benchmarks.

Enjoy playing with it. There are some more documented files in the package that you will discover, to help you to get fully acquainted with **Standard Prolog**.

This book describes precisely and completely **Standard Prolog** in a simplified manner. It is even more complete than the standard itself, thanks to the runnable specification: it contains potentially an infinite number of examples! However some features are not completely described in this book: the arithmetic corresponds essentially to the already standardised Language Independent Arithmetic.

It should be noted that the ISO standard specifies very precisely what the syntax and the semantics of the language are. For this purpose it uses a number of concepts which are carefully defined in it with no intention to standardise them. Therefore, in order to simplify its presentation, some of the concepts have been modified or simply abandoned. The fact that these concepts are not used or defined here does not mean that the description contains gaps. It means only that we adopted a more informal presentation than the standard when we thought it was clear enough, or that some concepts, resulting from long discussions over years and international compromises about an incompletely designed language, could be removed in an attempt to re-define it with a thorough knowledge of it.

It is also important to observe that the work on the standardisation has not been completely achieved. A second part concerning a module system is in progress, but will still require some years for its completion. Therefore this book does not describe any module system.

One may be unhappy with the design decisions made by the standardisers, sometimes after arduous discussions. The fact remains that the standard represents an exceptional effort of reflection in an attempt to describe comprehensively all features of a Prolog language. Most of the previous attempts remain to a large extent informal. The users are supposed to learn by practising some system and little effort has been devoted attempting to explain "full" Prolog. The result was that all dialects were different, not just due to creative variations, but also because of the informal descriptions, the language being finally defined by "what had been implemented".

Standard Prolog is the first logical programming language to be standardised and the first Prolog dialect to be described with such a precision. One may hope that this will help in comprehending, teaching, and learning it, and help to widen its dissemination.

Standard Prolog is also an attempt to facilitate the writing of portable applications. This has of course some intrinsic limits. The choice made by the standardisers has been to limit the standard to a "kernel". This means that existing processors may contain many other primitives. Moreover some features depend on the environment in which processors are run. In order to clarify these aspects different notions are used in the description of **Standard Prolog** which allow its limits to be understood. A natural question thus arises: to what extent does my "standard conforming" processor conform to the standard? The answer depends on the category to which the unspecified features belong. There are four categories, which are common to any standard.

– *Implementation defined feature* is a feature which must be documented with a processor. Example: the maximal integer.

- *Implementation dependent feature* is a feature which exists but does not need to be documented, hence a programmer should not rely on their specific properties. For example, the ordering of variables.
- *Undefined feature* is a feature which has no specification at all in the standard. Implementors are free to do "what they want". Portable programs should not rely on it.
- *Specific feature* is a feature which is considered as an allowed extension of the language. Of course programs using such feature are not portable without adaptation, or may not be portable at all. For example, definite clause grammars.

Such notions give an idea of what will be found in a conforming to the standard processor. Requirements that such a processor should fulfil are recalled in the annex.

Finally, notice that this book is a good complement to user's and reference manuals accompanying a standard-conforming Prolog dialect which contains many more primitives and specific features. Some references are given in the bibliography for the interested readers, in particular [3, 7, 6] are tutorial introductions. However, to read this book, no specific knowledge in logic programming is assumed; only some familiarity with programming language description (syntax rules) or with elementary mathematics is required.

Paris, January 1996

Pierre Deransart, Research Director, INRIA-Rocquencourt
AbdelAli Ed-Dhali, Associate Professor, University of Orléans
Laurent Cervoni, EDS International Senior Consultant, Paris

2. Prolog Data Structures

Basic abstract data structures, sufficient to understand the execution model and the meaning of the built-in predicates, are introduced. The full syntax of these data structures is given in Chapter 9.

2.1 Terms

In **Standard Prolog** a unique data structure is used: **terms**.

2.1.1 Definition

A term is defined recursively by applying a finite number of times the following syntax rules[1]:

Term	::=	Var | Atom | Integer | Float
	|	Compound-term

Compound-term	::=	Atom(Term {, Term }*)

A *term* is defined as a *variable*, an *atom*, a *number* (an *integer* or a *float*) or a *compound term*, i.e. a functor whose name is an atom together with its arguments (a non-empty sequence of terms between parentheses).

The objects used to build terms belong to the following disjoint sets:

- The *variables* denoted by a sequence of letters, digits or underscore characters, beginning with an upper case letter or by the underscore character. X1, _y2, Var, Atom, A_variable are examples of variables. Variables are used to refer to any object.

---

[1] Simplified notations are used for syntactic rules: "::=" holds for the defining symbol, "|" holds for alternative, "{...}*" holds for contents repeated zero or more times.

– The *atoms* denoted by a sequence of letters, digits or underscore characters beginning with a lower case letter or a sequence of arbitrary characters in single quotes. x1, atom, '1', 'This is a single atom', this_too are examples of atoms. The *null atom* is denoted ''. Atoms formed with any characters may be unquoted if there is no ambiguity (see Section 9.5.1 for details). The sequence of characters forming the atom between the delimiters is sometimes referred to as the *atom name*. Example 'aaa' and aaa denote the same atom whose atom name is aaa. Quotes may be necessary. For example, the atom '   ' whose atom name is a sequence of space characters cannot be unquoted[2].

Atoms are used in particular to denote names of predicates or functors.

– The *numbers* are, as usual, partitioned into *integers* (negative, null and positive integers) and *floating–point numbers*, or in short *floats* (see Section 6.1.2 for more details). They will be denoted as usual. 33, -33, 33.0, -0.33E+02 are examples of integers and floats.

– The *compound terms* are characterized by the name of their functor, called the *functor*, and the number of their arguments, called *arity*. The outermost functor of a term is called its *principal functor*.

Here are some compound terms:

.(.(t,e),.(r,m))	the functor '.' has arity 2.
+(X,1.0)	the functor '+' has arity 2.
f(_var1, g(_var2, a), b_c)	the functor 'f' has arity 3 and 'g' arity 2. 'f' is the principal functor.
':-'(legs(X,4), animal(X))	the functor 'animal' has arity 1, ':-' and 'legs' arity 2.

Atoms and numbers form the *constants* also called *atomic terms*. Atoms may be viewed as functors of arity 0. hahaha, foo, 'Bar', 1.2, -0.33E+02 are atomic terms.

A term is said to be *ground* if it has no variable in it. The (set of the) *variables of a term* is the set of all the variables occurring in a term. It is empty if the term is ground.

2.1.2 Order of the terms: the relation *term_precedes*

In **Standard Prolog** the terms are totally ordered according to the following rules which define the binary relation *term_precedes*.

---

[2] Atoms may also be written with graphic characters (11.3) and escape characters (\). For example @=, \+ are atoms. In a quoted atom the quote character (') and the escape character must be duplicated. So '''' is the atom consisting of a single quote and '\\/' is the atom \/. An atom may also be bracketed. For example \+ may be written (\+) or '\\+', the atom this_too may also be written (this_too) or 'this_too'.

- All variables precede all floating-point numbers, which precede all integers, which precede all atoms, which precede all compound terms.
- All variables are totally ordered but the order is **implementation dependent** and may vary during computations.
- All numbers (of the same type) are ordered according to the usual arithmetic.
- All atoms are ordered according to the characters forming their name and the character codes of the characters (an integer associated with each character). The null atom precedes all non-null atoms (hence z precedes z_a). An atom a1 precedes an atom a2 if the character code of the first character of a1 is less than the character code of the first character of a2. If these values are equal, the tail character sequences are compared.

  Notice that the order induced by the character codes is **implementation defined**, except that the alphabetical order must be respected and the digits must be sequential. More details are provided in Section 9.1.3.
- Compound terms are ordered according to their arity; if they have same arity, by the name of their functor. If they have same arity and same functor name, they are ordered by considering successively the order of their arguments starting from the first.

  Example: g(X) precedes f(X, Y), f(Z,b) precedes f(a,A), according to the ASCII table given in Annex 11.3, but is after f(Z,a). f(Z,Z) precedes f(X,X,X) but its comparison with f(X,X) depends on the processor (**implementation dependent**).

2.1.3 Operator notation

For simplicity, terms which use unary or binary functors may be written with a prefix, infix or postfix notation, with or without parentheses if there is no ambiguity. Such functors are called *operators*. The programmer may specify new operators by their *name*, *priority* and *class of associativity*, to avoid any ambiguity when using them without parenthesis. So non-bracketed subexpressions are in decreasing priorities.

Some of the predefined operators are shown in Table 2.1. The complete set of predefined operators as an explanation about priority and class are provided in Section 9.2.

For example (product(D) :- call(D), call(D)) corresponds to the term ':-'(product(D), ','(call(D), call(D))) because the priority of ':-' is greater than the priority of ','. Similarly, (1 * 2 + 3 * 4) is the term '+'('*'(1, 2), '*'(3, 4)) as the priority of '*' is less than the priority of '+'.

A dot may be sometimes used to mark the end of a term. When input by a Prolog processor, a term is called a read-term and must have a dot as an end delimiter.

Table 2.1. Some operators

Priority	Class	Operators
1200	xfx	:-
1100	xfy	;
1050	xfy	->
1000	xfy	,
700	xfx	= is
500	yfx	+ -
400	yfx	* /
200	fy	-

2.2 Some particular terms

2.2.1 Predicate indicator

A *predicate indicator* is used to denote predicates or functors. It is a ground term of the form `Name/Arity` where `Name` is an atom denoting the name of a predicate or a functor and `Arity` is a non-negative integer denoting the number of its arguments.

Examples: `sumlist/2`, `'.'/2`, `'/'/2`, `animal/1`, `'1'/0`.

It is necessary to indicate the arity together with the name of a predicate or a functor, since the same name may be used with different arities, denoting different objects. The *predicate indicator of a term* is the predicate indicator of its principal functor.

2.2.2 List and derived terms

The *list* constructors are the atom `[]` (empty list) and the functor `'.'/2`, where the first argument is a term and the second a list. A list of N elements is the term `.(a1, .(a2, .( ... .(aN,[]) ...)))`, but it may be written with a simpler notation: `[a1, a2, ..., aN]`[3].

One may also use a concatetation functor "`[_|_]/2`". By definition, writing `[a1, ..., aN | [b1, ..., bM]]` is equivalent to writing $N > 0$ and $M \geq 0$, or `[a1, ..., aN, b1, ..., bM]`.

`[a1, ..., aN | t]` is the term `.(a1, .(a2, .( ... .(aN, t) ...)))`. Terms formed with the list constructor `'.'/2`, but whose "last" subterm is not the empty list (t different from the empty list), will be called *list-terms*. Lists and list-terms are disjoint sets of terms.

List-terms whose last subterm is a variable, like `[a1, ..., aN | X]`, are called *partial lists*. List-terms and therefore partial lists have at least one element[4].

---

[3] The classical dot notation is not predefined infix because of its many uses in the representation of different objects (list, term end mark, floats).

[4] In the standard a slightly different notion of partial list is used in which a single variable is considered as a partial list. That is not the case here.

2.2.3 Clause, body and goal

Some terms represent clauses, bodies or goals. They are called *clause-terms*, *body-terms* or *goal-terms* and have a particular (abstract) syntax. In order to represent executable programs it is required in **Standard Prolog** that clauses and goals are *well-formed* . Well-formed clause-, body- and goal-terms satisfy the following (abstract) syntax:

Clause	::=	Head : – Body
	|	Predication
Head	::=	Predication

A *clause-term* is defined as a term, whose principal functor is `':-'/2` (it is thus called a *rule*), with a first argument, called the *head* and a second, called the *body*, or a term which is a predication (it is thus called a *fact*).

Predication	::=	Atom | Compound-term

A *predication* is defined as a term which is an atom or a compound term. It is also called a *callable term*.

Body	::=	(Body , Body)
	|	(Body ; Body)
	|	(Body -> Body)
	|	Variable
	|	Predication

A *body* is defined as a term, whose principal functor is `','/2` (a *conjunction* of bodies), `';'/2` (a *disjunction* of bodies), `'->'/2` (an *implication* of bodies), a variable or a predication whose principal functor is different from `','/2`, `';'/2` or `'->'/2`.

We will say that a body (of a clause or a goal) *contains* a given term, if this term occurs in the position of a predication using the rules defining a body.

For example, the clause

`p(X) :- ((cond(X) -> (then(X) , !)) ; else(X)) , cont(X).` contains a cut because the predication `!` occurs in such a position (second argument of a conjunction, itself second argument of an implication, etc). But the clause

`p(X) :- ((cond(X) -> call((q(X),!))) ; Y = !) , cont(Y).`
does not contain any cut (because the '!' only occurs as an argument).

Finally, a *goal-term* is a defined as a *body-term*:

Goal	::=	Body

A well-formed clause cannot have a number or a variable as head, and has a well-formed body. A well-formed body cannot contain a number. Examples of clause-terms:

    `product(A) :- A, A.` is a well-formed clause.

    `try_me :- (write(yes), fail, 1) ; write(no).` is not well-formed (because it contains the number 1).

(Well-formed) clauses and goals are aimed at describing programs (a sequence of clauses and directives), and well-formed goals at describing queries.

Example: if the first argument of the following predicate `sumlist/2` is a list of numerical expressions, then, after a successful execution, its second argument is the sum of the values of the elements of the list.

    `sumlist([], 0).`
    `sumlist([X,L],S) :- sumlist(L, R), S is R + X.`

With the goal: `sumlist([1, 2+3, 4*5], R)`, the computed value of R is the integer 26.

Some programs may have a clear logical meaning, for example the premises of the well-known syllogism:

    `human('Socrate').`
    `mortal(X) :- human(X).`

Clauses may thus be understood as logical assertions (in first order logic, interpreting `':-'/2` as the implication) with their variables universally quantified.

3. Prolog Unification

Unification is a basic device. Executions of goals result in so called "answer substitutions" which are usually displayed. Therefore we introduce the notions of substitution and unifier, and finally we define the unification in **Standard Prolog**.

3.1 Substitutions

A *substitution* is a mapping from variables to terms.

It is usually assumed that a substitution is the identity mapping with the exception of a finite number of variables. For representing such substitutions the notation { X1 <- t1, ..., Xn <- tn } is used, to denote that all variables, with the exception of X1, ..., Xn, are mapped to themselves, and each variable Xi is mapped to a term ti different from Xi, for i = 1, ..., n. The set { X1, ..., Xn } is called the *domain* of the substitution. The set { t1, ..., tn } is called the *range* of the substitution.

A substitution is *ground* if its range is ground (i.e. there is no variable in the terms of its range).

Examples:

    { X <- a, Y <- f(X, b), Z <- g(X, Y) }
    { X <- a, Y <- f(a, b) } is a ground substitution.

The *identity substitution* corresponds to the identity mapping. Therefore its (finite) representation is the empty set and it is called the *empty substitution* .

Substitutions denote *bindings*. Given a variable X and a term t , such that { X <- t } belongs to some substitution, the variable X is said to be *bound to* t by some substitution, whatever t may be. If t is different from a variable, one says that the variable X is *instantiated* (by some substitution).

A substitution σ is naturally extended to a function on terms by defining $\sigma($ f(t1, ..., tn)) to be f(σ(t1), ..., σ(tn)). In particular for any constant c, σ(c) is defined to be c. Substitutions will be represented by Greek letters acting as postfix operators, hence the application of a substitution σ to a term t is denoted: tσ (instead of σ(t)), and tσ is called an *instance* of

t. A term s is an instance of the term t if there exists a substitution σ such that s = tσ.

Examples: the application of the previous substitution to the term:

    f(Y, Z)

gives the term:

    f(f(X, b), g(X, Y)) which is an instance of it.

    f(a, b) is also an instance of the same term (applying, for example, the substitution { Y <- a, Z <- b }).

As substitutions are mappings they can be composed. Let θ and σ be the substitutions represented, respectively, by { X1 <- s1, ..., Xn <- sn } and by { Y1 <- t1, ..., Ym <- tm }. The representation of their composition can be obtained from the set { X1 <- s1σ, ..., Xn <- snσ, Y1 <- t1, ..., Ym <- tm } by removing all bindings Xi <- siσ for which Xi = siσ and all bindings Yj <- tj such that Yj $\in^1$ {X1, ..., Xn }.

Example: composing the previous substitution

    { X <- a, Y <- f(X, b), Z <- g(X, Y) } with:

    { X <- c, Y <- h(X), Z <- U, T <- i(Z) }, gives the substitution:

    { X <- a, Y <- f(c,b), Z <-g(c, h(X)), T <- i(Z) }

The notion of instance extends to substitutions. A substitution σ is an instance of the substitution θ if there exists a substitution μ such that $\sigma = \theta\mu$.

Example: the substitution:

    { X <- a, Y <- f(c,b), Z <-g(c, h(X)) } is an instance of

    { X <- a, Y <- f(X, b), Z <- g(X, Y) } by the substitution

    { X <- c, Y <- h(X) }.

A substitution is *idempotent* if successive applications to itself yield the same substitution (it is equivalent to saying that no variable of its domain occurs in the terms of its range).

Examples: a ground substitution is trivially idempotent; the following substitution is idempotent

    { X <- a, Y <- f(T, b), Z <- g(a, U) }.

A term s is a *variant* of a term t if s is obtained from t by mapping different variables into different variables[2].

Example: the term f(T, U, T) is a variant of the term f(X, Y, X), which is also a variant of f(Y, X, Y).

---

[1] "belongs to"

[2] "To be a variant of" is an equivalence relation on terms.

A term s is a *renaming* of the term t *with regard to (w.r.t.)* a set of variables V if s is obtained from t by mapping different variables into different variables and no variable of s belongs to V.

Example: the term f(T, U, T) is a renaming of the term f(X, Y, X) w.r.t. the set { X, Y, Z, W, P, Q }, but f(Y, U, Y) is not (it is only a renaming).

3.2 Unifiers

3.2.1 Definitions

A substitution σ is a unifier of two terms if the instances of these terms by the substitution are identical. Formally, σ is a unifier of t1 and t2 if t1σ and t2σ are identical. It is also a *solution* of the equation t1 = t2, and, by analogy, it is called the unifier of the equation. The notion of unifier extends straightforwardly to several terms or equations[3]. Terms or equations are called *unifiable* if there exists a unifier for them. They are *not unifiable* otherwise.

A unifier is a *most general unifier (MGU)* of terms if any unifier of these terms is an instance of it. A most general unifier always exists for terms if they are unifiable. There are infinitely many equivalent unifiers through renaming.

There is only one most general idempotent unifier for terms, whose domain is limited to the variables of the terms, up to a renaming. It is sometimes called the *"unique"* most general unifier.

Examples: the following equation f(X, Y) = f(g(Y), h(T)) has infinitely many solutions:

    { X <- g(h(T)), Y <- h(T) },
    { X <- g(h(a)), Y <- h(a) , T <- a },
    { X <- g(h(g(U))), Y <- h(g(U)) , T <- g(U) }, ...

The first one is the most general, as all the others are instances of it.

Considering the equation

    f(X, a) = f(a, X), its solution is:
    { X <- a }. As it is a ground substitution, it is also an *MGU*.

A more complex equation:

    f(X, Y, Z) = f(g(Y, Y), g(Z, Z), U) has a most general solution:
    { X <- g(g(U, U), g(U, U)), Y <- g(U, U), Z <- U }.

But the equation X = f(X) has no solution (no unifier for X and f(X)).

---

[3] All the terms or equation members become identical.

3.2.2 Computing a unifier

In **Standard Prolog** the unification algorithm is left undefined. However the meaning of a program is completely defined, in particular the unification is performed by a goal which is an equation (see the built-in predicate '='/2, *unify*). Instead of giving a direct definition of the unifiers that standard conforming programs and processors will produce, some conditions that such programs and goals must satisfy have been drawn up, which are independent of the implementation techniques. In order to define these conditions, a unification algorithm is given here. It is introduced with the purpose of helping the definition of the conditions only, and it may be used to find a most general idempotent unifier of two terms, if any exists.

The algorithm is described below by four equation transformation rules and by two failure conditions. At every step the state of the computation is characterised by a set of equations. The initial set is a set of one or more equations. The step consists in application of a transformation rule to one of the equations or in checking that an equation satisfies a failure condition. The computation terminates if an equation in the current set of equations satisfies a failure condition or if none of the rules is applicable to any equation.

– The transformation rules
  1. *Splitting*: Replace an equation of the form   f(s1, ..., sn) = f(t1, ..., tn), where n ≥ 0 by the equations s1 = t1, ..., sn = tn.
  2. *Identity removal*: Remove an equation of the form X = X, where X is a variable.
  3. *Swapping*: Replace an equation of the form t = X, where X is a variable and t is not a variable, by the equation X = t.
  4. *Variable elimination*: If there is an equation of the form X = u, where X is a variable, such that X does not appear in u (*negative occurs-check*) but X appears in some other equation then replace any other equation s = t by the equation s{X <- u} = t{X <- u}.
– The failure tests: halt and report failure if the set includes an equation in one of the following forms:
  1. *Disagreement*: f(s1, ..., sn) = g(t1, ...,tm) where f/n ≠ g/m, n,m ≥ 0.
  2. *Positive occurs-check*: X = t where X is a variable and t is a non-variable term including X.

This algorithm is called the *Herbrand algorithm*. Given two terms it always terminates in success (the remaining set of equations defines an MGU[4] of the two terms) or in failure (there is no unifier). The two actions corresponding to a negative or positive occurs-check correspond to the so called *occurs-check tests*.

---

[4] The Herbrand unification algorithm defines an idempotent MGU.

Examples: starting with one equation $f(X, Y) = f(g(Y), h(T))$, the *splitting* produces two equations:

$X = g(Y)$, $Y = h(T)$,

the first equation does not correspond to any transformation, but a *variable elimination* may be performed with the second, leading to the equations:

$X = g(h(T))$, $Y = h(T)$,

which corresponds to the substitution:

{ X <- g(h(T)), Y <- h(T) }, which is an idempotent *MGU*.

Notice that the equation: $X = f(X)$ corresponds to the positive occurs-check case and leads immediately to a failure.

3.3 The definition of the unification in Standard Prolog

3.3.1 A first definition

An easy first definition of the unification would be to require that the unifier of two terms is one of their *MGU*'s, if there are unifiable, and failure otherwise. This definition corresponds to the built-in predicate unify_with_occurs_check/2.

But this definition imposes implementing the occurs-check tests in the unification algorithm. It is easy to observe that these tests which are performed very frequently influence the performances of the algorithm[5]. Therefore, for efficiency reasons, a definition which is independent of any algorithm has been designed, which is in particular compatible with processors in which the unification algorithm does not perform occurs-check tests.

3.3.2 The occurs-check problem

Now if one omits the occurs-check tests, we are faced with different problems:

1. the behaviour of the Herbrand unification algorithm may be unsound: it may succeed when it should fail:
   Example: { $X = f(X)$, $Y = a$ } gives the (wrong) "solution"
   { X <- f(X), Y <- a }.
2. the Herbrand unification algorithm may not terminate:
   starting with the set of equations: { $X = f(Y, X)$, $Y = f(X, Y)$ } the fourth transformation rule may be applied indefinitely.
3. the result of the Herbrand unification algorithm is no longer independent of the way the transformation rules are applied:

---

[5] In some processors, which handle correctly the so called "rational terms", the occurs-check may be performed optionally at the end only once. However standard conforming processors may implement another unification algorithm.

starting with the set of equations: $\{$ X = f(Y), Y = f(X), Z = a, Z = b $\}$ the fourth transformation rule may be applied indefinitely on the first two equations instead of firstly considering the last two equations which immediately lead to a disagreement.

These depicted situations correspond to what may happen with processors which do not implement the occurs-check tests during the execution of a goal.

A way to avoid these problems is to restrict oneself to equations in which the occurs-check tests are never needed and to programs which never require such tests. In order to do so, one must be able to recognise the situations in which an occurs-check test is needed and to recognise the programs for which it is needed or not, or the places where the tests are needed.

For example, with the set of equations $\{$ X = f(Y), Y = f(Z), Z = a, Z = b $\}$ the Herbrand unification algorithm never needs to perform the occurs-check tests, whatever the way to proceed through the transformation steps may be.

Two concepts in **Standard Prolog** are aimed at capturing these ideas: *STO* and *NSTO*.

3.3.3 Subject to occurs-check and not subject to occurs-check

A set of equations (or two terms) is *subject to occurs-check* (*STO*) if there is a way to proceed through the steps of the Herbrand Algorithm such that the occurs-check happens.

A set of equations (or two terms) is *not subject to occurs-check* (*NSTO*) if there is no way to proceed through the steps of the Herbrand Algorithm such that the occurs-check happens.
For example, the set of equations
$\{$ a = b, X = f(X) $\}$ is STO, but the set:
$\{$ a = b, X = f(Y), Y = f(Z) $\}$ is NSTO.

STO and *NSTO* are decidable properties for a single unification.

A Prolog program (including goals) is *NSTO* if and only if all unifications, during the execution of its goals, are *NSTO*. It is *STO* otherwise.

The property *STO* (or *NSTO*) for a program is not decidable. Therefore these properties may be checked automatically only on subclasses of programs.

3.3.4 Normal unification in Standard Prolog

Unification of two terms is defined in **Standard Prolog** as:

- If two terms are *NSTO* and unifiable, then the result is one of their *MGU*s[6].
- If two terms are *NSTO* and the two terms are not unifiable, then the result is failure.
- If two terms are *STO* then the result is undefined.

This definition of unification applies both to the normal unification predicate '='/2 (*unify*) and also when unification is invoked implicitly in **Standard Prolog** as for example in '=..'/2 (*univ*).

So programs (with goals) are standard-conforming with respect to unification if one of the following conditions holds:

1. they are *NSTO* on a standard-conforming processor, or
2. they are *STO* but the programmer writes his program in such a way that all unifications are NSTO on a standard-conforming processor except in some places where occurs-check test is needed and the predicate unify_with_occurs_check/2 is explicitly used.

Although the NSTO condition is complex, writing NSTO programs does not seem too difficult: existing practice shows that most of the programs are "naturally" NSTO, except when the programmer wants to handle explicitly cyclic terms[7].

Unfortunately the NSTO property is required to preserve soundness of executions and portability, and in many cases it is not at all easy to verify this property or to always put the unify_with_occurs_check/2 predications in the right places.

There is no way to perform an automatic transformation because it would not preserve the behaviour of the program (the unification is modified). Therefore the programmer has to act by himself.

In Section 10.1, some guidelines are provided to help the programmers to identify the "risky" points where they should explicitly use the unification with occurs-check in order to preserve portability, and how to do it. The detection of the "risky" points may be performed automatically but the decision to introduce the predications must be controlled by the programmer[8].

---

[6] The standard does not specify any particular property of the *MGU* (but usually it is idempotent), nor how to display substitutions.

[7] It is not possible to handle cyclic terms in **Standard Prolog**. It may be possible in some extension.

[8] An automatic transformation would guarantee soundness and avoid loops during execution, but it may introduce unexpected failure (probably a mistake in the program but one which is extremely difficult to debug). A nice solution would be a processor which performs the transformation automatically, but raises a warning when a positive occurs-check has been detected during execution.

4. Prolog Execution Model

In this chapter, the execution model of **Standard Prolog** is described. It formalises its main characteristics: nondeterminism (multiplicity of the solutions), backtracking and control. Knowledge of this is needed in order to understand the meaning of many built-in predicates and the behaviour of a program.

A typical Prolog session consists of loading a program (in the form of a **Prolog text**) in order to include new user-defined procedures in the current database (this action is called *preparing for execution*), then of executing prepared goals.

It is not specified how Prolog texts and goals are prepared for execution, with the exception of some directives (see Chapter 7). If there are many prepared goals, the order in which they are processed is **implementation defined**.

Therefore the execution model describes only the execution of a single goal (called here the *initial goal*) in the context of a given **database** and a given environment, characterised by **sources and sinks, Prolog flags, operator table** and **character conversion table**

It takes into account multiple solutions of a goal (i.e. **re-execution**, also called **backtracking**). It also describes the control which makes it possible to understand how different side-effects, like successive I/O actions, are combined. However the standard does not specify how the results of the execution of an initial goal are displayed (**implementation defined**), nor how the system interacts with the user, when several solutions are obtained (**undefined**).

The execution model is first presented for a subset of **Standard Prolog** called **definite Prolog**. Then the model is extended to handle all the procedures.

4.1 Database and environment

In **Standard Prolog** many built-in predicates are aimed at using or updating objects of the environment. Four kinds of objects must be considered: the database, the sources and sinks, the flags, and the operator and character conversion tables. All are global objects in the execution model in which programs update them by *side-effects*.

4.1.1 The database

The *database*[1] is a set of procedures uniquely identified by their predicate indicator. It contains all the *user-defined procedures* and the system procedures called *built-in predicates*.

With each user-defined procedure is associated a sequence of clause-terms whose order corresponds to the order in which the clauses have been input (according to directives, Section 8.4). The final ordering of the clauses is **implementation defined**.

In a database all the clauses are well-formed (Section 2.2.3) and *transformed* , i.e. all variables X in the position of a predication in the body of the clauses have been replaced by call(X) and all the facts also have the form of a rule whose body is true. Thus all the clauses in a database have the form of a rule[2].

For example, the clause (in a Prolog text):

  product(A) :- A, A. is stored in the database after preparation for execution as the term:

  (product(A) :- call(A), call(A))

The fact spider(tarantula) is stored in the database prepared for execution as the term:

  (spider(tarantula) :- true)

Some built-in predicates may perform dynamic updates on procedures in the database (like asserta/1). In **Standard Prolog**, the so called "logical database update view" is adopted. It corresponds to the following principle: *the different alternatives which must be explored to execute completely a predication are not influenced by subsequent actions.* This principle also applies to re-executable built-in predicates. It is explained in more detail in Section 10.2.

In a database every procedure is either *dynamic* or *static*. A procedure is static by default and its clauses cannot be modified. A procedure may be declared "dynamic" using directives in a Prolog text (Section 8.4). All the built-in predicates are static.

Every procedure is also *public*, or *private* and cannot be inspected[3]. All the built-in predicates are private. All the dynamic user-defined procedures

---

[1] We present here the notion called *complete database* in the standard.

[2] The standard does not force a processor to perform this transformation. Nevertheless everything happens as with such transformation.

[3] It is **undefined** in the standard how a procedure should be declared public or private.

are public. Some static user-defined procedures may be public and can be inspected using the built-in predicate `clause/2`. Static user-defined procedures are private by default.

The partitioning of the procedures in a database is shown in Figure 4.1.

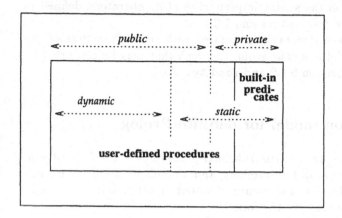

Fig. 4.1. Distribution of the procedures in a database

4.1.2 Sources and sinks

A program can output results to a sink or input Prolog data (called read-terms) from a source.

source/sinks may be a file, the user's terminal, or other **implementation defined** possibility permitted by the processor.

Each of them is associated with a finite or potentially infinite sequence of bytes or characters.

Sources and sinks are denoted "logically" by **streams**. It is specified as an **implementation dependent** ground term, a *handle*, that gets instantiated on opening the stream or its **alias** (a name given by the user to the stream). More details are given in Section 7.1.

4.1.3 Flags

A flag is an atom which is associated with a value that is either **implementation defined** or modifiable by the user.

Flags are parameters, specifying for example how the execution model should react if a called procedure does not exist (flag unknown) or what the maximal integer value is (flag `max_integer`). More details are given in Sections 8.1 and 8.2.

4.1.4 Operator and character conversion tables

Two tables are also global parameters: the operator table and the character conversion table.

Operator notation can be used for inputting or outputting terms in a form which depends on the syntactic properties of its operators, defined in the operator table (see Sections 7.4 and 9.2).

The character conversion table associates with some characters of the Extended Character Set one-char atoms to which they may be converted by inputting terms (see Section 9.1.2 and read_term/3).

4.2 The execution model for definite Prolog

In definite Prolog there are only user-defined procedures in the form of *definite clauses*, using terms all but numbers, and no built-in predicate; namely clauses in which the body is a sequence (denoted by conjunctions) of predications. So all the clauses have the form:

```
h(t0) :- p1(t1), p2(t2), ... , pN(tN). or
h(t0) :- true.
```

where the ti's are (possibly empty) sequences of terms.

Goals are definite bodies (i.e. a nonempty sequence of predications).

The execution model of definite Prolog is defined on the principle of a *general resolution algorithm*[4] whose input data are a single goal and a database.

4.2.1 The general resolution algorithm

The *general resolution* of a goal G with a database P is defined by the following algorithm:

1. Start with a *current goal* which is the initial definite goal G and a *current substitution* which is the empty substitution.
2. If G is true then stop (*success*), otherwise
3. Choose a predication A in G (*predication-choice*)
4. If A is true, delete it, and proceed to step (2), otherwise
5. If no freshly renamed clause in P has a head which unifies with A then stop (*failure*), otherwise
6. Choose in P a freshly renamed clause H :- B whose head unifies with A by substitution σ which is the *MGU* of H and A (*clause-choice*), and

---

[4] In definite Prolog, this algorithm corresponds to a proof procedure (a particular case of unit *resolution*), aimed at finding instances of the initial goal which are logical consequences of the definite program. A success corresponds to a successful proof and the instance of the initial goal by the answer substitution is a (more general) theorem.

7. Replace in G the predication A by the body B, flatten and apply the substitution σ to obtain the new current goal, let the new current substitution be the current substitution composed with σ, and proceed to step (2).

A *freshly renamed clause* means a clause which is renamed w.r.t. all the variables which have occurred in all the previous resolution steps.

The steps (3), (6), and (7) are called *resolution step*. The substitution σ is called the *local substitution*.

In the case of success (step 2), the current substitution restricted to the variables of the initial goal is the *answer substitution*.

This algorithm defines in an undeterminate manner successful, failed and possibly infinite computations. It is "indeterminate" because the order in which the computations may be considered is not fixed. It depends on the predication-choice (step 3) and the clause-choice (step 6). It is important to observe that the different successes do not depend on these choices, as long as all the clauses are considered in step (6.). But it also specifies all possible failed and infinite computations, while there is no need for all of them to be considered. Therefore in order to have a still precise but more efficient model it is useful to fix them in a way which will preserve the multiplicity of the potential successes[5], hence what is called the *non-determinism* of the solutions.

4.2.2 The Prolog computation rule

In **Standard Prolog** the choices are fixed as follows:

- The predication-choice consists of choosing the first predication in the sequence G (step 3).
- The clause-choice consists of choosing the "unifiable" clauses according to their sequential order (step 6).

This is called the *standard computation rule*[6] or *Prolog computation rule*.

With this rule a new algorithm may be designed. It uses the notion of search-tree.

---

[5] It retains the "completeness of the solutions" in the sense that any instance of the initial goal which is a logical consequence of the (definite) program P is an instance of the initial goal composed with the current substitution obtained by a successful computation.

[6] In the logic programming literature, *computation rule* denotes the predication choice only.

4.2.3 The Prolog search-tree

The different computations defined by the general resolution algorithm may be represented by a tree called the *Prolog search-tree* that we define as follows.

- Each node is labelled by the *local substitution* and the *current goal*.
- The labels of the root are the initial goal to be executed and the empty substitution.
- There are two kinds of leaf-nodes:
    - Nodes whose goal label is true, called *success nodes*.
    - Nodes with a goal label different from true such that there is no renamed clause whose head is unifiable with the chosen predication, called *failure nodes*.
- A non-leaf node has as many children as there are clauses whose head (with a suitable renaming) is unifiable with the chosen predication (the first predication in the current goal). If $B_1, \cdots, B_n$ is the goal associated with the node, B_1 being the chosen predication, and $A :\!\text{-} C_1, \ldots, C_m$ is a freshly renamed clause with B_1 and A unifiable, then the corresponding child is labelled with the local substitution which is the MGU σ of B_1 and A, and the current goal which is the sequence of predications obtained after flattening, $\sigma(C_1, \ldots, C_m, B_2, \ldots, B_n)$.
The children are in the same order as the clauses in the database. A *left-to-right order* of the children will be assumed.

There are three kinds of branches: *success*, *failed*, *infinite*.

- A *success branch* corresponds to a success node.
- A *failed branch* corresponds to a failure node.
- An *infinite branch* corresponds to a nonterminating computation following the Prolog computation rule.

If there is no infinite branch in a search-tree, it is a *finite search-tree*.

At every node a *current substitution* may be computed as the composition (see Section 3.1) of all the local substitutions along the path starting from the root up to that node (inclusive). To every success branch there corresponds an *answer substitution* which is the current substitution associated with the (success) leaf, restricted to the variables of the initial goal.

Notice that the notion of search-tree depends only on the predication-choice. The clause-choice specifies the way it is visited. Given a search-tree, the execution of a goal in the context of a database, with the Prolog computation rule, may be represented by a depth-first left-to-right visit of the search-tree. This visit defines the visit order of the nodes of the search-tree, hence the order of execution of goals and subgoals. If the search-tree has infinite branches, there is no way to visit beyond the first one, which will be explored indefinitely. This explains why the execution does not terminate

when the traversal visits an infinite branch. It also explains why not all solutions may be computed if there is an infinite branch with some success
branches afterwards.

4.2.4 A Prolog search-tree example

Consider the following database and the goal p(U, V)

```
p(X, Y) :- q(X), r(X, Y).   q(a) :- true.   r(b, b1) :- true.
p(X, Y) :- s(X).            q(b) :- true.   r(c, c1) :- true.
                            q(c) :- true.
s(d) :- true.
```

Figure 4.2 shows the corresponding Prolog search-tree with the chosen
predication underlined. Fresh renaming is denoted by new variables and local
substitutions are represented before the node, beside the incoming arc.

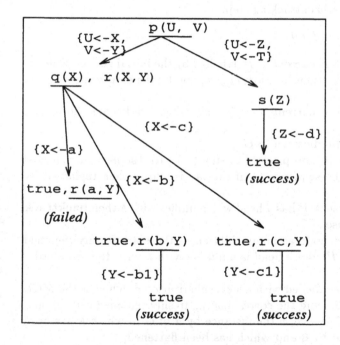

Fig. 4.2. A Prolog search-tree example.

The current substitution computed at the second success leaf is

   { U <- c, V <- c1, X <- c, Y <- c1 }

The corresponding answer substitution is

   { U <- c, V <- c1 }.

The tree walk produces the following answer substitutions, in this order:

```
{ U <- b, V <- b1 };
{ U <- c, V <- c1 };
{ U <- d }
```

4.2.5 The execution model of definite Prolog: search-tree visit and construction algorithm

Instead of describing the execution of a definite Prolog program by a non deterministic resolution algorithm and a Prolog search-tree representing all computations after fixing the choices, we synthetize both in a new algorithm describing the construction and visit of a search-tree simultaneously.

The algorithm describes the execution of a goal with a given database. It is defined in two parts: the "down walk" similar to the general resolution algorithm and the "backtracking" which corresponds to the choice of a not yet visited computation path. So, instead of simply "stopping", the algorithm will continue towards a backtracking step.

Let P be the *current database*.

1. Start from the root as *current node*, labelled by the initial goal G, which is a sequence of predications, as *current goal*, and by the empty substitution as *local substitution*,
2. If the goal G of the current node is **true** then **backtrack** (*success*), otherwise
3. Let A be the first predication in G,
4. If A is **true**, delete it, and proceed to step (2.) with the new current goal being the tail of the sequence G (if the tail is empty then replace it by **true**), otherwise
5. If no renamed clause in P has a head which unifies with A then **backtrack** (*failure*), otherwise
6. Add to the current node as many children as there are freshly renamed clauses H :- B in P whose head is unifiable with A with the same order as the clauses in P.
   The child nodes are labelled with a local substitution σ, which is the *MGU* of A and H (H :- B being the corresponding freshly renamed clause), and the current goal G' which is the instance by σ of G in which A has been previously replaced by B and which has been flattened,
7. The current node becomes the first child and proceed to step (2).

The new current substitution is obtained by composing all the local substitutions along the path from the root up to the current node (inclusive).

If a node has more than one child, it is *non-deterministic*. Such a node for which A is *re-executable* is called a *choice point*. If a node has only one child after its first visit it is a *deterministic node*. A node is said to be *completely visited* after all the branches issuing from it have been completely developed.

This algorithm describes how to walk down until success or failure is reached. The continuation (**backtrack**), which consists of visiting again a node which has not yet been completely visited, is called *backtracking*[7].

4.2.6 Backtracking

After constructing a success or failed branch, the possible nodes which may be visited are nodes with still non-visited children "on the right" of that branch (considering a left-to-right order of the children, this is illustrated in Figure 4.3). These nodes may be reached by seeking the first ancestor node with a not yet visited child.

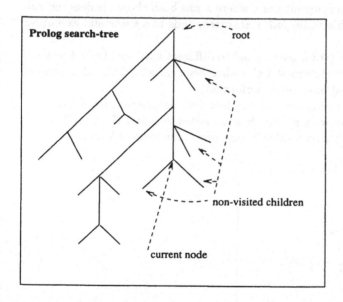

Prolog search-tree
root
non-visited children
current node

Fig. 4.3. A Prolog search-tree and its non-visited children.

The new current node is the first child not yet visited and the execution continues at step (2).

If there are no more non-visited children, the execution of the initial goal is achieved. What happens then is **implementation defined**.

4.2.7 An analogy with the box trace model

Comparing this model with the usual box trace model helps show how nodes are visited.

A box (Figure 4.4) represents what happens during the execution of the chosen predication A.

---

[7] "Backtracking" corresponds to the idea of re-execution of a goal. This is the reason for the name. It is, however, described here as a continuation of a tree walk.

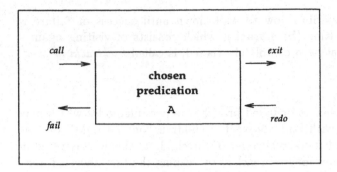

Fig. 4.4. Box trace model.

The first visit at the current node where A has been chosen is denoted *call* and the last visit to this node, *fail. exit* corresponds to a successful execution of A alone.

The different visits (*redo*) correspond to different attempts to find new solutions for A after an execution of A alone has been successful and all attempts to execute the tail goal have been performed.

Figure 4.5 shows the arrows of the box for the predication A from the search-tree point of view. A is the chosen predication and G the tail of the current goal. σ is the current substitution after a success of A alone.

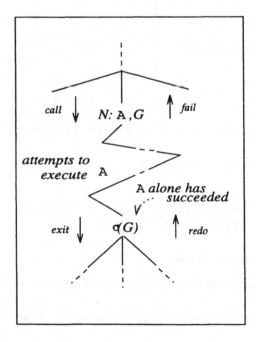

Fig. 4.5. Box trace model: a search-tree point of view.

The *"fail"* mark (last visit to the node N) must be distinguished from the "failure nodes" introduced previously. In fact many branches issued from N may be failed, whereas there is only one last visit.

4.3 The execution model for Standard Prolog

Up to now it has been assumed that the procedures were user-defined procedures. The model extends straightforwardly to built-in predicates: the search-tree is visited and constructed according to the Prolog search-tree visit and construction algorithm (Sections 4.2.5 and 4.2.6) as long as no built-in predicate is chosen.

This algorithm is thus adapted to describe the *execution of a goal* in the context of a given environment (database, sources and sinks, flags and tables).

Steps (5) and (6) of the search-tree visit and construction algorithm are modified as follows to take into account the built-in predicates and their side-effects.

Three cases have to be distinguished (Notice that A is different from true, since this case is already considered in steps (2) and (4)).

- A corresponds to a user-defined procedure which exists in the database (4.3.1).
- A does not correspond to any existing procedure (4.3.2).
- A corresponds to a built-in predicate defined in Chapter 5 or a system procedure (in an extension of **Standard Prolog**), (4.3.3).

4.3.1 The chosen predication corresponds to an existing user-defined procedure

The execution continues as indicated in steps (5) and (6) of the Prolog search-tree visit and construction algorithm.

4.3.2 The chosen predication does not correspond to any existing procedure

The action depends on the value of the flag unknown (Section 8.2). If its value is:

- error: an error is generated whose effect corresponds to the execution at the same node of the built-in predicate
    throw(existence_error(procedure, PI))[8],
  where PI is the predicate indicator of the chosen predication A

---

[8] The effect is defined in the description of the built-in predicate throw/1.

– **warning**: an **implementation dependent** warning is generated, and the current goal fails (*failure*).
– **fail**: the current goal fails (*failure*).

In both last cases the execution continues as indicated in backtracking (see 4.2.6).

4.3.3 The chosen predication is a built-in predicate

If the built-in predicate contains side-effects (modification of the search-tree, like **asserta/1** or **cut/0**, I/O action like **read_term/3**, or table update like **op/3**, ...), the side-effects described with the built-in predicate are performed and the computation continues according to one of the (mutually exclusive) following cases. The built-in predicates which provoque a specific side-effect on the search-tree without involving the database or play a particular role in the execution model are called here *logic and control* built-in predicates[9]; they are: **call/1, catch/3, ','/2, !/0, ';'/2** (Disjunction and If-then-else) , **fail/0, halt/0, halt/1, '->'/2, once/1, repeat/0, throw/1, true/0.**

– The built-in predicate is a *logic and control* built-in predicate not in error (**call/1** and **throw/1** only may raise an exception). It has a specific effect on the search-tree, specified in its description (adding at most two nodes). In all cases the execution continues at step (2) with the new (first) child as the current node (see 4.2.5) or with backtracking (see 4.2.6)[10].

– The built-in predicate is *deterministic* and succeeds with local substitution σ. Thus a new unique child is added whose labels are the local substitution and the instance by σ of the tail of the current goal. If the tail of the current goal is empty, the goal label is just **true** (hence there is a success branch). The execution continues at step (2) with the new child as the current node (see 4.2.5, step (2)).

– The built-in predicate is *re-executable* and has several possible successes with possibly different local substitutions[11]. Thus several children are created according to the order specified in the description of the built-in predicate. Each child is labelled with the corresponding local substitution as

---

[9] Some of them are called "control constructs" in the standard because they contribute to the construction and modification of the search-tree, thus producing control actions.

[10] **fail/0** and **true/0** only lead to backtracking, **halt/0, halt/1** and **throw/1** force a particular backtracking. The other logic and control built-in predicates create at least one child.

[11] This concerns: **atom_concat/3, bagof/3, clause/2, current_char_conversion/2, current_op/3, current_predicate/2, current_prolog_flag/2, retract/1, setof/3, stream_property/2, sub_atom/5.**

specified in the description of the built-in predicate and a goal which is the instance by the local substitution of the tail of the current goal. If the tail of the current goal is empty, the goal label is just **true** (hence it will be a success branch). The execution continues at step (2) with the first child as the current node (see 4.2.5, step (2)).

– The built-in predicate *fails* (*failure*). Thus the execution continues as indicated in backtracking (4.2.6).

– The built-in predicate generates an *error*. The execution is interrupted and an error is generated whose effect corresponds to the execution at the same node of built-in predicate **throw/1** whose argument is **error**(*error_term*, *impl_def*) where *error_term* in described with the error cases in the built-in predicate description and *impl_def* is an **implementation defined** term. The side-effect of **throw/1** is described with this built-in predicate.
If several errors are generated by a built-in predicate, the error that is reported is **implementation dependent**.

4.4 Additional error situations

4.4.1 System error

There may be a *system error* at any stage of execution. The conditions in which there is a system error, and the action taken by a processor after a system error are **implementation dependent**. The corresponding error-term is **system_error** (see, for example, the built-in predicate **throw/1**).

4.4.2 Resource error

There is a *resource error* at any stage of execution when the processor has insufficient resources to complete execution. The corresponding error-term is **resource_error**(*Resource*) where *Resource* is an **implementation dependent** atom (see, for example, the built-in predicate **close/2**).

4.5 The side-effects of cut

Finally we give some details of the built-in predicate "cut" (**!/0**) aimed at performing some control by pruning the search-tree.
"cut" always succeeds, but it has a drastic side-effect on the search-tree: it deletes some search-tree branches in order to force a predication to execute quickly without constructing and visiting all sub-search-trees.

For example if the first clause of the database (4.2.4) is replaced by
`p(X, Y):- q(X), !, r(X, Y).`
the clauses for p/2 become:

```
p(X, Y) :- q(X), !, r(X, Y).
p(X, Y) :- s(X).
```

Figure 4.6 shows that the search-tree corresponding to the goal p(U, V),
depicted in the Figure 4.2, now has only one failed branch.

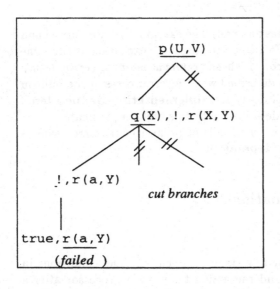

Fig. 4.6. A search-tree example showing the effect of cut.

The effect of the "cut" is thus to erase all the hanging nodes between the
current node and issued from the parent node of the goal which was containing
it (see also the built-in predicate !/0). Doing so, all the nodes which have
been made deterministic will be skipped when backtracking takes place.

Notice that many "embedded cuts" may increase the number of success
branches. This may be understood by the use of the "cut" to specify negation
by failure. The composition of two negations may increase the number of
successes (see the built-in predicate \+/1, not provable).

5. The Built-in Predicates

The built-in predicates are system procedures. They cannot be modified. All are static and private.

5.1 Presentation

The built-in predicates are presented in alphabetical order[1] with the following organisation:

---

0 **predicate indicator** : name   *The category to which it belongs*[2]

An informal introduction by a single sentence.

▷ **How to use it:**   `templates` (see below)

`One example of goal.` (normally a single predication)

▷ **Description:** `A predication used as a pattern`

— The complete definition: cases of success, failure, or other behaviours with the exception of the error cases.

The execution is performed as described is the Section 4.3.3 of the execution model for the corresponding case.

---

[1] The order follows the name and arity. If the name is symbolic, another name is also used.

[2] The category corresponds to the usual classsification also used in the standard with minor changes, see Annex 11.5. All related built-in predicates are grouped in the same category.

▷ **Error cases**   A complete table with all the error cases.

Conditions	Error-term
o error condition	`error_term`

With each error case is associated a not necessarily exclusive condition and an error-term. When a condition is satisfied, the execution is performed as described in Section 4.3.3 of the execution model ("the built-in predicate generates an *error*").

▷ **Examples**

A few examples to help understanding.

An example is normally a predication executing the built-in predicate as a goal, together with a statement whether the goal succeeds, fails or whether there is an error. The statement also describes any side-effect.

The examples are written assuming that the predefined operator table has not been altered.

In the case of success, the local substitution is also given. The word "local" may be omitted. If only **Succeeds** is mentionned, this is shorthand for **Succeeds with empty local substitution**.

In the case of several successes with different answer substitutions, the substitutions are separated by a semi-colon.

In the case of error, the error-term is given.

An example may also be a more complex goal term (i.e. a well-formed body-term different from a single predication) as a user may provide it to a processor. The result given is the one obtained by the execution model with this goal-term as initial goal.

With the examples an initial condition may be stated at the beginning (describing, for example, the initial state of the database). If there is such condition, it holds separately for every given goal.

5.2 Templates

A *template* is a piece of information provided as a traditional indication of the normal way of using a built-in predicate. Violation of this condition generates an error. It contains a *mode declaration* together with some *type information*. Here is a short description of the modes used and type information.

There may be several templates attached to one built-in predicate. In this case they are mutually exclusive.

5.2.1 Mode of an argument

The *mode of each argument* defines whether or not an argument shall be instantiated when the built-in predicate is executed.

The mode is one of the following atoms:

+ — the argument shall be instantiated (different from a variable),
? — the argument shall be instantiated or a variable,
@ — the argument shall remain unaltered (it is a compound term)[3],
- — the argument shall be a variable that will be instantiated (different from a variable) if the goal succeeds.

5.2.2 Type information

Type information[4] is denoted by one of the following atoms:

atom — an atom,
atom_or_atom_list — an atom or a list of atoms,
atomic — an atom or a number,
body_term — a well-formed body-term,
byte — a byte (see the Glossary),
callable_term — an atom or a compound term,
character — a one-char atom (9.1.1),
character_code — an integer which is a character code (9.1.3),
character_code_list — a list of character codes (9.1.3),
character_list — a list of one-char atoms (9.1.1),
clause_term — a well-formed clause-term,
close_options — a list of close-options (stream-options supported at stream closure),
compound_term — a compound term,
E_character — an element of **ECS** (9.1.1),
evaluable — an arithmetic expression evaluable without error,
flag — an atom denoting a flag name,
flag_value — an atom denoting a possible value for a given flag,
in_byte — a byte or the integer -1,
in_character — a one-char atom (9.1.1) or the atom end_of_file,
in_E_character — an element of **ECS** (9.1.1) or the atom end_of_file,
in_character_code — an integer which is the character code of a character in **ECS** (9.1.1) or the integer -1,
integer — an integer,

---

[3] When the argument is an atomic term, there is no difference between the modes + and @. The mode @ is therefore only used when the argument can be a compound term.

[4] **Standard Prolog** is a typeless language. This idea of "type" is used here for the sole purpose of describing templates. Most of the type information is the same as in the standard; some of it has been adapted.

io_mode — an I/O mode (7.3.1),
list — a list,
nonvar — an atom, a number or a compound term,
number — an integer or a floating-point number,
open_options — a list of stream-options supported at stream creation (7.3.2),

operator_specifier — one of the atoms: xf, yf, xfx, xfy, yfx, fx, fy,
predicate_indicator — a predicate indicator,
predicate_indicator_pattern — a predicate indicator pattern (see the Glossary),
read_options_list — a list of valid read-options (see the Glossary and 7.4.1),
source_sink — a source/sink term (an **implementation defined** ground term),
stream — a stream-term (an **implementation dependent** non atomic ground term),
stream_or_alias — a stream-term or an alias (an atom),
stream_position — a stream position (an **implementation dependent** ground term),
s　　am_property — a valid stream property (see the Glossary and 7.3.4),
term — a term,
write_options_list — a list of valid write-options (see the Glossary and 7.4.2).

5.3 The built-in predicates

The remaining part of this chapter contains the description of all the built-in predicates.

1 abolish/1   *Clause creation and destruction*

Removes the (dynamic) user defined procedure identified by its predicate indicator, leaving the database in the same state as if this procedure had never existed.

▷ **How to use it:**   abolish(@predicate_indicator)

Example: abolish(legs/2).

▷ **Description:** abolish(Pred)

- If Pred is a predicate indicator corresponding to a dynamic user-defined procedure in the database **then** removes all elements concerning this procedure and succeeds with empty local substitution.
- If Pred is a predicate indicator and does not correspond to any existing procedure in the database **then** succeeds with empty local substitution.

▷ **Error cases**

Conditions	Error-term
○ Pred is a variable, or Pred is a term Name/Arity and either Name or Arity is a variable	instantiation_error
○ Pred is neither a variable nor a term whose principal functor is (/)/2	type_error(predicate_indicator, Pred)
○ Pred is a term Name/Arity and Arity is neither a variable nor an integer	type_error(integer, Arity)
○ Pred is a term Name/Arity and Name is neither a variable nor an atom	type_error(atom, Name)
○ Pred is a term Name/Arity and Arity is an integer less than zero	domain_error(not_less_than_zero, Arity)
○ Pred is a term Name/Arity and Arity is an integer greater than the **implementation defined** integer *maxarity*	representation_error(max_arity)
○ The predicate indicator Pred is that of a static procedure	permission_error(modify, static_procedure, Pred)

▷ Examples

Assume the database initially contains the user-defined procedures:
    legs/2, insect/1, product/1
with the clauses (all dynamic):

```
                        ...
                        legs(A, 6)   :- insect(A).
                        legs(A, 4)   :- animal(A).
                        legs(A, 8)   :- spider(A).
                        insect(bee)  :- true.
                        insect(ant)  :- true.
                        product(A)   :- call(A), call(A).
                        ...
```

abolish(legs/2).   Succeeds, also removes legs/2,
                              leaving the database with the clauses:

```
                        ...
                        insect(bee)  :- true.
                        insect(ant)  :- true.
                        product(A)   :- call(A), call(A).
                        ...
```

insect(X), abolish(insect/1).
                      Succeeds twice, with substitutions:
                      { X <- bee} and removes the procedure insect/1;
                      { X <- ant}
                              leaving the database with the clauses:

```
                        ...
                        product(A)   :- call(A), call(A).
                        ...
```

abolish(product(_)). type_error(predicate_indicator,product(_01))

abolish(abolish/1). permission_error(modify,
                                      static_procedure, abolish/1)

2 arg/3   *Term creation and decomposition*

Relates a term (second argument) and its nth argument.

▷ **How to use it:**   arg(+integer, +compound_term, ?term)

Example: arg(2, foo(a, b, c), X).

▷ **Description:** arg(N, Term, Arg)

- If Term is a compound term, and N is an integer greater than zero and less than the arity of Term, and Arg and the Nth argument of Term are NSTO (3.3.3) **then** if Arg is unifiable with the Nth argument of Term by substitution σ **then** succeeds with local substitution σ **else** fails.
- If Term is a compound term, and N is an integer greater than zero and less than the arity of Term, and Arg and the Nth argument of Term are STO **then undefined.**
- If N is equal to zero, or Term is a compound term and N is an integer greater than the arity of Term **then** fails.

▷ **Error cases**

Conditions	Error-term
o N or Term is a variable	instantiation_error
o N is neither a variable nor an integer	type_error(integer, N)
o N is an integer less than zero	domain_error(not_less_than_zero, N)
o Term is neither a variable nor a compound term	type_error(compound, Term)

▷ **Examples**

arg(2, foo(a, b, c), X).   Succeeds with substitution:
                                          { X <- b }

arg(2, foo(a, f(X,b), c), f(a,Y)). Succeeds with substitution:
                                          { X <- a, Y <- b }

arg(1, foo(a, b, c), b).   Fails.

arg(1, foo(X, b, c), u(X)).   Undefined.

arg(a, foo(a, b, c), X).   type_error(integer, a)

3 (=:=)/2, (=\=)/2, (>)/2, (>=)/2, (<)/2, (=<)/2 :
arithmetic compare   *Arithmetic comparison*

Compares the values of the arguments according to the operations named as specified in Table 5.1 and defined in Section 6.2.2.

Table 5.1. The arithmetic comparison operators

Operator	Name
=:=	arithmetic equal
=\=	arithmetic not equal
>	arithmetic greater than
>=	arithmetic greater than or equal
<	arithmetic less than
=<	arithmetic less than or equal

▷ **How to use it:**   @evaluable *op* @evaluable

Arithmetic comparison operators are predefined infix operators. Their priority is 700 and they are non-associative (**xfx**).

Example: X = 1+2, X + 6 =:= X * 3.

▷ **Description:** Expression$_1$ *op* Expression$_2$

- If the *evaluations* (see Section 6.2) of **Expression$_1$** and **Expression$_2$** are errorless and the application of the right basic arithmetic operation corresponding to *op* to the obtained values is errorless (see 6.2.2 and 6.2.4) **then**
    - **if** the result of the application of the right basic arithmetic operation corresponding to *op* is **true then** succeeds with empty local substitution.
    - **if** the result of the application of the right basic arithmetic operation corresponding to *op* is **false then** fails.

▷ **Error cases**

See Section 6.2 for the exceptions raised by expressions evaluation.

▷ **Examples**

```
X = 1+2,  X + 6  =:=  X * 3 .
                    Succeeds with substitution       { X <- 1+2 }

'=:='(1.0, 1).      Succeeds.

=:=(3*2, 7-1).      Succeeds.

0.333 =:= 1/3 .         Succeeds or Fails.   (Implementation defined)
            (Depends on the definition of the rounding function)

'=:='(0, 1).        Fails.

1 =:= N+(3/0).      instantiation_error           or
                    evaluation_error(zero_divisor)
            (It is implementation dependent which error is raised.)

0.3 =:= n.
        where n is an integer which cannot be converted into a float.
                    evaluation_error(float_overflow)
--------------------------------------------------------------
X = 1+2, X+5 =\= X*3 . Succeeds with substitution      { X <- 1+2 }

'=\\='(0, 1).       Succeeds.

0.333 =\= 1/3 .         Succeeds or Fails.   (Implementation defined)
            (Depends on the definition of the rounding function)

=\=(1.0, 1).        Fails.

=\=(3*2, 7-1).      Fails.

'=\\='(X, 5).       instantiation_error

1 =\= N+(3/0).      instantiation_error           or
                    evaluation_error(zero_divisor)
            (It is implementation dependent which error is raised)

0.3 =\= n.
        where n is an integer which cannot be converted into a float.
                    evaluation_error(overflow)
--------------------------------------------------------------
X = 1+2, X+7 > X*3 .  Succeeds with substitution      { X <- 1+2 }

>(3*2, 6-1).        Succeeds.

>(1.0, 1).          Fails.
```

```
'>'(0, 1).              Fails.

0.333 > 1/3 .           Succeeds or Fails.   (Implementation defined)
                        (Depends on the definition of the rounding function)

'>'(X, 5).              instantiation_error

N > (3/0).              instantiation_error            or
                        evaluation_error(zero_divisor)
            (It is implementation dependent which error is raised.)


0.3 > n.
     where n is an integer which cannot be converted into a float.
                        evaluation_error(overflow)
------------------------------------------------------------------
X = 1+2, X+6 >= X*3 .   Succeeds with substitution    { X <- 1+2 }

>=(3*2, 7-1).           Succeeds.

>=(1.0, 1).             Succeeds.

'>='(0, 1).             Fails.

0.333 >= 1/3 .          Succeeds or Fails.   (Implementation defined)
                        (Depends on the definition of the rounding function)

'>='(X, 5).             instantiation_error

N >= (3/0).             instantiation_error            or
                        evaluation_error(zero_divisor)
             (It is implementation dependent which error is raised)

0.3 >= n.
     where n is an integer which cannot be converted into a float.
                        evaluation_error(overflow)
------------------------------------------------------------------
X = 1+2, X+5 < X*3 .    Succeeds with substitution    { X <- 1+2 }

'<'(0, 1).              Succeeds.

0.333 < 1/3 .           Succeeds or Fails.   (Implementation defined)
                        (Depends on the definition of the rounding function)

<(1.0, 1).              Fails.

'<'(3*2, 7-1).          Fails.

'<'(X, 5).              instantiation_error

1 < N + (3/0).          instantiation_error            or
                        evaluation_error(zero_divisor)
            (It is implementation dependent which error is raised.)
```

```
0.3 < n.
     where n is an integer which cannot be converted into a float.
                    evaluation_error(overflow).
---------------------------------------------------------------------
X = 1+2, X+6 =< X*3 .  Succeeds with substitution       { X <- 1+2 }

'=<'(0, 1).            Succeeds.

=<(1.0, 1).            Succeeds.

0.333 =< 1/3 .         Succeeds or Fails.    (Implementation defined)
                  (Depends on the definition of the rounding function)

=<(3*2, 6-1).          Fails.

'=<'(X, 5).            instantiation_error

N =< (3/0).           instantiation_error            or
                      evaluation_error(zero_divisor)
             (It is implementation dependent which error is raised)

0.3 =< n.
     where n is an integer which cannot be converted into a float.
                    evaluation_error(overflow)
```

4 asserta/1   *Clause creation and destruction*

Adds a new clause as the first clause of a procedure.

▷ **How to use it:**   asserta(@clause_term)

Example: asserta((legs(A, 4) :- animal(A))).

▷ **Description:** asserta(Clause)

Let ':-'(Head,Body) be the term built as follows:

- if Clause is an atom or a compound term whose principal functor is different from ':-'/2 then Head is Clause and Body is true,
- if Clause is a compound term ':-'(t1, t2) where t1 is a callable term and t2 is a well-formed body-term then Head is t1 and Body is t2 transformed (4.1.1),

the clause Head :- Body, freshly renamed, is added before all existing clauses of the procedure whose predicate is the functor of Head, and succeeds with empty local substitution.

▷ **Error cases**

Conditions	Error-term
○ Clause is a variable	instantiation_error
○ Head is a variable	instantiation_error
○ Head is neither a variable nor a predication	type_error(callable, Head)
○ Body is not a well-formed body-term	type_error(callable, Body)
○ The predicate indicator Pred of Head is that of a static procedure	permission_error(modify, static_procedure, Pred)

▷ **Examples**

```
Assume the database contains the user-defined procedures:
                              moose/1, legs/2, insect/1, elk/1
with the clauses:   static:  elk(X)      :- moose(X).
                    dynamic: legs(A, 6)  :- insect(A).
                             legs(A, 7)  :- fail.
                             insect(bee) :- true.
                    . . .
```

```
asserta(insect(ant)).    Succeeds.
    The database of the dynamic user-defined procedures now has the
    two clauses for insect/1:
                          insect(ant)  :- true.
                          insect(bee)  :- true.

insect(X),asserta(insect(ant)),insect(Y).
                      Succeeds twice with the substitutions:
                                      { X <- bee, Y <- ant };
                                      { X <- bee, Y <- bee }.

asserta((legs(A, 4) :- animal(A))).
                      Succeeds.
    The database of the dynamic user-defined procedures now has the
    three clauses for legs/2:
                      legs(_01, 4) :- animal(_01).
                      legs(A, 6)   :- insect(A).
                      legs(A, 7)   :- fail.

asserta((foo(X) :- X)). Succeeds.
    The database of the dynamic user-defined procedures now has one
    clause for foo/1:
                      foo(_01)     :- call(_01).

asserta((bar(X) :- X)), clause(bar(X), B).
                      Succeeds with substitution: { B <- call(X) }
    The database of the dynamic user-defined procedures now has one
    clause for bar/1:
                      bar(_01)     :- call(_01).

asserta((bar(X) :- X)), clause(bar(X), foo(Y)).
                      Fails.
    The database of the dynamic user-defined procedures now has one
    clause for bar/1:
                      bar(_01)     :- call(_01).

asserta(X).                instantiation_error

asserta(4).                type_error(callable, 4)

asserta((foo :- (true; 4))).
                      type_error(callable, (true; 4))

asserta( (atom(_) :- true) ).
                  permission_error(modify,
                                  static_procedure, atom/1)
```

5 assertz/1

Adds a new clause as the last clause of a procedure.

▷ **How to use it:**   `assertz(@clause_term)`

Example: `assertz((legs(A, 4) :- animal(A)))`.

▷ **Description:** `assertz(Clause)`

Let `':-'(Head,Body)` be the term built as follows:

- if `Clause` is an atom or a compound term whose principal functor is different from `':-'/2` then `Head` is `Clause` and `Body` is `true`,
- if `Clause` is a compound term `':-'(t1, t2)` where `t1` is a callable term and `t2` is a well-formed body-term then `Head` is `t1` and `Body` is `t2` transformed (4.1.1),

the clause `Head :- Body`, freshly renamed, is added after all existing clauses of the procedure whose predicate is the functor of `Head`, and succeeds with empty local substitution.

▷ **Error cases**

Conditions	Error-term
∘ `Clause` is a variable	`instantiation_error`
∘ `Head` is a variable	`instantiation_error`
∘ `Head` is neither a variable nor a predication	`type_error(callable, Head)`
∘ `Body` is not a well-formed body-term	`type_error(callable, Body)`
∘ The predicate indicator `Pred` of `Head` is that of a static procedure	`permission_error(modify, static_procedure, Pred)`

▷ **Examples**

```
Assume the database contains the user-defined procedures:
                          moose/1, legs/2, insect/1, elk/1
with the clauses:  static:   elk(X)       :- moose(X).
                   dynamic:  legs(A, 6)   :- insect(A).
                             legs(A, 7)   :- fail.
                             insect(bee)  :- true.
                   ...
```

```
assertz(insect(ant)).    Succeeds.
    The database of the dynamic user-defined procedures now has the
    two clauses for insect/1:
                            insect(bee)   :- true.
                            insect(ant)   :- true.

insect(X),assertz(insect(ant)),insect(Y).
                        Succeeds twice with the substitutions:
                                        { X <- bee, Y <- bee };
                                        { X <- bee, Y <- ant }.

assertz((legs(A, 4) :- animal(A))).
                        Succeeds.
    The database of the dynamic user-defined procedures now has the
    three clauses for legs/2:
                        legs(A, 6)    :- insect(A).
                        legs(A, 7)    :- fail.
                        legs(_01, 4) :- animal(_01).

assertz((foo(X) :- X)). Succeeds.
    The database of the dynamic user-defined procedures now has one
    clause for foo/1:
                        foo(_01)       :- call(_01).

assertz((bar(X) :- X)), clause(bar(X),B).
                        Succeeds with substitution: { B <- call(X) }
    The database of the dynamic user-defined procedures now has one
    clause for bar/1:
                        bar(_01)       :- call(_01).

assertz((bar(X) :- X)), clause(bar(X), foo(Y)).
                        Fails.
    The database of the dynamic user-defined procedures now has one
    clause for bar/1:
                        bar(_01)       :- call(_01).

assertz(X).               instantiation_error

assertz(4).               type_error(callable, 4)

assertz((foo :- (true; 4))).
                        type_error(callable, (true; 4))

assertz( (atom(_) :- true) ).
                        permission_error(modify,
                                        static_procedure, atom/1)
```

6 at_end_of_stream/0   *Stream selection and control*

Tests whether the current input stream has stream position end-of-stream or past-end-of-stream.

▷ **How to use it:**   at_end_of_stream

Example: at_end_of_stream.

▷ **Description:** at_end_of_stream

− **if** the current input stream has current stream-property end_of_stream(at) or end_of_stream(past) **then** succeeds with empty local substitution **else** fails.

▷ **Error cases**
None.

▷ **Examples**

```
Assume the current input stream is completely scanned.

at_end_of_stream.          Succeeds.

Assume the current input stream is the user_input.

at_end_of_stream.          Fails.
```

7 at_end_of_stream/1 *Stream selection and control*

Tests whether a given open stream has stream position end-of-stream or past-end-of-stream.

▷ **How to use it:**   at_end_of_stream(@stream_or_alias)

Example: at_end_of_stream(mickey).

▷ **Description:** at_end_of_stream(Stream_or_alias)

– If Stream_or_alias is a stream-term or alias associated with an open stream then if it has the property end_of_stream(at) or end_of_stream(past) then succeeds with empty local substitution else fails.

▷ **Error cases**

Conditions	Error-term
o Stream_or_alias is a variable	instantiation_error
o Stream_or_alias is neither a variable nor a stream-term or alias	domain_error(stream_or_alias, Stream_or_alias)
o Stream_or_alias is not associated with an open stream	existence_error(stream, Stream_or_alias)

▷ **Examples**

Assume there is an input stream with alias 'mickey' which has been completely scanned.

at_end_of_stream(mickey).   Succeeds.

at_end_of_stream(user_input).   Fails.

at_end_of_stream(X).   instantiation_error

8 atom/1

Tests whether the argument is an atom.

▷ **How to use it:**   atom(?term)

Example: atom('Yeti').

▷ **Description:** atom(Term)

− If Term is an atom **then** succeeds with empty local substitution.
− If Term is not an atom **then** fails.

▷ **Error cases**
    None.

▷ **Examples**

atom('Yety').   Succeeds.

atom([]).   Succeeds.

atom(f(X)).   Fails.

atom(10.01).   Fails.

9 atom_chars/2

Explodes an atom name into a list of one-char atoms and conversely.

▷ **How to use it:**   atom_chars(+atom, ?character_list)
atom_chars(-atom, +character_list)

Example: atom_chars(X, [a,n,n,a]).

▷ **Description:** atom_chars(Atom, List)

− If Atom is an atom **then** let L be the list of one-char atoms identical to the sequence of characters of the name of Atom, and
if L and List are unifiable by substitution σ **then** succeeds with local substitution σ **else** fails.
− If Atom is a variable and List is a list of one-char atoms **then** let A be the atom whose name is the sequence of the one-char atoms in List, and succeeds with local substitution { Atom ← A }.

▷ **Error cases**

Conditions	Error-term
○ Atom is neither a variable nor an atom	type_error(atom, Atom)
○ Atom is a variable and List is a variable or a partial list, or a list with an element which is a variable	instantiation_error
○ Atom is a variable and List is neither a variable nor a partial list nor a list	type_error(list, List)
○ Atom is a variable and an element E of the list List is neither a variable nor a one-char atom	type_error(character, E)

▷ **Examples**

atom_chars(X, [a,n,n,a]).	Succeeds with substitution: { X <- anna }
atom_chars(anna, 4).	Fails.
atom_chars(X, [a | X])	instantiation_error

10 atom_codes/2   *Atomic term processing*

Explodes an atom name into a list of the atom codes corresponding to the one-char atoms forming its name and conversely.

▷ **How to use it:**   atom_codes(+atom, ?character_code_list)
                        atom_codes(-atom, +character_code_list)

Example: atom_codes(X, [0'a, 0'n, 0'n, 0'a]).

▷ **Description:** atom_codes(Atom, List)

— If Atom is an atom then let L be the list of atom codes whose corresponding one-char atoms form the name of Atom, and
  if L and List are unifiable by substitution σ **then** succeeds with local substitution σ **else** fails.
— If Atom is a variable and List is a list of atom codes then let A be the atom whose name is the sequence of the one-char atoms whose atom codes are in List, and succeeds with local substitution { Atom ← A }.

▷ **Error cases**

Conditions	Error-term
○ Atom is neither a variable nor an atom	type_error(atom, Atom)
○ Atom is a variable and List is a variable or a partial list, or a list with an element which is a variable	instantiation_error
○ Atom is a variable and List is neither a variable nor a partial list nor a list	type_error(list, List)
○ Atom is a variable and an element E of the list List is neither a variable nor a character code	representation_error(character_code)

▷ Examples

atom_codes(X, [0'a, 0'n, 0'n, 0'a]).   **Succeeds with substitution:**
                                        { X <- anna }

atom_codes([], L).   **Succeeds with substitution:**
                      { L <- [0'[, 0']] }

atom_codes(anna, [0'a, X, 0'n, X]).   **Fails.**

atom_codes(X, [0'a | X]).   **instantiation_error**

11 atom_concat/3   *Atomic term processing*

Atom concatenation and splitting.

▷ **How to use it:**   atom_concat(?atom, ?atom, +atom)
                        atom_concat(+atom, +atom, -atom)

Example: atom_concat('hello', ' world', S3).

▷ **Description:** atom_concat(Atom_1, Atom_2, Atom_12)

– If (1) Atom_12 is an atom and Atom_1 and Atom_2 are variables or atoms,
  or (2) Atom_12 is a variable and Atom_1 and Atom_2 are atoms **then**
  let S be the sorted list[5] of all triples (A1, A2, A3) such that A3 is the atom
  formed with the characters forming A1 followed by the characters forming A2, and (A1, A2, A3) and (Atom_1, Atom_2, Atom_12) are unifiable
  then
  – if S is empty **then** fails.
  – if S is not empty **then** **if** (Atom_1, Atom_2, Atom_12) and the first not
    already chosen element (A1, A2, A3) of S are unifiable by substitution
    σ **then** succeeds with local substitution σ.

NOTE — atom_concat/3 is re-executable as many times as there are elements in S.
The order of the solutions follows the order of the elements in the sorted list S.

▷ **Error cases**

Conditions	Error-term
○ Atom_1 and Atom_12, or Atom_2 and Atom_12 are variables	instantiation_error
○ Atom_1 is neither a variable nor an atom	type_error(atom, Atom_1)
○ Atom_2 is neither a variable nor an atom	type_error(atom, Atom_2)
○ Atom_12 is neither a variable nor an atom	type_error(atom, Atom_12)

---

[5] The ordering on the variables is **implementation dependent** but constant.

▷ Examples

```
atom_concat('hello', ' world', S3).    Succeeds with substitution
                                       { S3 <- 'hello world' }

atom_concat(T, ' world', 'small world').
                                       Succeeds with substitution
                                       { T <- 'small' }

atom_concat(T1, T2, 'hello').          Succeeds 6 times,
                 with substitutions    { T1 <- '', T2 <- 'hello' };
                                       { T1 <- 'h', T2 <- 'ello' };
                                       { T1 <- 'he', T2 <- 'llo' };
                                       { T1 <- 'hel', T2 <- 'lo' };
                                       { T1 <- 'hell', T2 <- 'o' };
                                       { T1 <- 'hello', T2 <- '' }.

atom_concat('hello', ' world', 'small world').
                                       Fails.

atom_concat(small, S2, S4).            instantiation_error
```

12 atom_length/2

Relates an atom and the number of characters forming that atom.

▷ **How to use it:**   atom_length(+atom, ?integer)

Example: atom_length('enchanted evening', N).

▷ **Description:** atom_length(Atom, Length)

— **If** Atom is an atom and Length is a variable or a non-negative integer, **then**
let n be the number of characters forming Atom, and **if** Length and n are
unifiable (3.2) by substitution σ **then** succeeds with local substitution σ
else fails.

▷ **Error cases**

Conditions	Error-term
○ Atom is a variable	instantiation_error
○ Atom is neither a variable nor an atom	type_error(atom, Atom)
○ Length is neither a variable nor an integer	type_error(integer, Length)
○ Length is an integer that is less than zero	domain_error(not_less_than_zero, Length)

▷ **Examples**

atom_length('enchanted evening', N).	Succeeds with substitution { N <- 17 }
atom_length('enchanted\ evening', N).	Succeeds with substitution { N <- 17 }
atom_length('', N).	Succeeds with substitution { N <- 0 }
atom_length('scarlet', 5).	Fails.
atom_length(1.23, 4).	type_error(atom, 1.23)

13 atomic/1

Tests whether the argument is an atom or a number.

▷ **How to use it:**   atomic(?term)

Example: atomic(10.01).

▷ **Description:** atomic(Term)

- **If** Term is a constant (an atom or a number) **then** succeeds with empty local substitution.
- **If** Term is not a constant (it is a variable or a compound term) **then** fails.

▷ **Error cases**
  None.

▷ **Examples**

atomic(10.01).	Succeeds.
atomic('Yeti').	Succeeds.
atomic((;)).	Succeeds.
atomic(X).	Fails.
atomic(f(X,Y)).	Fails.

14 bagof/3

Assembles a list of the solutions of a goal for each different instantiation of the free variables in that goal. The elements of each list are in order of solution, but the order in which each list is found is **undefined**.

▷ **How to use it:**   bagof(@term, +body_term, ?list)

Example: bagof(A, legs(A,N), B).

▷ **Description:** bagof(Template, Bgoal, Blist)

– If the bagof-subgoal[6] G of Bgoal is a well-formed body-term different from a variable,
  let W be a witness of the free variables[6] of (Template ^ Bgoal), and
  let S be the list, solution of findall([W,Template], G, S),
  – If S is the empty list, **then** fails.
  – If S is a non-empty list, **then** let Lp be the list of pairs (L, ϕ) such that:
    - assuming S' is a sublist of (not already used) elements of S, formed by one element of S (the choice is **undefined**), say [w, t], and all the other elements of S, [w', t'], such that w and w' are variants. The order of the elements in S' is the same as in S (solution order), and
    - ϕ is a unifier (3.2) of all terms w's in S' and W (it always exists), and L is the list formed with the terms tϕ such that the [w, t]'s are elements of S', in the same order, and Blistϕ and L are NSTO and unifiable.
    • If Lp is the empty list, **then** fails.
    • If Lp is a non-empty list, **then** succeeds with local substitution $\phi\sigma$ where σ is the unifier of Blistϕ and L and (L, ϕ) is an element of Lp not yet used.

NOTES:

1– According to the definition of findall/3, the transformed bagof-subgoal is executed.
2– **bagof/3** is re-executable as long as Lp is not empty, using not already chosen elements of the list Lp (**undefined** order).
3– The number of elements of the list Lp, as the behaviour of **bagof/3**, may be **undefined** if some tried pairs are STO.
4– If (Template ^ Bgoal) has no free variable and call(G) has at least one solution the predicate succeeds with one solution only.

---

[6] See the Glossary.

5— The variables of `Template` and the non free variables of `Bgoal` remain uninstantiated after each success of `bagof(Template, Bgoal, Blist)`.
6— In most applications, the free variables are bound to ground terms after each success of the bagof-subgoal. In this case there is no need to consider the substitution ϕ in the definition, which becomes simpler.

▷ **Error cases**

Conditions	Error-term
○ The bagof-subgoal G of `Bgoal` is a variable	`instantiation_error`
○ The bagof-subgoal G of `Bgoal` is neither a variable nor a callable term nor a well-formed body-term	`type_error(callable, G)`
○ `Blist` is neither a variable nor a partial list nor a list	`type_error(list, Blist)`

▷ **Examples**

```
Assume the database contains the user-defined procedures:
        legs/2, insect/1, animal/1, spider/1
```

```
with the clauses:       legs(A, 6)        :- insect(A).
                        legs(A, 4)        :- animal(A).
                        legs(A, 8)        :- spider(A).
                        insect(bee)       :- true.
                        insect(ant)       :- true.
                        animal(horse)     :- true.
                        animal(cat)       :- true.
                        animal(dog)       :- true.
                        spider(tarantula) :- true.
```

```
bagof(A, legs(A,N), B).
        Succeeds three times (undefined order) with substitutions:
                        { N <- 4, B <- [horse, cat, dog] };
                        { N <- 8, B <- [tarantula]       };
                        { N <- 6, B <- [bee, ant]        }.
                (the free variable set is {N}, A remains unbound)

bagof(X, (X=Y ; X=Z ; Y=1), S).
        Succeeds twice (undefined order) with substitutions:
                        { S <- [Y, Z]       };
                        { S <- [_01], Y <- 1 }.
                (the free variable set is {Y, Z}, X remains unbound)

bagof(X, X = f(Y, Y), [f(Z, g(Z))]).
        Undefined.

bagof(X, X ^ (true ; 4), L).
        type_error(callable, 1)
```

15 call/1 : metacall

Executes a goal, restricting the scope of the cuts to this goal.

▷ **How to use it:**   call(+body_term)

Example: X = write('hello'), call(X).

▷ **Description:** call(G)

– **If** G is a well-formed body-term different from a variable (2.2.3), **then** executes transformed G (4.1.1).

More precisely (see Section 4.3.3), if the current goal is (call(G),Cont)[7], a new child is created whose labels are the empty substitution and the goal (G',Cont), where G' is transformed G.

NOTE — The effect of a cut occurring inside the goal G is limited to this goal; it has no effect outside of call/1. call/1 is said to be *opaque* (or *not transparent*) *to cut.*

▷ **Error cases**

Conditions	Error-term
○ G is a variable	instantiation_error
○ G is neither a variable nor a callable term nor a well formed body-term	type_error(callable, G)

▷ **Examples**

```
Assume the database contains the clauses:
                        a(1) :- true.
                        a(2) :- true.

X = write('hello'), call(X). Succeeds with substitution:
                    { X <- write('hello') },
                            after outputting 'hello'.
```

---

[7] If Cont is empty, then one assumes Cont = true.

```
call(!) ; true.                Succeeds twice with empty substitution.

Z = !, call( (Z=!, a(X), Z) ).
                               Succeeds once with local substitution:
                                  { X <- 1, Z <- ! }

call( (Z=!, a(X), Z) ).
                               Succeeds twice
                                         with local substitutions:
                                  { X <- 1, Z <- ! };
                                  { X <- 2, Z <- ! }.

call(fail).                    Fails.

call((write(3), X)).           Outputs '3', then
                               instantiation_error

call((write(3), fail, 1)).
                               type_error(callable,
                                               (write(3), fail, 1))
```

---

16 catch/3 : Exception handling: error catching *Logic and control*

Captures errors generated during the execution of a given goal (first argument) either explicitly in the program (see throw/1) or implicitly when an error is raised by the processor, and executes a recover goal (third argument after instantiation).

▷ **How to use it:**   catch(+body_term, ?term, ?term)

Example: catch(p, X,
         (write('warning: error raised when executing p'),nl)).

▷ **Description:** catch(Goal, Catcher, Recovergoal)

The meaning must be considered with the built-in predicate throw/1.

– **If** Goal is a well-formed body-term different from a variable, the goal call(Goal) is executed. If an error occurs during its execution which is caught by Catcher, the resulting instance of Recovergoal is executed (see throw/1 definition).

More precisely (see Section 4.3.3), if the current goal is (catch(Goal, Catcher, Recovergoal), Cont)[8], it creates a new child whose labels are the empty substitution and the goal (call(Goal),Cont).

NOTE — If a ball is thrown (see throw/1 definition) in the sub-seach-tree issued from that node, there are two possibilities: either it is thrown during the execution of call(Goal), and the ball can be caught by Catcher. Or it is thrown during the execution of Cont and the ball is not caught by Catcher.

▷ **Error cases**

Conditions	Error-term
○ Goal is a variable	instantiation_error
○ Goal is neither a variable nor a well-formed body-term	type_error(callable, Goal)

---

[8] If Cont is empty, then one assumes Cont = true.

▷ Examples

Assume the database contains the user-defined procedures:

p/0, q/0, r/1

with the clauses: p :- true.   r(X) :- throw(X).
                  p :- throw(b).

                  q :- catch(p, B, write('hellop')), r(c).

catch(p, X, (write('warning: error raised when executing p'),nl)).
                        Succeeds twice:
                        first time with empty substitution;
                        second time with substitution:
{ X <- b}
                            after outputting:
                    warning: error raised when executing p

catch(q, C, write(helloq)).   Succeeds with substitution {C <- c}
                        after outputting: helloq

17 char_code/2   *Atomic term processing*

Relates a character and its character code (an integer).

▷ **How to use it:**   char_code(+E_character, ?character_code)
                        char_code(-E_character, +character_code)

Example: char_code('1', Y).

▷ **Description:** char_code(Char, Code)

- If **Char** is a variable and **Code** is the character code of a character in **ECS** (9.1.3) whose name is **A**, **then** succeeds with local substitution {Char ← A}.
- If **Char** is a character in **ECS** whose character code is **C then if** Code and C are unifiable (3.2) by the substitution σ **then** succeeds with local substitution σ **else** fails.

▷ **Error cases**

Conditions	Error-term
○ Char and Code are variables	instantiation_error
○ Char is neither a variable nor a character in **ECS**	type_error(character, Char)
○ Code is neither a variable nor an integer	type_error(integer, Code)
○ Code is an integer which is not a character code	representation_error-(character_code)

▷ **Examples**

```
char_code('1', Y).          Succeeds with substitution: { Y <- 49 }
      (assuming the character code for the character '1' is 49)

char_code(X, 163).          Succeeds with substitution: { X <- 'UU'}
   (if there is an extended character UU whose character code is 163)
                            representation_error(character_code)
   (if there is no extended character whose character code is 163)

char_code('1', 0'2).        Fails.

char_code(1, 0'1).          type_error(character, 1)
```

18 char_conversion/2   *Term input/output*

Updates the character conversion table used by inputting terms (see read_term/3) or during the preparation of Prolog texts.

▷ **How to use it:**   char_conversion(@E_character, @E_character)

Example: char_conversion('&', ',')

▷ **Description:** char_conversion(In_char, Out_char)

— **If** In_char and Out_char are characters in **ECS** (9.1)
then updates the character conversion table by replacing the value associated with In_char in the table by Out_char and succeeds with empty substitution.

NOTES:

1– Originally each character in **ECS** is associated with itself. Exceptions to this rule are **implementation defined**.
2– When In_char and Out_char are the same, the effect of char_conversion/2 is to remove any conversion of a character In_char.
3– The character conversion table has exactly one entry per character.
4– The characters In_char and Out_char should be quoted in order to ensure that they have not been converted by a character-conversion directive when the Prolog text was prepared for execution.
5– char_conversion/2 affects only characters read by inputting read-terms. When it is necessary to convert characters read by character input/output built-in predicates (11.5), it will be necessary to program the conversion explicitly using current_char_conversion/2.

▷ **Error cases**

Conditions	Error-term
○ In_char is a variable	instantiation_error
○ Out_char is a variable	instantiation_error
○ In_char is neither a variable nor a character in **ECS**	representation_error(character)
○ Out_char is neither a variable nor a character in **ECS**	representation_error(character)

▷ Examples

char_conversion('&', ','). Succeeds with empty substitution,
                    after updating the character conversion table with:
                        , associated with the entry &

char_conversion('&', '&')} Succeeds with empty substitution,
                    after updating the character conversion table with:
                        & associated with itself (identity).
                (& is not converted anymore)

NOTE — After the following goal:
    char_conversion('&', ','), char_conversion('''', ''''),
                    char_conversion('a', a).
    when the value associated with flag char_conversion is on, all occurrences of &,
', and a as unquoted characters read by term input built-in predicates are converted
to , ' and a respectively. For example, the three characters a&a are converted to the
characters a,a. However the characters 'a&a' represent an atom a&a because
they are enclosed by the single quotes, and the characters 'a&a' form an atom
'a,a'.

19 clause/2

Clause retrieval and information

Selects clauses of the public user-defined procedures in the database.

▷ **How to use it:**   clause(+callable_term, ?callable_term)

Example: clause(reverse(X,Y),B).

▷ **Description:** clause(Head, Body)

- If Head is a callable term (an atom or a compound term) and Body is a variable or a callable term, let S be the sequence of all the terms (H, B) obtained by a sequential search in the database (procedures, followed by clauses) such that H :- B is a freshly renamed copy of the clause of a public user-defined procedure and (Head, Body) and clause(H,B) are NSTO (3.3.3) and unifiable,
  then
  - if S is empty **then** fails.
  - if S is not empty **then if** the first element not yet selected of S and (Head, Body) are unifiable (3.2) by substitution σ **then** succeeds with local substitution σ.

NOTES:

1– clause/2 is re-executable as many times as the size of S. The order of the solutions corresponds to the order of the elements in the sequence S.
2– Dynamic procedures and public static procedures are inspected.
3– The number of elements of the sequence S may be **undefined** if some tried pairs are STO.

▷ **Error cases**

Conditions	Error-term
○ Head is a variable	instantiation_error
○ Head is neither a variable nor a callable term	type_error(callable, Head)
○ Body is neither a variable nor a callable term	type_error(callable, Body)
○ The predicate indicator Predind of Head is that of a private procedure	permission_error(access, private_procedure, Predind)

▷ Examples

```
Assume the database contains the user-defined procedures:
            reverse/2, append/3, legs/2, insect/1, elk/1, moose/1
with the clauses:
  static, public: elk(X)            :- moose(X).
                  reverse([],[])    :- true.
                  reverse([E|L],R)  :- reverse(L,Q), append(Q,[E],R).

  dynamic:        legs(A, 6)        :- insect(A).
                  legs(A, 7)        :- fail.
                  insect(ant)       :- true.
                  insect(bee)       :- true.
                  ...
```

```
clause(reverse(X,Y),B).  Succeeds twice with substitutions:
              { X <- [], Y <- [], B <- true                      };
              { X <- [_01|_02], Y <- _03,
                B <- (reverse(_02,_04), append(_04,[_01],_03)) }.
```

```
clause(elk(N), Body).     Succeeds with substitution:
              { N <- _01, Body <- moose(_01) }              or
              { Body <- moose(N) }    (implementation defined)
```

```
clause(x, Body).          Fails.
```

```
clause(insect(X), (true ; 1)).
                          Fails.
```

```
clause(reverse(X, Y, Z), T).
                          Fails.
```

```
abolish(reverse/2), clause(reverse(X, Y), B).
                          Fails.
```

```
retract(elk/1), clause(elk(X), B).
                          Fails.
```

```
clause(legs(A, 6), insect(f(A))).
                          Undefined.
```

```
clause(X, B).             instantiation_error
```

```
clause(insect(X), 1).     type_error(callable, 1)
```

```
clause(atomic(_), Body). permission_error(access,private_procedure,
                                                        atomic/1)
```

20 close/1
Stream selection and control

Closes a source/sink according to the default list of close-options (7.3.3).

▷ **How to use it:**   close(@stream_or_alias)

Example: close(mickey).

▷ **Description:** close(Stream_or_alias)

It behaves like:
close(Stream_or_alias, []).,   or equivalently:
close(Stream_or_alias, [force(false)]).

▷ **Error cases**

Conditions	Error-term
o Stream_or_alias is a variable	instantiation_error
o Stream_or_alias is neither a variable nor a stream-term or alias	domain_error(stream_or_alias, Stream_or_alias)
o Stream_or_alias is not associated with an open stream	existence_error(stream, Stream_or_alias)

▷ **Examples**

Assume that the current output stream has alias 'mickey'.

close(mickey).   closes the stream if there is no resource or
                                 system error condition and
                      succeeds with empty substitution,
               after flushing any buffered information to that stream.

close(user_input).   Succeeds.

close(mouse(X)).   domain_error(stream_or_alias, mouse(X))

21 close/2 *Stream selection and control*

Closes a source/sink according to a list of close-options (7.3.3).

▷ **How to use it:**   close(@stream_or_alias, @close_options)

Example: close(mickey, [force(true)]).

▷ **Description:** close(Stream_or_alias, Options)

- If Stream_or_alias is a stream-term or alias associated with an open stream, and Options is a list of close-options (7.3.3),
  then performs (1) and (2)
  (1) **if** there is a close-option force(true), **then** ignores any resource error condition or system error condition that may be satisfied (4.4),
  (2) **if** the stream associated to Stream_or_alias is an output stream, sends to that stream any output which is currently buffered by the processor for the stream associated with Stream_or_alias, and
  - **if** the stream associated to Stream_or_alias is the standard input or output stream **then** succeeds with empty local substitution.
  - **if** the stream associated to Stream_or_alias is not the standard input or output stream, and is the current input (resp. output) stream **then** closes the current input (resp. output) stream, deletes any alias associated with that stream, the current input (resp. output) stream becomes the standard one, and succeeds with empty local substitution.
  - **if** the stream associated to Stream_or_alias is neither the standard input or output stream, nor the current input or output stream **then** closes the stream associated with Stream_or_alias, deletes any alias associated with that stream, and succeeds with empty local substitution.

NOTES:
1- If Options contains contradictory close-options, the rightmost stream-option is the one which applies.
2- force(false) is the default option.
3- force(true): data and results may be lost and the stream may be left in an inconsistent state.

▷ Error cases

Conditions	Error-term
○ Options is a variable or a list with an element E which is a variable	instantiation_error
○ Options is neither a variable nor a list	type_error(list, Options)
○ An element E of the Options list is neither a variable nor a close-option	domain_error(close_option, E)
○ Stream_or_alias is a variable	instantiation_error
○ Stream_or_alias is neither a variable nor a stream-term or alias	domain_error(stream_or_alias, Stream_or_alias)
○ Stream_or_alias is not associated with an open stream	existence_error(stream, Stream_or_alias)

▷ Examples

Assume that the current output stream has alias 'mickey', and 'mouse' does not correspond to any open stream.

```
close(mickey, [force(true)]). closes the stream and
                            succeeds with empty substitution,
         after flushing any buffered information to that stream,
      independently of the existence of resource or system errors.

close(user_input).          Succeeds.

close(mouse, [X]).          instantiation_error or
                            existence_error(stream, mouse)
            (it is implementation dependent which error is raised)

close(mouse(X),[]).         domain_error(stream_or_alias,mouse(X))
```

22 compound/1   *Type testing*

Tests whether the argument is a compound term.

▷ **How to use it:**   compound(?term)

Example: compound(f(X,Y)).

▷ **Description:** compound(Term)

- **If Term** is a compound term **then** succeeds with empty local substitution.
- **If Term** is not a compound term (it is a variable, an atom or a number) **then** fails.

▷ **Error cases**
   None.

▷ **Examples**

compound(f(X,Y)).	Succeeds.
compound([a]).	Succeeds.
compound(-a).	Succeeds.
compound(-1).	Fails.
compound(10.01).	Fails.
compound('ok').	Fails.
compound([]).	Fails.

23 (,)/2 : conjunction   *Logic and control*

Sequential execution of two goals.

▷ **How to use it:**   (+body_term , +body_term)

',' /2 is a predefined infix operator. Its priority is 1000 and it is right associative (**xfy**).

Example: (insect(X), fly(X)); (legs(X,6), fly(X)).

▷ **Description:** (G_1 , G_2)

– If G_1 and G_2 are two well-formed transformed (2.2.3) goals **then** executes G_1 and executes G_2 in sequence each time G_1 is satisfied.

More precisely (see Section 4.3.3) if the current goal is ((G_1 , G_2),Cont)[9] a new child is created whose labels are the empty substitution and the goal (G_1, (G_2, Cont)).

NOTE — The conjunction also satisfies the following obvious properties:
($goal$, **true**) = (**true**, $goal$) = $goal$ and
(($goal_1$, $goal_2$), $goal_3$) = ($goal_1$, ($goal_2$, $goal_3$)) = ($goal_1$, $goal_2$, $goal_3$)
(**true**, **true**) = **true**, (**true**, **fail**)= **fail**, and (**fail**, **true**) = **fail**.

It is always possible to "flatten" conjunctions of goals or to simplify goals according to these rules.

▷ **Error cases**

There is no error because in **Standard Prolog** only well-formed transformed goals are executed.

▷ **Examples**

```
Assume the database contains the user-defined procedures:
                                    insect/1, fly/1, legs/2
with the clauses:  legs(A, 6) :- insect(A). insect(bee) :- true.
                   legs(A, 4) :- animal(A). insect(ant) :- true.
                   fly(bee) :- true.

(insect(X) ; legs(X,6)) , fly(X).  Succeeds twice
                          with the same substitution:  { X <- bee }
```

---
[9] If Cont is empty, then one assumes Cont = true.

24 copy_term/2   *Term creation and decomposition*

Term duplication: unifies the second argument with a freshly renamed copy of the first.

▷ **How to use it:**   copy_term(?term, ?term)

Example: copy_term(f(X,Y),Z).

▷ **Description:** copy_term(Term₁, Term₂)

- **If** a freshly renamed copy of **Term₁** and **Term₂** are *NSTO* (3.3.3) and unifiable by the substitution σ **then** succeeds with local substitution σ.
- **If** a freshly renamed copy of **Term₁** and **Term₂** are *NSTO* and not unifiable, **then** fails.
- **If** a freshly renamed copy of **Term₁** and **Term₂** are *STO* , **then** the result is **undefined** (success, failure, loop or error are standard conforming behaviours).

▷ **Error cases**
  None.

▷ **Examples**

```
copy_term(f(X, Y),Z).        Succeeds with substitution
                                          { Z <- f(U, V) }

copy_term(X, -10).           Succeeds.

copy_term(f(a,X), f(X,b)).   Succeeds with substitution { X <- a }

copy_term(f(X,X), f(A,B)).   Succeeds with substitution { A <- B }
                             (or { B <- A }, implementation dependent)

copy_term(a, 'ok').          Fails.

X = f(Y,Z), copy_term(X,U), U == f(Y,Z).
                             Fails.

copy_term(f(a,X), f(X,b)), copy_term(f(a,X), f(X,b)).
                             Fails.

copy_term(f(X,X), f(Y, g(Y))). Undefined.
```

25 current_char_conversion/2

Finds the elements of the character conversion table used by term input, different from identity.

▷ **How to use it:**   current_char_conversion(?E_character,
                        ?character)

Example: current_char_conversion(C, a).

▷ **Description:** current_char_conversion(In_char, Out_char)

– If In_char is a variable or a character in **ECS** (9.1) and In_char is a variable or a one-char atom **then**
  let S be the set of all the terms (In, Out) of the character conversion table such that In and Out are different and (In, Out) is unifiable with (In_char, Out_char),
  – If S is empty **then** fails.
  – If S is not empty **then** succeeds with local substitution σ which is the unifier of (In_char, Out_char) and one of the elements of S not already chosen (the choice is **implementation dependent**).

NOTE — current_char_conversion/2 is re-executable as many times as the size of S. The order of the solutions is **implementation dependent**.

▷ **Error cases**

Conditions	Error-term
o In_char is neither a variable nor a character in **ECS**	type_error(character, In_char)
o Out_char is neither a variable nor a one-char atom	type_error(character, Out_char)

▷ Examples

Assume the character conversion table contains the pairs:
  a , a
  a , a
and 'UU' is not a character in ECS.
current_char_conversion(C, a).   Succeeds twice with substitutions:
                                  { C <- a };
                                  { C <- *a* }.
        (The order of solutions is implementation dependent)

current_char_conversion(a, a).   Fails.

current_char_conversion(c, 'UU'). type_error(character, 'UU')

26 current_input/1 *Stream selection and control*

Identifies the current input stream.

▷ **How to use it:**   current_input(?stream)

Example: current_input(S).

▷ **Description:** current_input(Stream)

– If Stream is a variable or a stream-term **then**
  let *ST* be the current input stream-term,
  – **If** *ST* and Stream are unifiable (3.2) by unifier σ **then** succeeds with
    local substitution σ
  – **If** *ST* and Stream are not unifiable **then** fails.

NOTES:
1– Stream cannot be an atom, hence it cannot be an alias.
2– By default the current input stream is the standard input stream.

▷ **Error cases**

Conditions	Error-term
o Stream is neither a variable nor a stream-term	domain_error(stream, Stream)

▷ **Examples**

Assume the current input stream is 'user_input'.

current_input(S).   Succeeds with substitution:
                              { S <- '$stream'(132464) }
                   (an implementation dependent non atomic ground term)

current_input(user_input).   domain_error(stream, user_input)

---

27 current_op/3   *Term input/output*

Finds the elements of the current operator table (the predefined operators are in Table 9.2.2 in Chapter 9).

▷ **How to use it:**   current_op(?integer, ?operator_specifier, ?atom)

Example: current_op(P, xfy, OP).

▷ **Description:** current_op(Priority, Op_specifier, Operator)

— **If** Priority is a variable or an integer between 1 and 1200 inclusive, and Op_specifier is a variable or an operator specifier as in Table 9.1, and Operator is a variable or an atom,
then
let S be the set of all the terms (P,Spec,Op) corresponding to operators defined in the current operator table which are unifiable with (Priority, Op_specifier, Operator),
   — **If** S is empty **then** fails.
   — **If** S is not empty **then** succeeds with local substitution σ which is the unifier of (Priority, Op_specifier, Operator) and one of the elements of S not already chosen (the choice is **implementation dependent**).

NOTE — current_op/3 is re-executable as many times as the size of S. The order of the solutions is **implementation dependent**.

▷ **Error cases**

Conditions	Error-term
○ Priority is neither a variable nor an integer between 1 and 1200 inclusive	domain_error(operator_priority, Priority)
○ Op_specifier is neither a variable nor an operator specifier	domain_error(operator_specifier, Op_specifier)
○ Operator is neither a variable nor an atom	type_error(atom, Operator)

▷ Examples

```
current_op(P, xfy, OP).
          If the default operator table has not been altered, then
                    Succeeds 4 times with substitutions:
                          { P <- 1100, OP <- ';'  };
                          { P <- 1050, OP <- '->' };
                          { P <- 1000, OP <- ','  };
                          { P <-  200, OP <- '^'  }.
          (The order of solutions is implementation dependent)

current_op(0, X, Y).    domain_error(operator_priority, 0)
```

28 current_output/1   *Stream selection and control*

Identifies the current output stream.

▷ **How to use it:**   current_output(?stream)

Example: current_output(S).

▷ **Description:** current_output(Stream)

- **If Stream** is a variable or a stream-term **then**
  let *ST* be the current output stream-term,
  - **If** *ST* and **Stream** are unifiable (3.2) by unifier σ **then** succeeds with
    local substitution σ
  - **If** *ST* and **Stream** are not unifiable **then** fails.

NOTES:

1– **Stream** cannot be an alias.
2– By default the current output stream is the standard output stream.

▷ **Error cases**

Conditions	Error-term
o **Stream** is neither a variable nor a stream-term	domain_error(stream, Stream)

▷ **Examples**

Assume the current output stream is user_output.

current_output(S).   Succeeds with substitution:
                                        { S <- stream-term }
            (an implementation dependent non atomic ground term)

current_input('user_output').   domain_error(stream, user_output)

29 current_predicate/1
Clause retrieval and information

Finds the predicate indicators of the user-defined procedures (dynamic or static) in the database.

▷ **How to use it:** current_predicate(?predicate_indicator_pattern)

Example: current_predicate(reverse/X).

▷ **Description:** current_predicate(Term)

– If Term is a variable or a predicate indicator pattern, let S be the set of all the terms A/N such that
(1) the database contains a user-defined procedure (static or dynamic, not abolished) whose predicate indicator is A/N, and
(2) A/N and Term are unifiable (3.2).
then
  – If S is empty **then** fails.
  – If S is not empty **then** succeeds with local substitution σ which is the unifier of Term and one of the elements of S not already chosen (the choice is **implementation dependent**).

NOTES:

1– current_predicate/2 is re-executable as many times as the size of S. The order of the solutions is **implementation dependent**.
2– A user-defined procedure is still found even when all its clauses have been retracted.
3– It is **undefined** whether private procedures are found.

▷ **Error cases**

Conditions	Error-term
○ Term is neither a variable nor a predicate indicator pattern	type_error(predicate_indicator, Term)

▷ Examples

Assume the database contains the user-defined procedures:
reverse/2, reverse/3 and plus/3.

```
current_predicate(reverse/X). Succeeds twice with substitutions:
                                        { X <- 2 };
                                        { X <- 3 }.
                        (the order is implementation dependent)

current_predicate(X).           Succeeds 3 times with substitutions:
                                        { X <- plus/3    };
                                        { X <- reverse/2 };
                                        { X <- reverse/3 }.
                        (the order is implementation dependent)

current_predicate(reverse/1). Fails.

current_predicate(4).           type_error(predicate_indicator, 4)
```

30 current_prolog_flag/2

Finds the pairs $< flag, value >$ where *flag* is a flag supported by the processor and *value* the value currently associated with it.

▷ **How to use it:**   current_prolog_flag(?atom, ?term)

Example: current_prolog_flag(unknown, V).

▷ **Description:** current_prolog_flag(Flag, Value)

− If Flag is a variable or an atom, let S be the set of all the terms (F, V) such that
(1) F is a flag supported by the processor (including standard ones and extensions) and V is the value currently associated with it,
(2) (F, V) and (Flag, Value) are unifiable (3.2).
then
  − If S is empty **then** fails.
  − If S is not empty **then** succeeds with local substitution σ which is the unifier of (Flag, Value) and one of the elements of S not already chosen (the choice is **implementation dependent**).

NOTES:

1− current_prolog_flag/2 is re-executable as many times as the size of S. The order of the solutions is **implementation dependent**.
2− If the flag **bounded** is **false**, there is no value for the flags min_integer and max_integer, hence current_prolog_flag(min_integer,N) or current_prolog_flag(max_integer,N) fails.

▷ **Error cases**

Conditions	Error-term
∘ Flag is neither a variable nor an atom	type_error(atom, Flag)

▷ Examples

Assume the current value of the flag 'unknown' is 'error', there is
no flag 'flag' supported by the processor and the flag 'bounded' has
value 'false'.

```
current_prolog_flag(unknown, V).     Succeeds with substitution:
                                                { V <- error }

current_prolog_flag(unknown, fail).  Fails.

current_prolog_flag(flag, error).    Fails.

current_prolog_flag(min_integer, N). Fails.

current_prolog_flag(flag(unknown), V).
                                     type_error(atom, flag(unknown))
```

31 !/0 : cut

Logic and control

Prunes alternative solutions (cuts unexplored hanging branches in the search-tree).

▷ **How to use it:**   !.

Example: insect(X),!.

▷ **Description:** !

— Succeeds with empty local substitution, after cutting some alternatives.

More precisely (see Sections 4.3.3 and 4.5) the effect of '!'/0 is to make deterministic all the nodes[10] between the node (inclusive), where the predication, head of the clause whose body contains this cut, has been chosen, and the current node where this cut is executed.
If the current goal is (!,G), a new child is thus created whose labels are the empty substitution and the goal G[11].

▷ **Error cases**
None.

▷ **Examples**

```
Assume the database contains the user-defined procedures:
                                        insect/1, animal/1

with the clauses:  insect(bee)   :- true.    animal(horse) :- true.
                   insect(ant)   :- true.    animal(cat)   :- true.
                                             animal(dog)   :- true.

insect(X),!.              Succeeds once with substitution:
                                                  { X <- bee }

(insect(X); animal(Y)),!. Succeeds once with substitution:
                                                  { X <- bee }

insect(X), !, animal(Y).  Succeeds three times with substitutions
                   { X <- bee, Y <- horse }; { X <- bee, Y <- cat  };
                                             { X <- bee, Y <- dog  }.
```

---

[10] This means that all the branches corresponding to not yet visited children of these nodes are deleted.

[11] If G is empty, then one assumes G = true.

32 (;)/2 : disjunction   *Logic and control*

Alternative execution of two goals.

▷ How to use it: (+body_term ; +body_term)

';'/2 is a predefined infix operator. Its priority is 1100 and it is right associative (**xfy**).

Example: (insect(X), fly(X)); (legs(X,6), fly(X)).

▷ Description: $(G_1 ; G_2)$

– If G_1 and G_2 are two well-formed transformed (2.2.3) goals and the principal functor of G_1 is not '->'/2 **then**
  executes G_1 and skips G_2 each time G_1 is satisfied, and executes G_2 when G_1 fails if this alternative has not been cut by the execution of G_1.

  More precisely (see Section 4.3.3) if the current goal is $((G_1 ; G_2),\text{Cont})$[12] then two children are created whose labels are the empty substitution and the goal (G_1,Cont) for the first, (G_2,Cont) for the second.

NOTE — The disjunction corresponds to a non-deterministic node. It may also be defined by the two meta clauses ("meta" because the variables G1, G2 stands for subgoals):
    ';'(G1, G2) :- G1.
    ';'(G1, G2) :- G2. if the principal functor of G1 is not '->'/2.

▷ Error cases
There is no error because in **Standard Prolog** only well-formed transformed goals are executed.

▷ Examples

```
Assume the database contains the clauses:
  legs(A, 6)      :- insect(A). insect(bee) :- true.  fly(bee) :- true.
  legs(horse, 4) :- true.       insect(ant) :- true.

(insect(X), fly(X)) ; (legs(X,6), fly(X)).
                Succeeds twice with the same substitution: { X <- bee }
```

---

[12] If Cont is empty, then one assumes Cont = true.

33 fail/0

Forced failure.

▷ How to use it: fail

Example: (X =1 ; Y = 2), write(X), fail.

▷ Description: fail

− Fails.

More precisely fail can be viewed as a user defined predicate with no definition at all. Hence its execution defines a failed branch and the execution continues with backtracking (Section 4.2.6).

NOTE — In contrast to the execution of a predication which does not correspond to any existing user defined procedure[13], no message is raised by executing fail/0.

▷ Error cases
None.

▷ Examples

(X = 1 ; X = 2), write(X), fail.
                    Outputs on the current output stream 12 and fails.

repeat, write(1), fail.
                    Outputs infinitely on the current output stream 111...

---

[13] Its behaviour depends on the value of the flag unknown.

34 findall/3

Collects all the solutions of a goal in a list (solution order) according to a given pattern.

▷ **How to use it:**   findall(@term, @body_term, ?list)

Example: findall(X, insect(X), S)

▷ **Description:** findall(Term, Goal, Bag)

- **If** Goal is a well-formed body-term different from a variable,
  let S be the sequence of the substitutions obtained by successive re-execution of call(Goal) and
  let L be the list whose elements are freshly renamed copies of Termμ for all μ in S in the same order (if there is no element in S, L is the empty list).
  Then
  - **If** Bag and L are NSTO (3.3.3) and unifiable by substitution σ, **then** succeeds with local substitution σ.
  - **If** Bag and L are NSTO and not unifiable **then** fails.
  - **If** Bag and L are STO **then undefined.**

▷ **Error cases**

Conditions	Error-term
○ Goal is a variable	instantiation_error
○ Goal is neither a variable nor a callable term nor a well-formed body-term	type_error(callable, Goal)
○ Bag is neither a variable nor a partial list nor a list	type_error(list, Bag)

▷ Examples

Assume the database contains the clauses:

```
legs(A, 6)  :- insect(A).
legs(A, 4)  :- animal(A).
legs(A, 8)  :- spider(A).
insect(bee) :- true.
insect(ant) :- true.
```

findall(X, insect(X), S).   Succeeds with substitution:
                                       { S <- [bee, ant] }

findall(X, (X=1; X=2), S).   Succeeds with substitution:
                                        { S <- [1, 2] }

findall(X, (X = Y ; X = Y), S).   Succeeds with substitution:
                                      { S <- [_01, _02] }

findall(X, fail, S).   Succeeds with substitution:
                                        { S <- [] }

findall(X, legs(_,X), [X, Y, Z]). Succeeds with substitution:
                             { X <- 6, Y <- 4, Z <- 8 }

findall(X, insect(X), [ant, bee]). Fails.

findall(X, X = f(Y,Y), [f(X,g(X))]). Undefined.

findall(X, G, S).   instantiation_error

findall(X, (true; 4), S).   type_error(callable, (true; 4))

35 float/1   *Type testing*

Tests whether the argument is a floating–point number.

▷ **How to use it:**   float(?term)

Example: float(10.01).

▷ **Description:** float(Term)

— **If Term** is a floating–point number **then** succeeds with empty local substitution.
— **If Term** is not a floating–point number **then** fails.

▷ **Error cases**
   None.

▷ **Examples**

float(10.01).	Succeeds.
float(-10.01).	Succeeds.
float(- -10.01).	Fails.
float(10).	Fails.
float(X).	Fails.

36 flush_output/0   *Stream selection and control*

Flushes any buffered information to the current output stream.

▷ **How to use it:**   flush_output

Example: flush_output.

▷ **Description:** flush_output

− Succeeds with empty local substitution after flushing any buffered information to the current output stream.

NOTE — Behaves like:
  current_output(S), flush_output(S).

▷ **Error cases**
  None.

▷ **Examples**

Assume that the current output stream has alias 'mickey'.

flush_output.   Succeeds with empty substitution,
      after flushing any buffered information to the stream 'mickey'.

37 flush_output/1   *Stream selection and control*

Flushes any buffered information to an output stream.

▷ **How to use it:**   flush_output(@stream_or_alias)

Example: flush_output(mickey).

▷ **Description:** flush_output(Stream_or_alias)

– **If** Stream_or_alias is a stream-term or alias associated to an open non-input stream, **then** sends to that stream any output which is currently buffered by the processor for the stream associated with Stream_or_alias, and succeeds with empty local substitution.

▷ **Error cases**

Conditions	Error-term
○ Stream_or_alias is a variable	instantiation_error
○ Stream_or_alias is neither a variable nor a stream-term or alias	domain_error(stream_or_alias, Stream_or_alias)
○ Stream_or_alias is not associated with an open stream	existence_error(stream, Stream_or_alias)
○ Stream_or_alias is associated with an input stream	permission_error(output, stream, Stream_or_alias)

▷ **Examples**

Assume that the current output stream has alias 'mickey' and 'mouse' does not correspond to any open stream.

flush_output(mickey).   Succeeds with empty substitution,
              after flushing any buffered information to that stream.

flush_output(mouse).   existence_error(stream, mouse)

38 functor/3   *Term creation and decomposition*

Relates a term (the first argument) with the name and the arity of its principal functor.

▷ **How to use it:**   functor(-term, +atomic, +integer)
functor(@nonvar, ?atomic, ?integer)

Example: functor(foo(aa,X), Y, Z).

▷ **Description:** functor(Term, Name, Arity)

- **If Term** is a compound term $f(t_1, t_2, \ldots, t_n)$, $n > 0$ **then** if (f, n) is unifiable (3.2) with (Name, Arity) by substitution σ **then** succeeds with local substitution σ **else** fails.
- **If Term** is an atomic term c (an atom or a number) **then** if $(c, 0)$ is unifiable with (Name, Arity) by substitution σ **then** succeeds with local substitution σ **else** fails.
- **If Term** is a variable and Name is an atomic term c and Arity is the integer 0, **then** succeeds with local substitution $\{$ Term $\leftarrow c\}$.
- **If Term** is a variable and Name is an atom f and Arity is an integer $n, 0 < n <maxarity$, **then** succeeds with local substitution: $\{$ Term $\leftarrow f(X_1, \ldots, X_n)\}$, where $X_1, \ldots, X_n$ are distinct **implementation dependent** fresh variables.

▷ **Error cases**

Conditions	Error-term
○ Term and Name are both variables	instantiation_error
○ Term and Arity are both variables	instantiation_error
○ Term is a variable and Name is neither a variable nor an atomic term	type_error(atomic, Name)
○ Term is a variable and Arity is neither a variable nor an integer	type_error(integer, Arity)
○ Term is a variable, Name is a number and Arity is not 0	type_error(atom, Name)
○ Term is a variable and Arity is an integer greater than the **implementation defined** integer *maxarity*	representation_error(max_arity)

○ Term is a variable and Arity is an integer   domain_error(not_less_than_ze-
that is less than zero   ro, Arity)

▷ Examples

functor(foo(aa,X), Y, Z).   Succeeds with local substitution:
                                        { Y <- foo, Z <- 2 }

functor(X, foo, 3).   Succeeds with local substitution:
                                        { X <- foo(X1,X2,X3) }
              where X1, X2, X3 are different implementation
                                    dependent fresh variables.

functor(F, 1.5, 1).   type_error(atom, 1.5)

39 get_byte/1

Reads from the current input stream a single byte (stream altered).

▷ **How to use it:**   get_byte(?in_byte)

Example: get_byte(Byte).

▷ **Description:** get_byte(Byte)

– If the current input stream is neither a text stream nor has properties
  end_of_stream(past) together with eof_action(error), and Byte is a
  variable or an in-byte (a byte or the number -1),
  then it behaves like:
  current_input(S), get_byte(S, Byte).

▷ **Error cases**

Conditions	Error-term
∘ Byte is neither a variable nor an in-byte	type_error(in_byte, Byte)
∘ The current input stream is associated with a text stream IS	permission_error(input, binary_stream, IS)
∘ The current input stream IS has stream properties end_of_stream(past) and eof_action(error)	permission_error(input, past_end_of_stream, IS)

▷ **Examples**

```
Assume the current input stream has contents:  113,119,101,114, ...

get_byte(Byte).    Succeeds with substitution: { Byte <- 113 }
            and the current input stream is left as: 119,101,114, ...

get_byte(117).    Fails.
            and the current input stream is left as: 119,101,114, ...

get_byte('az').    type_error(in_byte, az)
```

40 get_byte/2   *Byte input/output*

Reads from a binary stream a single byte (stream altered).

▷ **How to use it:**   get_byte(@stream_or_alias, ?in_byte)

Example: get_byte(mickey, Byte).

▷ **Description:** get_byte(Stream_or_alias, Byte)

− **If** Stream_or_alias is a stream-term or alias of an open stream which is neither an output stream nor a text stream nor has properties end_of_stream(past) together with eof_action(error), and Byte is a variable or an in-byte (a byte or the number -1),
then
  − **if** the stream position of the stream associated with Stream_or_alias is past-end-of-stream without the property eof_action(error) **then** performs the action specified in 7.3.2 appropriate to the value of A where the stream associated with Stream_or_alias has stream property eof_action(A).
  − **if** the stream position of the stream associated with Stream_or_alias is end-of-stream, **then** sets the stream position so that it is past-end-of-stream, **if** the number -1 and Byte are unifiable (3.2) by substitution σ **then** succeeds with local substitution σ **else** fails.
  − **if** the stream position of the stream associated with Stream_or_alias is neither past-end-of-stream nor end-of-stream **then** let B be the next byte to be read from the stream associated with Stream_or_alias, advances the stream position of the stream associated with Stream_or_alias by one byte, **if** B and Byte are unifiable by substitution σ **then** succeeds with local substitution σ **else** fails.

▷ **Error cases**

Conditions	Error-term
∘ Byte is neither a variable nor an in-byte	type_error(in_byte, Byte)
∘ Stream_or_alias is a variable	instantiation_error
∘ Stream_or_alias is neither a variable nor a stream-term or alias	domain_error(stream_or_alias, Stream_or_alias)
∘ Stream_or_alias is not associated with an open stream	existence_error(stream, Stream_or_alias)

○ Stream_or_alias is an output stream	permission_error(input, stream, Stream_or_alias)
○ Stream_or_alias is associated with a text stream	permission_error(input, text_stream, Stream_or_alias)
○ Stream_or_alias has stream properties end_of_stream(past) and eof_action(error)	permission_error(input, past_end_of_stream, Stream_or_alias)

▷ Examples

```
Assume there is an input stream with alias 'mickey'
                  whose contents are:       113,119,101,114, ...
and 'mouse' is not an open stream.

get_byte(mickey, Byte).  Succeeds with substitution: { Byte <- 113 }
                         and the stream is left as: 119,101,114, ...

get_byte(mickey, 117).   Fails,
                         and the stream is left as: 119,101,114, ...

get_byte(mouse, Byte).   existence_error(stream, mouse)
```

41 get_char/1   *Character input/output*

Reads from the current input stream a single character (stream altered).

▷ **How to use it:**   get_char(?in_E_character)

Example: get_char(Char).

▷ **Description:** get_char(Char)

— If the current input stream is neither a binary stream nor has properties
end_of_stream(past) together with eof_action(error), and Char is a
variable or a character in **ECS** (9.1) or the atom 'end_of_file',
then it behaves like:
current_input(S), get_char(S, Char).

▷ **Error cases**

Conditions	Error-term
○ Char is neither a variable nor a character nor the atom end_of_file	type_error(in_character, Char)
○ The current input stream is associated with a binary stream IS	permission_error(input, binary_stream, IS)
○ The current input stream IS has stream properties end_of_stream(past) and eof_action(error)	permission_error(input, past_end_of_stream, IS)
○ The entity input from the stream is not a character in **ECS**	representation_error(character)

▷ **Examples**

```
Assume the current input stream has contents:                qverty ...

get_char(Char).  Succeeds with substitution: { Char <- 'q' }
                      and the current input stream is left as: werty ...

get_char('a').   Fails.
                      and the current input stream is left as: werty ...

get_char('az').  type_error(in_character, 'az')
```

42 get_char/2   *Character input/output*

Reads from a text stream a single character (stream altered).

▷ **How to use it:**   get_char(@stream_or_alias, ?in_E_character)

Example: get_char(mickey, Char).

▷ **Description:** get_char(Stream_or_alias, Char)

- If Stream_or_alias is a stream-term or alias of an open stream which
  is neither an output stream nor a binary stream nor has properties
  end_of_stream(past) together with eof_action(error), and Char is a
  variable or a character in **ECS** (9.1) or the atom 'end_of_file',
  then
  - **if** the stream position of the stream associated with Stream_or_alias
    is past-end-of-stream without the property eof_action(error) **then**
    performs the action specified in 7.3.2 appropriate to the value of A
    where the stream associated with Stream_or_alias has stream property
    eof_action(A).
  - **if** the stream position of the stream associated with Stream_or_alias is
    end-of-stream, **then** sets the stream position so that it is past-end-of-
    stream, **if** the atom end_of_file and Char are unifiable (3.2) by substi-
    tution σ **then** succeeds with local substitution σ **else** fails.
  - **if** the stream position of the stream associated with Stream_or_alias
    is neither past-end-of-stream nor end-of-stream **then** let C be the next
    entity to be read from the stream associated with Stream_or_alias,
    advances the stream position of the stream associated with Stream_or_a-
    lias by one character, **if** C is a character in **ECS** and C and Char are
    unifiable by substitution σ **then** succeeds with local substitution σ **else**
    fails.

▷ **Error cases**

Conditions	Error-term
○ Char is neither a variable nor a character nor the atom end_of_file	type_error(in_character, Char)
○ Stream_or_alias is a variable	instantiation_error
○ Stream_or_alias is neither a variable nor a stream-term or alias	domain_error(stream_or_alias, Stream_or_alias)

○ Stream_or_alias is not associated with an open stream	existence_error(stream, Stream_or_alias)
○ Stream_or_alias is an output stream	permission_error(input, stream, Stream_or_alias)
○ Stream_or_alias is associated with a binary stream	permission_error(input, binary_stream, Stream_or_alias)
○ Stream_or_alias has stream properties end_of_stream(past) and eof_action(error)	permission_error(input, past_end_of_stream, Stream_or_alias)
○ The entity input from the stream is not a character in ECS	representation_error(character)

▷ Examples

```
Assume there is an input stream with alias 'mickey'
                            whose contents are:      qwerty ...
and there is an input stream with alias 'mouse'
                            whose contents are:    'qwerty' ...
and 'donald' is not an open stream.

get_char(mickey, Char). Succeeds with substitution:  { Char <- 'q' }
                            and the stream is left as:   werty ...

get_char(mouse, Code).  Succeeds with substitution: { Char <- '''' }
                            (the atom containing just a single quote)
                            and the stream is left as: qwerty' ...

get_char(mickey, 'a'). Fails, and the stream is left as:  werty ...

get_char(donald, Char). existence_error(stream, donald)
```

43 get_code/1

Reads from the current input stream the character code of a single character (stream altered).

▷ **How to use it:**   get_code(?in_character_code)

Example: get_code(Code).

▷ **Description:** get_code(Code)

− If the current input stream is neither a binary stream nor has properties end_of_stream(past) together with eof_action(error), and Code is a variable or an in-character code (a character code or the integer −1), then it behaves like:
current_input(S), get_code(S, Code).

▷ **Error cases**

Conditions	Error-term
∘ Code is neither a variable nor an integer	type_error(integer, Code)
∘ Code is an integer but not an in-character code	representation_error(in_character_code)
∘ The current input stream IS is associated with a binary stream	permission_error(input, binary_stream, IS)
∘ The current input stream IS has stream properties end_of_stream(past) and eof_action(error)	permission_error(input, past_end_of_stream, IS)
∘ The entity input from the stream is not a character in **ECS**	representation_error(character)

▷ **Examples**

```
Assume the current input stream has contents:              qwerty ...

get_code(Code). Succeeds with substitution: { Code <- 113 }
                    (the value is implementation defined)
                and the current input stream is left as:   werty ...

get_code('a').  type_error(integer, a)
```

44 get_code/2   *Character input/output*

Reads from a text stream the character code of a single character (stream altered).

▷ **How to use it:**   get_code(@stream_or_alias,
?in_character_code)

Example: get_code(mickey, Code).

▷ **Description:** get_code(Stream_or_alias, Code)

- If Stream_or_alias is a stream-term or alias of an open stream which is neither an output stream nor a binary stream nor has properties end_of_stream(past) together with eof_action(error), and Code is a variable or a in-character code (a character code or the integer -1), **then**
  - if the stream position of the stream associated with Stream_or_alias is past-end-of-stream without the property eof_action(error) **then** performs the action specified in 7.3.2 appropriate to the value of A where the stream associated with Stream_or_alias has stream property eof_action(A).
  - if the stream position of the stream associated with Stream_or_alias is end-of-stream, **then** sets the stream position so that it is past-end-of-stream, if the integer -1 and Code are unifiable (3.2) by substitution σ **then** succeeds with local substitution σ **else** fails.
  - if the stream position of the stream associated with Stream_or_alias is neither past-end-of-stream nor end-of-stream **then** let C be the next entity to be read from the stream associated with Stream_or_alias, advances the stream position of the stream associated with Stream_or_alias by one character, if C is a one-char atom and the character code of C and Code are unifiable by substitution σ **then** succeeds with local substitution σ **else** fails.

▷ **Error cases**

Conditions	Error-term
○ Code is neither a variable nor an integer	type_error(integer, Code)
○ Code is an integer but not an in-character code	representation_error(in_character_code)

o Stream_or_alias is a variable	instantiation_error
o Stream_or_alias is neither a variable nor a stream-term or alias	domain_error(stream_or_alias, Stream_or_alias)
o Stream_or_alias is not associated with an open stream	existence_error(stream, Stream_or_alias)
o Stream_or_alias is an output stream	permission_error(input, stream, Stream_or_alias)
o Stream_or_alias is associated with a binary stream	permission_error(input, binary_stream, Stream_or_alias)
o Stream_or_alias has stream properties end_of_stream(past) and eof_action(error)	permission_error(input, past_end_of_stream, Stream_or_alias)
o The entity input from the stream is not a character in ECS	representation_error(character)

▷ Examples

```
Assume there is an input stream with alias 'mickey'
                        whose contents are:              qwerty ...
and there is an input stream with alias 'mouse'
                        whose contents are:            'qwerty' ...
and 'donald' is not an open stream.

get_code(mickey, Code).  Succeeds with substitution: { Code <- 113 }
                              (the value is implementation defined)
                                   and the stream is left as: werty ...

get_code(mouse, Code).   Succeeds with substitution:  { Code <- 39 }
                              (the value is implementation defined)
                                   and the stream is left as: qwerty' ...

get_code(mickey, 0'p).   Fails, and the stream is left as: werty ...

get_code(donald, Code).  existence_error(stream, donald)
```

45 halt/0   *Logic and control*

Stops the execution of the user top-level goal.

▷ **How to use it:**   halt

Example: halt.

▷ **Description:** halt

– Exits from the execution of the (initial) top-level goal; the behaviour of
the processor is thus **implementation defined**.

▷ **Error cases**
None.

▷ **Examples**

```
halt.        Stops the execution of the initial top level goal.
             The behaviour of the processor is implementation defined.

catch((read(G),G), X, (write('SOS!'), halt)).
             If the execution of the goal  G raises an exception, it
             will be caught, and  SOS!  will be output  on the current
             output stream before the execution stops.
```

46 halt/1

Stops the execution of the user top-level goal, passing some information to the processor.

▷ **How to use it:**   halt(+integer)

Example: halt(1).

▷ **Description:** halt(Int)

– If Int is an integer **then** exits from the execution of the (initial) top-level goal, passing the value Int as a message to the processor whose behaviour is thus **implementation defined**.

NOTE — This built-in predicate never succeeds or fails.

▷ **Error cases**

Conditions	Error-term
○ Int is a variable	instantiation_error
○ Int is neither a variable nor an integer	type_error(integer, Int)

▷ **Examples**

```
halt(1).        Stops the execution of the initial top level goal.
                The behaviour of the processor is implementation defined,
                according to the value 1 passed to the processor.

halt(a).        type_error(integer, a)
```

Assume rescue/2 is a relation between caught error-terms and integers in the range of the implementation defined argument values of halt/1.

```
catch((read(G),G), X, (write('SOS!'), rescue(X,Y), halt(Y))).
                If the execution of the goal G raises an exception, it will
                be caught, and SOS! will be output on the current output
                stream before some implementation defined action is performed
                according to the value Y passed to the processor.
```

47 (->)/2 : if-then

Prolog implication.

▷ **How to use it:**   +body_term -> +body_term

'->'/2 is a predefined infix operator. Its priority is 1050 and it is right associative (**xfy**).

Example: (X = 0 -> write('null')).

▷ **Description:** Cond -> Then

- **If** Cond and Then are two well-formed transformed (2.2.3) goals and '->'(Cond, Then) is defined out of the context of a disjunction (i.e. it is not the first argument of ';'/2) **then**
  - **if** Cond succeeds **then** cuts the choice points issued from Cond only and executes **Then.**
  - **if** Cond fails **then** fails [14].

More precisely (see Section 4.3.3), if the current goal is ((Cond -> Then), Cont)[15], it adds a new child whose labels are the empty substitution and the goal ((call(Cond),!,Then), Cont).

NOTES:

1– Cond is not transparent to cut.
2– Its behaviour is equivalent to the meta-clause ("meta" because the variables COND, THEN stands for subgoals) :
   '->'(COND, THEN) :- COND,!,THEN.

▷ **Error cases**
There is no error because in **Standard Prolog** only well-formed transformed goals are executed.

---

[14] Therefore if-then/2 cannot be interpreted as a logical implication (otherwise it should succeed when the first argument fails); (Cond -> Then; true) could be used instead.
[15] If Cont is empty, then one assumes Cont = true.

▷ Examples

Assume the database contains the user-defined procedures:

                                                    legs/2, insect/1

with the clauses: legs(A, 6)   :- insect(A).
                     legs(horse, 4) :- true.
                     insect(bee)   :- true.
                     insect(ant)   :- true.

X = 0 -> write('null').   Succeeds with substitution:
                                 { X <- 0 }   after outputting: null

legs(A,6) -> write(insect(A)).   Succeeds once with substitution
                 { A <- bee }   after outputting: insect(bee)

X \= 0 -> write('positive').   Fails.

fail -> (true ; true).   Fails.

48 (;)/2 : if-then-else

Prolog alternative implication.

▷ **How to use it:**   (+body_term -> +body_term ; +body_term)

' ; '/2 is a predefined infix operator. Its priority is 1100 and it is right associative (**xfy**).

->/2 is a predefined infix operator. Its priority is 1050 and it is right associative (**xfy**).

Example: (X = 0 -> write('null'); write('non-null')).

▷ **Description:** (Cond -> Then; Else)

− **If** Cond, Then and Else are well-formed transformed (4.1.1) goals **then**
  − **if** Cond succeeds **then** cuts the choice points issued from Cond only and executes Then, ignoring Else.
  − **if** Cond fails **then** executes Else.

More precisely (see Section 4.3.3) if the current goal is ((Cond -> Then; Else), Cont)[16] then two children are created whose labels are the empty substitution and the goal (Call(Cond),!, Then, Cont) for the first and (Else, Cont) for the second.

NOTES:

1− Cond is not transparent to cut.
2− Its behaviour is equivalent to the meta-clause ("meta" because the variables COND, THEN, ELSE stands for subgoals) :
    ((COND -> THEN); ELSE) :- (Call(COND),!,THEN);ELSE.
3− If-then-else satisfies the property:
    (Cond -> fail; true) = \+(Cond)

▷ **Error cases**
    There is no error because in **Standard Prolog** only well-formed transformed goals are executed.

---

[16] If Cont is empty, then one assumes Cont = true.

▷ Examples

```
(X = 0 -> write('null'); write('positive')).
```
　　　　　　　　　　　　　　Succeeds with substitution
　　　　　　　　　{ X <- 0 }　　　after outputting: null

```
(X = 1, (X = 0 -> write('null'); write('positive'))).
```
　　　　　　　　　　　　　　Succeeds with substitution
　　　　　　　　　{ X <- 1 } after outputting: positive

```
(((!, X=1, fail) -> true; fail); X=2).
```
　　　　　　　　　　　　　　Succeeds with substitution
　　　　　　　　　{ X <- 2 }

```
fail -> true ; true.                    Succeeds.
```

```
((!, X=1, fail) -> true; fail).     Fails.
```

49 integer/1   *Type testing*

Tests whether the argument is an integer.

▷ **How to use it:**   integer(?term)

Example: integer(10).

▷ **Description:** integer(Term)

– **If** Term is an integer **then** succeeds with empty local substitution.
– **If** Term is not an integer **then** fails.

▷ **Error cases**
      None.

▷ **Examples**

integer(10).	Succeeds.
integer(-10).	Succeeds.
integer(- -10).	Fails.
integer(10.01).	Fails.
integer(X).	Fails.
integer('o_k').	Fails.

---

50 is/2 : evaluate expression   *Arithmetic evaluation*

Unifies the first argument and the value of the second argument.

▷ **How to use it:**   is(?nonvar, @evaluable)

is/2 is a predefined infix operator. Its priority is 700 and it is non-associative (**xfx**).

Example: X = atan(1.0), Y is cos(X)**2 + sin(X)**2 .

▷ **Description:** Result is Expression

– **If** the evaluation of **Expression** is errorless (see Section 6.2) and produces the value V **then**
  if Result and V are unifiable (3.2) by the substitution σ **then** succeeds with local substitution σ **else** fails.

▷ **Error cases**
See Section 6.2 the exceptions raised by expression evaluation.

▷ **Examples**

```
X = atan(1.0), Y is cos(X)**2 + sin(X)**2 .
                    Succeeds with substitution   (approximate value)
                               { X <- atan(1.0), Y <- 1.000 }

X = 1+2, Y is X*3.  Succeeds with substitution  { X <- 1+2, Y <- 9 }

Result is 3+11.0.   Succeeds with substitution    { Result <- 14.0 }

is(foo, 77).        Fails.

1.0 is 1.           Fails.

X is (N+1)+(3/0).   instantiation_error             or
                    evaluation_error(zero_divisor)
                (it is implementation dependent which one is raised)
```

---

51 nl/0

Outputs to the current output text stream the **implementation depen-dent** new-line character.

▷ **How to use it:**   nl

Example: nl, put_char(t).

▷ **Description:** nl

- **If** the current output stream is not a binary stream,
  then outputs the **implementation dependent** new-line character to the current output stream, changes the stream position on the current output stream, and
  succeeds with empty local substitution.

▷ **Error cases**

Conditions	Error-term
○ The current output stream OS is associated with a binary stream	permission_error(output, binary_stream, OS)

▷ **Examples**

```
Assume the current output stream has contents:                  >... qwer

nl, put_char(t).     Succeeds with empty substitution
               and the current output stream is left as:  >... qwer
                                                          >t

Assume the current output stream is a binary stream with alias
                                                         'mickey'.

nl.                    permission_error(output, binary_stream, mickey)
```

52 nl/1

Outputs to a text stream the **implementation dependent** new-line character.

▷ **How to use it:**   nl(@stream_or_alias)

Example: nl(mickey), put_char(mickey, t).

▷ **Description:** nl(Stream_or_alias)

— If Stream_or_alias is a stream-term or alias of an open stream which is neither an input stream nor a binary stream,
  then
  outputs the **implementation dependent** new-line character to the stream associated with stream-term or alias Stream_or_alias,
  changes the stream position on the stream associated with Stream_or_alias,
  succeeds with empty local substitution.

▷ **Error cases**

Conditions	Error-term
○ Stream_or_alias is a variable	instantiation_error
○ Stream_or_alias is neither a variable nor a stream-term or alias	domain_error(stream_or_alias, Stream_or_alias)
○ Stream_or_alias is not associated with an open stream	existence_error(stream, Stream_or_alias)
○ Stream_or_alias is an input stream	permission_error(output, stream, Stream_or_alias)
○ Stream_or_alias is associated with a binary stream	permission_error(output, binary_stream, Stream_or_alias)

▷ **Examples**

```
Assume there is an output stream  with alias 'mickey'
                                  whose contents are:   >... qwer

nl(mickey), put_char(mickey, t).   Succeeds with empty substitution,
                and the current output stream is left as: >... qwer
                                                          >t
```

53 nonvar/1   *Type testing*

Tests whether the argument is not a variable.

▷ **How to use it:**   nonvar(?term)

Example: nonvar('ok').

▷ **Description:** nonvar(Term)

— **If** Term is not a variable **then** succeeds with empty local substitution.
— **If** Term is a variable **then** fails.

▷ **Error cases**
   None.

▷ **Examples**

nonvar('ok').	Succeeds.
nonvar(33.3).	Succeeds.
nonvar(foo).	Succeeds.
nonvar(a(b)).	Succeeds.
foo = Foo, nonvar(Foo).	Succeeds.
nonvar(Foo).	Fails.
nonvar(_).	Fails.

54 (\+)/1 : not provable   *Logic and control*

Negation by failure: if the goal succeeds then fails else succeeds.

▷ **How to use it:**   \+(@body_term)

(\+)/1 is a predefined infix operator (its priority is 900 and it is right associative **fy**).

Example: X = 3, \+((X = 1 ; X = 2)).

▷ **Description:** \+(Goal)

- If Goal is a well-formed body-term different from a variable and succeeds **then** fails.
- If Goal is a well-formed body-term different from a variable and fails **then** succeeds with empty local substitution.

More precisely (see Section 4.3.3), if the current goal is (\+(Goal), Cont)[17], two new children are created whose labels are the empty substitution and the goal (call(Goal),!,fail) for the first and Cont for the second.

▷ **Error cases**

Conditions	Error-term
○ Goal is a variable	instantiation_error
○ Goal is neither a variable nor a callable term nor a well-formed body-term	type_error(callable, Term)

▷ **Examples**

X = 3, \+((X = 1 ; X = 2)).	Succeeds with substitution { X <- 3 }
\+(fail).	Succeeds.
\+(!); X = 1.	Succeeds with substitution { X <- 1 }
\+((X = 1 ; X = 2)), X = 3.	Fails.

---

[17] If Cont is empty, then one assumes Cont = true.

```
X = 1, \+((X = 1 ; X = 2)).      Fails.

\+((fail, 1)).                   type_error(callable, (fail, 1))
```

Assume the following definition of the "barber paradox":
```
            shave(barber,X) :- \+ shave(X, X).
```

```
shave(barber, 'Donald').         Succeeds.
```

```
shave(barber, barber).           Loops.
```

The following program tests whether the arguments are unifiable:
```
            test_Prolog_unifiable(X, Y) :- \+ \+ X = Y.
```

```
test_Prolog_unifiable(f(a,X), f(X, a)).    Succeeds.
```

```
test_Prolog_unifiable(f(a,X), f(X, b)).    Fails.
```

```
test_Prolog_unifiable(X, f(X)).            Undefined.
```

The following two programs show that adding cuts in a program may increase the number of successes:

```
        p1 :- \+ q1.          p2 :- \+ q2.

        q1 :- fail.          q2 :- !, fail.
        q1 :- true.          q2 :- true.
```

```
p1.        Fails.

p2.        Succeeds.
```

55 number/1   *Type testing*

Tests whether the argument is a number.

▷ **How to use it:**   number(?term)

Example: number(10.01).

▷ **Description:** number(Term)

- **If** Term is a number **then** succeeds with empty local substitution.
- **If** Term is not a number (an atom, a compound term or a variable) **then** fails.

▷ **Error cases**
   None.

▷ **Examples**

number(10.01).	Succeeds.
number(-10).	Succeeds.
number('ok').	Fails.
number(X).	Fails.
number(f(X, Y)).	Fails.

56 number_chars/2   *Atomic term processing*

Relates a number and the list of the one-char atoms forming its writable representation.

▷ **How to use it:**   number_chars(+number, ?character_list)
                       number_chars(-number, +character_list)

Example: number_chars(X, ['3', '.', '3', 'E', +, '0', '1']).

▷ **Description:** number_chars(Number, List)

- If List is a list of one-char atoms parsable as a number of value N **then if** Number and N are unifiable (3.2) by the substitution σ **then** succeeds with local substitution σ **else** fails.
- If Number is a number and List is not a list **then** let L be the list of one-char atoms whose names correspond to the sequence of characters which would be output by writing Number by write_canonical(Number) (as described in 7.4.3 in the items 2 and 3 (with option quoted(true)), the result is **implementation dependent**), and
  if List and L are unifiable by the substitution σ **then** succeeds with local substitution σ **else** fails.

▷ **Error cases**

Conditions	Error-term
○ Number is neither a variable nor a number	type_error(number, Number)
○ Number is a variable and List is a variable or a partial list or a list with an element which is a variable	instantiation_error
○ Number is a variable and List is neither a variable nor a partial list nor a list	type_error(list, List)
○ List is a list and one of its elements E is not a one-char atom	type_error(character, E)
○ List is a list of one-char atoms and it is not parsable as a number	syntax_error(*imp_dep_atom*)

▷ Examples

```
number_chars(X, ['3', '.', '3', 'E', +, '0', '1']).
                        Succeeds with substitution: { X <- 33.0 }

number_chars(33.0, ['3', '.', '3', 'E', +, '0', '1']).
                        Succeeds.

number_chars(33.0, Y).    Succeeds with substitution:
                          { Y <- ['3', '.', '3', 'E', +, '0', '1'] }
                          (the list is implementation dependent)

X = 33.0, number_chars(X, C), number_chars(Y, C), X == Y.
                        Succeeds.

number_chars(A, ['\n', ' ', '3']).
                        Succeeds with substitution:   { A <- 3 }

number_chars(4.2, ['4', '2' | X]).
                        Fails or
                        Succeeds with some substitutions:
                          { X <- ['.', '0', 'E', '-', '1'] } or
                          { X <- ['0', '.', '0', 'e', '-', '2'] }
                        or ...
                        (The result is implementation dependent)

number_chars(A, ['0', '''', a]).
                        Succeeds with substitution:   { A <- 97}
                        (The result is implementation defined)

number_chars(3.33, ['3', '.', '3', 'E', +, '0']).
                        Fails.

number_chars(4.2, ['a', '2', '.', '0', 'e', '-', '1']).
                        syntax_error(imp_dep_atom)
```

57 number_codes/2   *Atomic term processing*

Relates a number and the list of character codes whose characters form its writable representation.

▷ **How to use it:**   number_codes(+number, ?character_code_list)
                        number_codes(-number, +character_code_list)

Example: number_codes(33, [0'3, 0'3]).

▷ **Description:** number_codes(Number, List)

– **If** Number is a variable and List is a list of character codes corresponding to a character sequence of one-char atoms parsable as a number of value N **then**
  if Number and N are unifiable (3.2) by the substitution σ **then** succeeds with local substitution σ **else** fails.
– **If** Number is a number and List is a variable or a list of character codes corresponding to a character sequence of one-char atoms parsable as a number **then** let L a list of character codes corresponding to the sequence of characters which would be output by writing Number by write_canonical(Number) (as described in 7.4.3 in the items 2 and 3 (with option quoted(true)), the result is **implementation dependent**), and **if** List and L are unifiable by the substitution σ **then** succeeds with local substitution σ **else** fails.

▷ **Error cases**

Conditions	Error-term
o Number and List are variables	instantiation_error
o Number is neither a variable nor a number	type_error(number, Number)
o List is neither a variable nor a list of character codes	domain_error(character_code_list, List)
o List is a list and an element E of List is not a character code	representation_error(character_code)
o List is a list of character codes and it is not parsable as a number	syntax_error(*imp_dep_atom*)

▷ Examples

number_codes(33, [0'3, 0'3]). Succeeds.

number_codes(X, [0'3, 0'3]).   Succeeds with substitution:
                                                    { X <- 33 }

number_codes(33, Y).   Succeeds with substitution:
                                                { Y <- [0'3, 0'3] }

number_codes(33.0, Y).   Succeeds with substitution:
                    { Y <- [0'3, 0'., 0'3, 0'E, 0'+, 0'0, 0'1] }
                        (the list is implementation dependent)

X = 3.3e+01, number_codes(X, C), number_codes(Y, C), X == Y.
                        Succeeds with substitution:
                    { X <- 3.3, Y <- 3.3, C <- [0'3, 0'., 0'3] }
                        (the list is implementation dependent)

number_codes(3.3, [0'3, 0'., 0'3, 0'E, 0'+, 0'0]).
                            Succeeds or
                            Fails.
                                        (implementation dependent)

number_codes(4.2, ['a', '2', '.', '0', 'e', '-', '1']).
                            domain_error(character_code_list,
                            ['a', '2', '.', '0', 'e', '-', '1'])

58 once/1

Executes a goal once only, whatever may be the number of solutions.

▷ **How to use it:**   once(+body_term)

Example: once((X = 1 ; X = 2)).

▷ **Description:** once(Goal)

− **If** Goal is a well-formed body-term different from a variable **then** executes Goal only once (until the first success, if any).

More precisely (see Section 4.3.3), if the current goal is (once(Goal), Cont)[18], a new child is created whose labels are the empty substitution and the goal (Goal,!, Cont).

NOTE — once(Goal) behaves like call(Goal,!).

▷ **Error cases**

Conditions	Error-term
o Goal is a variable	instantiation_error
o Goal is neither a variable nor a callable term nor a well-formed body-term	type_error(callable, Goal)

▷ **Examples**

once((X = 1 ; X = 2)).	Succeeds with substitution:	{ X <- 1 }
once(repeat).	Succeeds.	
once(fail).	Fails.	
once(X = f(X)).	Undefined.	
once((fail; 1)).	type_error(callable, (fail; 1))	

---

[18] If Cont is empty, then one assumes Cont = true.

59 op/3

Updates the operator table used by inputting and outputting terms. The table specifies which atoms will be regarded as operators when a sequence of tokens is parsed or written by the I/O built-in predicates , or when a prolog text is prepared for execution.

▷ **How to use it:**   op(@integer, @operator_specifier, @atom_or_atom_list)

Example: op(30, xfy, ++).

▷ **Description:** op(Priority, Op_specifier, Operator)

– **If** Priority is an integer between 0 and 1200 inclusive,   and
  Operator is an atom or a list of atoms such that no atom is ',',   and
  Op_specifier is an operator specifier such that inclusion of the operators of Operator in the current operator table would not breach its validity (9.2.4),
  then updates the operator table as follows:
  for every atom Op in Operator,
  – **if** Op is currently an operator with the same operator class (prefix, infix or postfix)[19] as Op_specifier **then** if Priority = 0 then Op is removed, so that Op is no longer an operator of that class, else (Priority > 0) the priority of the operator Op with specifier Op_specifier is updated to Priority,
  – **if** Op is not currently an operator with the same operator class **then** if Priority is different from 0 then Op is made an operator with specifier Op_specifier and priority Priority,
  and succeeds with empty local substitution.

NOTES:

1– In the event of an error being detected in an **Operator** list argument, it is **undefined** which, if any, of the atoms in the list is made an operator.
2– A Priority of zero can be used to remove an operator from the operator table.
3– It does not matter if the same atom appears more than once in an **Operator** list; this is not an error and the duplicates simply have no effect.
4– In general, except for ',', any operator can be removed from the operator table and its priority or specifier can be changed.
5– op/3 never fails.

---

[19] See Table 9.1.

▷ Error cases

Conditions	Error-term
o Priority is a variable	instantiation_error
o Priority is neither a variable nor an integer	type_error(integer, Priority)
o Priority is an integer but not between 0 and 1200 inclusive	domain_error(operator_priority, Priority)
o Op_specifier is a variable	instantiation_error
o Op_specifier is neither a variable nor an atom	type_error(atom, Op_specifier)
o Op_specifier is not an operator specifier	domain_error(operator_specifier, Op_specifier)
o Op_specifier is a specifier such that inclusion of the operators of Operator in the current operator table would breach its validity	permission_error(create, operator, Operator)
o Operator is a variable or a list with an element E which is a variable	instantiation_error
o Operator is neither a variable nor an atom nor a list	type_error(list, Operator)
o An element E of the Operator list is neither a variable nor an atom	type_error(atom, E)
o Operator is ',' or an element of the Operator list is ','	permission_error(modify, operator, ',')

▷ Examples

```
Assuming the predefined operator table is unaltered.

op(30, xfy, ++).    Succeeds, making ++ a right associative
                                infix operator with priority 30.

op(0, yfx, ++).     Succeeds,  making ++ no longer an infix operator.

op(30, xfy, ++), op(40, xfx, ++).
                    Succeeds, making ++ a non-associative
                                infix operator with priority 40.

op(1201, xfy, ++). domain_error(operator_priority, 1201)

op(30, XFY, ++).    instantiation_error

op(30, xfy, ++), op(50, yf, ++).
                        permission_error(create, operator, ++)
(there cannot be an infix and a postfix operator with the same name)
```

60 open/3 *Stream selection and control*

Opens a source/sink which is a text stream with the default options.

▷ **How to use it:**   open(@source_sink, @io_mode, -stream)

Example: open('/user/peter/data', read, D).

▷ **Description:** open(Source_sink, Mode, Stream)

− **If** Source_sink is a source/sink-term and corresponds to a source/sink which may be opened, and
Mode is an I/O mode atom (7.3.1), and
Stream is a variable,
then opens the source/sink Source_sink for input or output as indicated by Mode, and succeeds with local substitution: { Stream ← *stream-term* } (where *stream-term* is an **implementation dependent** non atomic ground term).

NOTES:

1− open(Source_sink, Mode, Stream) behaves like:
            open(Source_sink, Mode, Stream, []).
2− A permission error when Mode is write or append means that Source_sink does not specify a sink that can be created, for example, a specified disk or directory does not exist. If Mode is read then it is also possible that the file specification is valid but the file does not exist.
3− The effect of opening more than once a source/sink is **undefined**.

▷ **Error cases**

Conditions	Error-term
○ Source_sink is a variable	instantiation_error
○ Source_sink is neither a variable nor a source/sink-term	domain_error(source_sink, Source_sink)
○ The source/sink specified by Source_sink does not exist	existence_error(source_sink, Source_sink)
○ The source/sink specified by Source_sink cannot be opened	permission_error(open, source_sink, Source_sink)
○ Mode is a variable	instantiation_error
○ Mode is neither a variable nor an atom	type_error(atom, Mode)
○ Mode is an atom but not an I/O mode	domain_error(io_mode, Mode)

∘Stream is not a variable   type_error(variable,
                                                   Stream)

▷ Examples

Assuming '/user/peter/data' is the path name of an existing file.

open('/user/peter/data', read, D).
       opens the file '/user/peter/data' as text stream for input, then
       Succeeds with substitution: { D <- '$stream'(132464) }
                    (an implementation dependent non atomic ground term)

61 open/4

Opens a source/sink.

▷ **How to use it:** open(@source_sink, @io_mode, -stream,
                           @open_options)

Example: open('/user/peter/data', read, D, [type(binary)]).

▷ **Description:** open(Source_sink, Mode, Stream, Options)

– If Source_sink is a source/sink term (an **implementation defined**
ground term) and corresponds to a source/sink which may be opened,
Mode is an I/O mode atom (7.3.1),
Stream is a variable,
Options is a list of stream-options supported at stream creation (7.3.2)
with no variable as element, such that, if one of its elements is alias(A),
A is not already associated with an open stream, or if one of its elements
is reposition(true), it is possible to reposition this stream[20],
then opens the source/sink Source_sink for input or output as indicated
by Mode and Options, and succeeds with local substitution: { Stream ←
stream-term } (where *stream-term* is an **implementation dependent**
non atomic ground term).

NOTES:

1– A permission error when Mode is **write** or **append** means that Source_sink does
not specify a sink that can be created, for example, a specified disk or directory
does not exist. If Mode is **read** then it is also possible that the file specification
is valid but the file does not exist.

2– The effect of opening more than once a source/sink is **undefined**.

3– If Options contains contradictory stream-options, the rightmost stream-option
is the one which applies.

▷ **Error cases**

Conditions	Error-term
○ Source_sink is a variable	instantiation_error
○ Source_sink is neither a variable nor a source/sink-term	domain_error(source_sink, Source_sink)

---

[20] A stream may have several aliases.

o The source/sink specified by Source_sink does not exist	`existence_error(source_sink, Source_sink)`
o The source/sink specified by Source_sink cannot be opened	`permission_error(open, source_sink, Source_sink)`
o Mode is a variable	`instantiation_error`
o Mode is neither a variable nor an atom	`type_error(atom, Mode)`
o Mode is an atom but not an I/O mode	`domain_error(io_mode, Mode)`
o Stream is not a variable	`type_error(variable, Stream)`
o Options is a variable	`instantiation_error`
o Options is a list with an element E which is a variable	`instantiation_error`
o Options is neither a variable nor a list	`type_error(list, Options)`
o An element E of the Options list is neither a variable nor a valid stream-option	`domain_error(stream_option, E)`
o An element E of the Options list is alias(A) and A is already associated with an open stream	`permission_error(open, source_sink, alias(A))`
o An element E of the Options list is reposition(true) and it is not possible to reposition this stream	`permission_error(open, source_sink, reposition(true))`

▷ Examples

```
Assuming '/user/peter/data' is the path name of an existing file.

open('/user/peter/data', read, D, [type(binary)]).
        The stream corresponding to the file '/user/peter/data' is
        opened as binary for input, then
     Succeeds with substitution          { D <- '$stream'(132464) }
                    (an implementation dependent non atomic ground term)

Assuming '/user/ali/data' is the path name of an existing file.

open('/user/ali/data', read, DD, []).
        The stream corresponding to the file  '/user/ali/data' is
        opened as text for input, then
     Succeeds with substitution              { D <- '$stream'(142464) }
                    (an implementation dependent non atomic ground term)
```

62 peek_byte/1   *Byte input/output*

Reads from the current input binary stream a single byte leaving the stream position unaltered.

▷ **How to use it:**   peek_byte(?in_byte)

  Example: peek_byte(Byte).

▷ **Description:** peek_byte(Byte)

– **If** the current input stream is neither a text stream nor has properties end_of_stream(past) together with eof_action(error), and Byte is a variable or an in-byte (a byte or the number -1),
then it behaves like:
current_input(S), peek_byte(S, Byte).

▷ **Error cases**

Conditions	Error-term
o **Byte** is neither a variable nor an in-byte	type_error(in_byte, Byte)
o The current input stream IS is associated with a text stream	permission_error(input, text_stream, IS)
o The current input stream IS has stream properties end_of_stream(past) and eof_action(error)	permission_error(input, past_end_of_stream, IS)

▷ **Examples**

```
Assume the current input stream has contents:  113,119,101,114, ...

peek_byte(Byte).    Succeeds with substitution:  { Byte <- 113 }
        and the current input stream is left as: 113,119,101,114, ...

peek_byte(119).     Fails.
                    and the stream is left as: 113,119,101,114, ...

peek_byte(a).       type_error(in_byte, a)
```

63 peek_byte/2   *Byte input/output*

Reads from a binary stream a single byte leaving the stream position unaltered.

▷ **How to use it:**   peek_byte(@stream_or_alias, ?in_byte)

Example: peek_byte(mickey, Byte).

▷ **Description:** peek_byte(Stream_or_alias, Byte)

- If Stream_or_alias is a stream-term or alias of an open stream which is neither an output stream nor a text stream nor has properties end_of_stream(past) together with eof_action(error), and Byte is a variable or an in-byte (a byte or the number -1),
  then
  - **if** the stream position of the stream associated with Stream_or_alias is past-end-of-stream without the property eof_action(error) **then** performs the action specified in 7.3.2 appropriate to the value of A where the stream associated with Stream_or_alias has stream property eof_action(A).
  - **if** the stream position of the stream associated with Stream_or_alias is end-of-stream, **then if** the number -1 and Byte are unifiable (3.2)by substitution σ **then** succeeds with local substitution σ **else** fails.
  - **if** the stream position of the stream associated with Stream_or_alias is neither past-end-of-stream nor end-of-stream **then** let B be the next byte to be read from the stream associated with Stream_or_alias, **if** B and Byte are unifiable by substitution σ **then** succeeds with local substitution σ **else** fails.

▷ **Error cases**

Conditions	Error-term
◦ Byte is neither a variable nor an in-byte	type_error(in_byte, Byte)
◦ Stream_or_alias is a variable	instantiation_error
◦ Stream_or_alias is neither a variable nor a stream-term or alias	domain_error(stream_or_alias, Stream_or_alias)
◦ Stream_or_alias is not associated with an open stream	existence_error(stream, Stream_or_alias)

○ `Stream_or_alias` is an output stream

`permission_error(input, stream, Stream_or_alias)`

○ `Stream_or_alias` is associated with a text stream

`permission_error(input, text_stream, Stream_or_alias)`

○ `Stream_or_alias` has stream properties `end_of_stream(past)` and `eof_action(error)`

`permission_error(input, past_end_of_stream, Stream_or_alias)`

▷ Examples

```
Assume there is an input binary stream with alias 'mickey
                          whose contents are:  113,119,101,114, ...
and 'mouse' is not an open stream.

peek_byte(mickey, Byte).
                Succeeds with substitution:    { Byte <- 113 }
                    and the stream is left as: 113,119,101,114, ...

peek_byte(mickey, 119).
                Fails,
                    and the stream is left as: 113,119,101,114, ...

peek_byte(mouse, Char).
                existence_error(stream, mouse)

peek_byte(user_output, X).
                permission_error(input, stream, user_output)
```

64 peek_char/1

Reads from the current input text stream a single character leaving the stream position unaltered.

▷ **How to use it:**   peek_char(?in_E_character)

Example: peek_char(Char).

▷ **Description:** peek_char(Char)

– **If** the current input stream is neither a binary stream nor has properties
   end_of_stream(past) together with eof_action(error), and Char is a
   variable or a character in **ECS** or the atom 'end_of_file',
   then it behaves as:
   current_input(S), peek_char(S, Char).

▷ **Error cases**

Conditions	Error-term
○ **Char** is neither a variable nor a character in **ECS** nor the atom **end_of_file**	type_error(in_character, Char)
○ The next entity to be read from the stream is not a one-char atom	representation_error(character)
○ The current input stream IS is associated with a binary stream	permission_error(input, binary_stream, IS)
○ The current input stream IS has stream properties end_of_stream(past) and eof_action(error)	permission_error(input, past_end_of_stream, IS)

▷ **Examples**

```
Assume the current input stream has contents:              qwerty ...

peek_char(Char). Succeeds with substitution: { Char <- q }
                 and the current input stream is left as: qwerty ...

peek_char('a'). Fails.

peek_char(1).    type_error(in_character, 1)
```

65 peek_char/2   *Character input/output*

Reads from a text stream a single character leaving the stream position unaltered.

▷ **How to use it:**   peek_char(@stream_or_alias, ?in_E_character)

Example: peek_char(mickey, Char).

▷ **Description:** peek_char(Stream_or_alias, Char)

- If Stream_or_alias is a stream-term or alias of an open stream which is neither an output stream nor a binary stream nor has properties end_of_stream(past) together with eof_action(error), and Char is a variable or a character in **ECS** or the atom 'end_of_file',
  then
  - **if** the stream position of the stream associated with Stream_or_alias is past-end-of-stream without the property eof_action(error) **then** performs the action specified in 7.3.2 appropriate to the value of A where the stream associated with Stream_or_alias has stream property eof_action(A).
  - **if** the stream position of the stream associated with Stream_or_alias is end-of-stream, **then if** the atom end_of_file and Char are unifiable (3.2) by substitution σ **then** succeeds with local substitution σ **else** fails.
  - **if** the stream position of the stream associated with Stream_or_alias is neither past-end-of-stream nor end-of-stream **then** let C be the next entity to be read from the stream associated with Stream_or_alias, and if C is a character in **ECS** then **if** C and Char are unifiable by substitution σ **then** succeeds with local substitution σ **else** fails.

▷ **Error cases**

Conditions	Error-term
○ Stream_or_alias is a variable	instantiation_error
○ Stream_or_alias is neither a variable nor a stream-term or alias	domain_error(stream_or_alias, Stream_or_alias)
○ Stream_or_alias is not associated with an open stream	existence_error(stream, Stream_or_alias)
○ Stream_or_alias is an output stream	permission_error(input, stream, Stream_or_alias)

○ Stream_or_alias is associated with a binary stream	permission_error(input, binary_stream, Stream_or_alias)
○ Stream_or_alias has stream properties end_of_stream(past) and eof_action(error)	permission_error(input, past_end_of_stream, Stream_or_alias)
○ Char is neither a variable nor a character in ECS nor the atom end_of_file	type_error(in_character, Char)
○ The next entity to be read from the stream is not a character in ECS	representation_error(character)

▷ Examples

```
Assume there is an input stream with alias 'mickey'
                          whose contents are:          qwerty ...
and there is an input stream with alias 'mouse'
                          whose contents are:          'qwerty'...
and 'donald' is not an open stream.


peek_char(mickey, Char). Succeeds with substitution:   { Char <- q }
                         and the stream is left as:     qwerty ...

peek_char(mouse, Code).  Succeeds with substitution: { Char <- '''' }
                           (the atom consisting of a single quote)
                         and the stream is left as:    'qwerty'...

peek_char(mickey, a).    Fails,
                           and the stream is left as:   qwerty ...

peek_char(mickey, 1).    type_error(in_character, 1)

peek_char(donald, Char). existence_error(stream, donald)
```

66 peek_code/1

Reads from the current input text stream the character code of a single character leaving the stream position unaltered.

▷ **How to use it:** peek_code(?in_character_code)

Example: peek_code(Code).

▷ **Description:** peek_code(Code)

– **If** the current input stream is neither a binary stream nor has properties end_of_stream(past) together with eof_action(error), and Code is a variable or an in-character code (a character code or the integer -1), **then** it behaves like:
current_input(S), peek_code(S, Code).

▷ **Error cases**

Conditions	Error-term
○ Code is neither a variable nor an integer	type_error(integer, Code)
○ Code is neither a variable nor an in-character code	representation_error(in_character_code)
○ The current input stream IS is associated with a binary stream	permission_error(input, binary_stream, IS)
○ The current input stream IS has stream properties end_of_stream(past) and eof_action(error)	permission_error(input, past_end_of_stream, IS)
○ The next entity to be read from the stream is not a character in **ECS**	representation_error(character)

▷ **Examples**

```
Assume the current input stream has contents:            qwerty ...


peek_code(Code). Succeeds with substitution:      { Code <- 113 }
                            (the value is implementation defined)
                  and the current input stream is left as: qwerty ...

peek_code(0'p).  Fails.
```

67 peek_code/2   *Character input/output*

Reads from a text stream the character code of a single character leaving the stream position unaltered.

▷ **How to use it:**   peek_code(@stream_or_alias,
                                   ?in_character_code)

Example: peek_code(mickey, Code).

▷ **Description:** peek_code(Stream_or_alias, Code)

– If Stream_or_alias is a stream-term or alias of an open stream which is neither an output stream nor a binary stream nor has properties end_of_stream(past) together with eof_action(error), and Code is a variable or an in-character code (a character code or the integer -1), **then**
  – if the stream position of the stream associated with Stream_or_alias is past-end-of-stream without the property eof_action(error) **then** performs the action specified in 7.3.2 appropriate to the value of A where the stream associated with Stream_or_alias has stream property eof_action(A).
  – if the stream position of the stream associated with Stream_or_alias is end-of-stream, **then if** the integer -1 and Code are unifiable (3.2) by substitution σ **then** succeeds with local substitution σ **else** fails.
  – if the stream position of the stream associated with Stream_or_alias is neither past-end-of-stream nor end-of-stream **then** let C be the next entity to be read from the stream associated with Stream_or_alias, and if C is a character in **ECS then if** the character code of C and Code are unifiable by substitution σ **then** succeeds with local substitution σ **else** fails.

▷ **Error cases**

Conditions	Error-term
○ Code is neither a variable nor an integer	type_error(integer, Code)
○ Code is neither a variable nor an in-character code	representation_error(in_character_code)
○ Stream_or_alias is a variable	instantiation_error

o Stream_or_alias is neither a variable nor a stream-term or alias	domain_error(stream_or_alias, Stream_or_alias)
o Stream_or_alias is not associated with an open stream	existence_error(stream, Stream_or_alias)
o Stream_or_alias is associated with an output stream	permission_error(input, stream, Stream_or_alias)
o Stream_or_alias is associated with a binary stream	permission_error(input, binary_stream, Stream_or_alias)
o Stream_or_alias has stream properties end_of_stream(past) and eof_action(error)	permission_error(input, past_end_of_stream, Stream_or_alias)
o The next entity to be read from the stream is not a character in **ECS**	representation_error(character)

▷ Examples

```
Assume there is an input stream with alias 'mickey'
                              whose contents are:  qwerty ...
and there is an input stream with alias 'mouse'
                              whose contents are: 'qwerty'...
and 'donald' is not an open stream.


peek_code(mickey, Code). Succeeds with substitution: { Code <- 113 }
                         (the value is implementation defined)
              and the current input stream is left as: qwerty ...

peek_code(mouse, Code).  Succeeds with substitution: {Code <- 0''' }
                              and the stream is left as:  'qwerty'...

peek_code(mickey, 0'p).  Fails,
                              and the stream is left as: qwerty ...

peek_code(donald, Code). existence_error(stream, donald)
```

68 put_byte/1   *Byte input/output*

Outputs to the current output stream a single byte.

▷ **How to use it:**   put_byte(+byte)

Example: put_byte(84).

▷ **Description:** put_byte(Byte)

- **If** the current output stream is not a text stream and Byte is a byte,
  then it behaves like:
  current_output(S), put_byte(S, Byte).

▷ **Error cases**

Conditions	Error-term
o **Byte** is a variable	instantiation_error
o **Byte** is neither a variable nor a byte	type_error(byte, Byte)
o The current output stream OS is associated with a text stream	permission_error(output, text_stream, OS)

▷ **Examples**

Assume the current output stream has contents:
```
                                    ..., 113,119,101,114
```

```
put_byte(84).     Succeeds with empty substitution,
    and the current output stream is left as: ..., 113,119,101,114,84

put_byte('t').    type_error(byte, t)
```

69 put_byte/2

Outputs to a binary stream a single byte.

▷ **How to use it:**   put_byte(@stream_or_alias, +byte)

Example: put_byte(mickey, 113).

▷ **Description:** put_byte(Stream_or_alias, Byte)

− If Stream_or_alias is a stream-term or alias of an open stream which is
neither an input stream nor a text stream and Byte is a byte,
then outputs Byte to the stream associated with Stream_or_alias, changes
the stream position to take account of the byte which has been output, and
succeeds with empty local substitution.

▷ **Error cases**

Conditions	Error-term
o Byte is a variable	instantiation_error
o Byte is neither a variable nor a byte	type_error(byte, Byte)
o Stream_or_alias is a variable	instantiation_error
o Stream_or_alias is neither a variable nor a stream-term or alias	domain_error(stream_or_alias, Stream_or_alias)
o Stream_or_alias is not associated with an open stream	existence_error(stream, Stream_or_alias)
o Stream_or_alias is associated with an input stream	permission_error(output, stream, Stream_or_alias)
o Stream_or_alias is associated with a binary stream	permission_error(output, text_stream, Stream_or_alias)

▷ **Examples**

```
Assume there is an output stream with alias 'mickey'
                        whose contents are:    ..., 113,119,101,114

put_byte(mickey, 84).       Succeeds with empty substitution,
                        and the stream is left as: 113,119,101,114,84

put_byte(mickey, 't').       type_error(byte, t)

put_byte(mickey, C).         instantiation_error
```

70 put_char/1
Character input/output

Outputs to the current output text stream a single character.

▷ **How to use it:**   put_char(+E_character)

Example: put_char(t).

▷ **Description:** put_char(Char)

− **If** the current output stream is not a binary stream and Char is a character
in **ECS**,
then it behaves like:
current_output(S), put_char(S, Char).

▷ **Error cases**

Conditions	Error-term
○ Char is a variable	instantiation_error
○ Char is neither a variable nor a character	type_error(character, Char)
○ Char is neither a variable nor a character in **ECS**	representation_error(character)
○ The current output stream OS is associated with a binary stream	permission_error(output, binary_stream, OS)

▷ **Examples**

Assume the current output stream has contents: ... qwer

put_char(t).   Succeeds with empty substitution,
                and the current output stream is left as: ... qwert

put_char(1).   type_error(character, 1)

put_char('UUU').   representation_error(character)
                                (assuming 'UUU' is not a character in ECS)

71 put_char/2   *Character input/output*

Outputs to a text stream a single character.

▷ **How to use it:**   put_char(@stream_or_alias, +E_character)

Example: put_char(mickey, t).

▷ **Description:** put_char(Stream_or_alias, Char)

– If Stream_or_alias is a stream-term or alias of an open stream which is
neither an input stream nor a binary stream and Char is a character in
ECS, then outputs the character Char to the stream associated with
Stream_or_alias, changes the stream position, and succeeds with empty
local substitution.

▷ **Error cases**

Conditions	Error-term
○ Char is a variable	instantiation_error
○ Char is neither a variable nor a character	type_error(character, Char)
○ Char is neither a variable nor a character in **ECS**	representation_error(character, Char)
○ Stream_or_alias is a variable	instantiation_error
○ Stream_or_alias is neither a variable nor a stream-term or alias	domain_error(stream_or_alias, Stream_or_alias)
○ Stream_or_alias is not associated with an open stream	existence_error(stream, Stream_or_alias)
○ Stream_or_alias is not associated with an input stream	permission_error(output, stream, Stream_or_alias)
○ Stream_or_alias is associated with a binary stream	permission_error(output, binary_stream, Stream_or_alias)

▷ **Examples**

```
Assume there is an output stream with alias 'mickey'
                            whose contents are:       ... qwer

put_char(mickey, t).        Succeeds with empty substitution,
                                  and the stream is left as: ... qwert

put_char(mickey, 1).        type_error(character, 1)
```

72 put_code/1

Outputs to the current output stream a single character corresponding to a given character code.

▷ **How to use it:**   put_code(+character_code)

Example: put_code(Code).

▷ **Description:** put_code(Code)

— **If** the current output stream is not a binary stream and Code is a character code,
then it behaves like:
current_output(S), put_code(S, Char).

▷ **Error cases**

Conditions	Error-term
○ Code is a variable	instantiation_error
○ Code is neither a variable nor an integer	type_error(integer, Code)
○ Code is an integer but not a character code	representation_error(charac-ter_code)
○ The current output stream is associated with a binary stream OS	permission_error(output, binary_stream, OS)

▷ **Examples**

```
Assume the current output stream has contents:              ... qwer

put_code(0't).      Succeeds with empty substitution,
                    and the current output stream is left as: ... qwert

put_code('ty').     type_error(integer, ty)
```

---

73 put_code/2   *Character input/output*

Outputs to a text stream a single character corresponding to the given character code.

▷ **How to use it:**   put_code(@stream_or_alias, +character_code)

Example: put_code(mickey, 0't).

▷ **Description:** put_code(Stream_or_alias, Code)

– **If** Stream_or_alias is a stream-term or alias of an open stream which is neither an input stream nor a binary stream and Code is a character code, **then**
outputs the character whose character code is Code to the stream associated with Stream_or_alias, changes the stream position, and succeeds with empty local substitution.

▷ **Error cases**

Conditions	Error-term
○ Code is a variable	instantiation_error
○ Code is neither a variable nor an integer	type_error(integer, Code)
○ Code is an integer but not a character code	representation_error(character_code)
○ Stream_or_alias is a variable	instantiation_error
○ Stream_or_alias is neither a variable nor a stream-term or alias	domain_error(stream_or_alias, Stream_or_alias)
○ Stream_or_alias is not associated with an open stream	existence_error(stream, Stream_or_alias)
○ Stream_or_alias is not associated with an input stream	permission_error(output, stream, Stream_or_alias)
○ Stream_or_alias is associated with a binary stream	permission_error(output, binary_stream, Stream_or_alias)

▷ **Examples**

```
Assume there is an output stream with alias 'mickey'
                                  whose contents are:       ... qwer

put_code(mickey, 0't).       Succeeds with empty substitution,
                                  and the stream is left as: ... qwert
```

74 read/1

Reads from the current input stream a single term.

▷ **How to use it:**   read(?term)

Example: read(T).

▷ **Description:** read(Term)

– **If** the current input stream is not a binary stream and does not have
properties end_of_stream(past) together with eof_action(error), then
it behaves like:
current_input(Stream), read_term(Stream, Term, [ ]).

NOTE — The number of characters which are input is **undefined** if an error occurs
during the execution of **read/1**.

▷ **Error cases**

Conditions	Error-term
o The current input stream IS is associated with a binary stream	permission_error(input, binary_stream, IS)
o The current input stream IS has stream properties end_of_stream(past) and eof_action(error)	permission_error(input, past_end_of_stream, IS)
o The term to be read breaches an **implementation defined** limit specified by Flag where Flag is the flag max_arity, max_integer, or min_integer	representation_error(Flag)
o The sequence of tokens cannot be parsed as a term using the current operator table	syntax_error(*imp_dep_atom*)

▷ **Examples**

```
read(T).
   If the contents of the current input stream are:
                                  foo(A+B, A+C).term2. ...
                  Succeeds with substitution:
                      { T <- foo(_01 + _02, _01 + _03) }
```

The current input stream is left as: term2. ...

```
read(foo(X,a)).
```
   If the contents of the current input stream are:
                                        foo(a,a).term2. ...
                Succeeds with substitution: { X <- a }
        The current input stream is left as: term2. ...

```
read(foo(X,a)).
```
   If the contents of the current input stream are:
                                        foo(a,b).term2. ...
                Fails.
        The current input stream is left as: term2. ...

```
read(foo(X,f(X))).
```
   If the contents of the current input stream are:
                                        foo(Y,Y).term2. ...
                Undefined.
        The current input stream is left as: term2. ...

```
read(T).
```
   If the contents of the current input stream are: 3.1
                        syntax_error(violation)
   where 'violation' is an implementation dependent atom.
   The current input stream is left with position past-end-of-stream.

75 read/2

Reads from a text stream a single term.

▷ **How to use it:**   read(@stream_or_alias, ?term)

Example: read(mickey, T).

▷ **Description:** read(Stream_or_alias, Term)

— If Stream_or_alias is a stream-term of an open stream which is neither output nor binary stream and does not have properties end_of_stre-
am(past) together with eof_action(error),
then it behaves like:
read_term(Stream_or_alias, Term, [ ]).

NOTE — The number of characters which are input is **undefined** if an error occurs
during the execution of **read/2**.

▷ **Error cases**

Conditions	Error-term
o Stream_or_alias is a variable	instantiation_error
o Stream_or_alias is neither a variable nor a stream-term or alias	domain_error(stream_or_alias, St)
o Stream_or_alias is not associated with an open stream	existence_error(stream, St)
o Stream_or_alias is an output stream	permission_error(input, stream, St)
o Stream_or_alias is associated with a bi- nary stream	permission_error(input, binary_stream, St)
o Stream_or_alias has stream properties end_of_stream(past) and eof_action(error)	permission_error(input, past_end_of_stream, St)
o The term to be read breaches an **imple- mentation defined** limit specified by Flag where Flag is the flag max_arity, max_integer, or min_integer	representation_error(Flag)
o The sequence of tokens cannot be parsed as a term using the current operator table	syntax_error(*imp_dep_atom*)

▷ **Examples**

```
read(mickey, T).
```
If the contents of the stream associated with mickey are:
```
                              foo(A+B, A+C).term2. ...
```
Succeeds with substitution:
```
                        { T <- foo(_01 + _02, _01 + _03) }
```
The stream associated with mickey is left as: term2. ...

```
read(mickey, foo(X,a)).
```
If the contents of the stream associated with mickey are:
```
                                       foo(a,a).term2. ...
```
Succeeds with substitution: { X <- a }
The stream associated with mickey is left as: term2. ...

```
read(mickey, foo(X,a)).
```
If the contents of the stream associated with mickey are:
```
                                       foo(a,b). term2. ...
```
Fails
The stream associated with mickey is left as: term2. ...

```
read(mickey, foo(X,f(X))).
```
If the contents of the stream associated with mickey are:
```
                                       foo(Y,Y). term2. ...
```
Undefined.
The stream associated with mickey is left as: term2. ...

```
read(mickey, T).
```
If the contents of the stream associated with mickey are:
```
                                                   'a'a ...
```
```
                        syntax_error(violation)
```
where 'violation' is an implementation dependent atom.
The stream associated with mickey is left in an undefined position.

76 read_term/2

Reads from the current input stream a single term and instantiates accordingly the read-options list.

▷ **How to use it:**   read_term(?term, +read_options_list)

Example: read_term(T, [variables(U)]).

▷ **Description:** read_term(Term, Options)

− **If** the current input stream is not a binary stream and does not have properties end_of_stream(past) together with eof_action(error), and Options is a list of valid read-options[21] with no variable as element, **then** it behaves like:
read_term(Stream, Term, Options).

NOTES:

1− The number of characters which are input is **undefined** if an error occurs during the execution of **read_term/2**.
2− The behaviour of **read_term/2** is **undefined** if Term and Options share some variables.

▷ **Error cases**

Conditions	Error-term
○ Options is a variable	instantiation_error
○ Options is a list with an element E which is a variable	instantiation_error
○ Options is neither a variable nor a list	type_error(list, Options)
○ An element E of the Options list is neither a variable nor a valid read-option	domain_error(read_option, E)
○ The term to be read breaches an **implementation defined** limit specified by Flag where Flag is the flag max_arity, max_integer, or min_integer	representation_error(Flag)
○ The sequence of tokens cannot be parsed as a term using the current operator table	syntax_error(*imp_dep_atom*)
○ The current input stream IS is associated with a binary stream	permission_error(input, binary_stream, IS)

---

[21] See the Glossary.

○The current input stream IS has   permission_error(input,
  stream properties end_of_stream(past)   past_end_of_stream, IS)
  and eof_action(error)

▷ Examples

```
read_term(T, [variables(U)]).
```
  If the contents of the current input stream are:
                                    foo(A+_, A+_).term2. ...
                  Succeeds with substitution:
                    { T <- foo(_01+_02, _01+_03) ,
                      U <- [_01, _02, _03]   }.
  The stream associated with the current input stream is left as:
                                                  term2. ...

```
read_term(T, [variables(VL), variable_names(VN), singletons(VS)]).
```
  If the contents of the current input stream are:
                                    foo(A+_, A+C).term2. ...
                  Succeeds with substitution:
                    { T <- foo(X1+X2, X1+X3)   ,
                      VL <- [X1, X2, X3]   ,
                      VN <- ['A' = X1, 'C' = X3] ,
                      VS <- ['C' = X3]   }.
  The stream associated with the current input stream is left as:
                                                  term2. ...
```
read_term(foo(X,a), [variables(U)]).
```
  If the contents of the current input stream are:
                                    foo(a,b).term2. ...
                  Fails.

```
read_term(foo(X,f(X)), [variable(U)]).
```
  If the contents of the current input stream are:
                                    foo(Y,Y). term2. ...
                  Undefined.
  The stream associated with the current input stream is left as:
                                                  term2. ...

```
read_term(T, [variable(X)]).
```
                  domain_error(read_option, variable(X))

```
read_term(T, []).
```
  If the contents of the current input stream are: 3.1
                  syntax_error(violation)
  where 'violation' is an implementation dependent atom.
  The current input stream is left with position past-end-of-stream.

77 read_term/3   *Term input/output*

Reads from a text stream a single term and instantiates accordingly the read-option list.

▷ **How to use it:**   read_term(@stream_or_alias, ?term, +read_options_list)

Example: read_term(mickey, T, [variables(V)]).

▷ **Description:** read_term(Stream_or_alias, Term, Options)

– **If** Stream_or_alias is the stream-term of an open stream which is neither output nor binary stream and does not have properties end_of_stream(past) together with eof_action(error), and Options is a list of valid read-options[22] with no variable as element,
then let S be the sequence of the characters in Stream_or_alias such that:
the last character of the sequence is the first end token on the stream, and each character of the sequence is the same corresponding character $Char$ on Stream_or_alias if the char_conversion flag is off or $Char$ is a quoted character, otherwise it is the corresponding character according to the current character conversion table (9.1.2).

if S is parsable as a term T', **then** let T be T', freshly renamed, and μ be the substitution denoting the instantiation of the variables of Options for the term T as described for the read-options (7.4.1), and

– **if** T and Term are $NSTO$ (3.3.3) and unifiable by the substitution σ **then** succeeds with local substitution $\mu\sigma$.
– **if** T and Term are $NSTO$ and not unifiable **then** fails.
– **if** T and Term are STO **then undefined.**

NOTES:

1– The number of characters which are input is **undefined** if an error occurs during the execution of read_term/3.
2– The behaviour of read_term/3 is **undefined** if Term and Options share some variables.

---

[22] See the Glossary.

▷ Error cases

Conditions	Error-term
○ Options is a variable	instantiation_error
○ Options is a list with an element E which is a variable	instantiation_error
○ Options is neither a variable nor a list	type_error(list, Options)
○ An element E of the Options list is neither a variable nor a valid read-option	domain_error(read_option, E)
○ Stream_or_alias is a variable	instantiation_error
○ Stream_or_alias is neither a variable nor a stream-term or alias	domain_error(stream_or_alias, Stream)
○ Stream_or_alias is not associated with an open stream	existence_error(stream, Stream)
○ Stream_or_alias is an output stream	permission_error(input, stream, Stream_or_alias)
○ Stream_or_alias is associated with a binary stream	permission_error(input, binary_stream, Stream_or_alias)
○ Stream_or_alias has stream properties end_of_stream(past) and eof_action(error)	permission_error(input, past_end_of_stream, St)
○ The term to be read breaches an **implementation defined** limit specified by Flag where Flag is the flag max_arity, max_integer, or min_integer	representation_error(Flag)
○ The sequence of tokens cannot be parsed as a term using the current operator table	syntax_error(*imp_dep_atom*)

▷ Examples

```
read_term(mickey, T, [variables(V)]).
    If the contents of the stream associated with mickey are:
                                    foo(A+_, A+_).term2. ...
                    Succeeds with substitution:
                    { T <- foo(_01+_02, _01+_03) ,
                      V <- [_01, _02, _03]        }.
    The stream associated with the current input stream is left as:
                                    term2. ...


read_term(mickey, T,
            [variables(VL), variable_names(VN), singletons(VS)]).
    If the contents of the stream associated with mickey are:
                                    foo(A+B, A+_). term2. ...
                    Succeeds with substitution:
                    { T  <- foo(X1+X2, X1+X3)    ,
                      VL <- [X1, X2, X3]          ,
                      VN <- ['A' = X1, 'B' = X2] ,
                      VS <- ['B' = X2]            }.
```

```
                    The stream associated with mickey is left as: term2. ...

read_term(mickey, foo(X,a), [variables(VL), variable_names(VN),
                                               singletons(VS)]).
    If the contents of the stream associated with mickey are:
                                          foo(a,b). term2. ...
                      Fails
         The stream associated with mickey is left as: term2. ...

read_term(mickey, foo(X,f(X)), [variables(VL)]).
    If the contents of the stream associated with mickey are:
                                          foo(Y,Y). term2. ...
                    Undefined.

read_term(mickey, T, [variables(VL), _]).
                      instantiation_error

read_term(mickey, T, [variable(X)]).
                      domain_error(read_option, variable(X))

read_term(mickey, T, []).
    If the contents of the stream associated with mickey are:       3.1
                      syntax_error(violation)
    where 'violation' is an implementation dependent atom.
    The stream associated with mickey is left with position
    past-end-of-stream.
```

---

78 repeat/0   *Logic and control*

Succeeds repeatedly and indefinitely.

▷ **How to use it:**   `repeat.`

Example: `repeat, write('hello '), fail.`

▷ **Description:** repeat

— It has the same behaviour as if it were defined by the two clauses:

```
repeat :- true.
repeat :- repeat.
```

▷ **Error cases**
    None.

▷ **Examples**

```
repeat, write('hello '), fail.
```
                        Outputs indefinitely:
                            hello hello hello hello ...

```
repeat, !.
```              Succeeds.

```
repeat, !, fail.
```          Fails.

```
repeat, X = f(X), !.
```      Undefined.

```
repeat, fail.
```              Loops.

```
repeat, f(X,Y,X) = f(g(X),g(Y),Y), fail.
```
                        Loops, repeating an undefined action.

# 79 retract/1

*Clause creation and destruction*

Retracts from the database the clauses which are unifiable with the argument.

▷ **How to use it:**    retract(+clause_term)

Example: retract(insect(X)).

▷ **Description:** retract(Clause)
Let (Head,Body) be the term built as follows:

- if Clause is not a compound term whose principal functor is :-/2 then Head is Clause and Body is true,
- if Clause is a compound term ':-'(H, B) then Head is H and Body is B.

- If Head is a callable term (an atom or a compound term) **then**
  Let $S$ be the sequence of all the terms (A, C) obtained by a sequential search in the database such that
  (1) the database contains a clause in a dynamic user-defined procedure of the form A' :- C', such that A :- C is a freshly renamed copy, and
  (2) (Head,Body) and (A, C) are NSTO (3.3.3) and unifiable.
  **then**
  - if $S$ is empty **then** fails.
  - if $S$ is not empty **then** succeeds with local substitution $\sigma$ which is the unifier of (Head,Body) and the first element of $S$ not yet used.

NOTES:

1- retract/1 is re-executable as many times as the size of $S$. The order of the solutions corresponds to the order of the elements in the sequence $S$.
2- The number of elements of the sequence $S$ may be **undefined** if some tried pairs are STO.

▷ **Error cases**

| Conditions | Error-term |
|---|---|
| ∘ Head is a variable | instantiation_error |
| ∘ Head is not a callable term | type_error(callable, Head) |
| ∘ The predicate indicator PI of Head is that of a static procedure | permission_error(access, static_procedure, PI) |

## ▷ Examples

Assume the database contains the user-defined procedures:
      moose/1, legs/2, insect/1, elk/1
with the clauses: (dynamic:)  legs(A, 6)   :- insect(A).
                              legs(A, 4)   :- animal(A).
                              legs(A, 8)   :- spider(A).
                              insect(bee) :- true.
                              insect(ant) :- true.
                              product(A)   :- call(A), call(A).
                              ...

```
retract(insect(X)).   Succeeds twice with the substitutions:
                                  { X <- bee };
                                  { X <- ant }.
```
  After the last success, all the clauses of insect/1
  have been removed.

```
insect(X), (retract(insect(Y)); true).
                               Succeeds 4 times with the substitutions:
                                  { X <- bee, Y <- bee };
                                  { X <- bee, Y <- ant };
                                  { X <- bee };
                                  { X <- ant }.
```
  All the clauses of insect/1 have been removed after the second
  success.

```
retract((legs(A, 4) :- X)). Succeeds with the substitution:
                                  { X <- insect(A) }
```
  and removes the clause 'legs(A, 4) :- animal(A).'.
  Other possible substitution:  { A <- _01, X <-insect(_01) }
                                              (undefined)

```
retract((product(X) :- call(X), call(X))).
                               Succeeds with empty substitution.
```
  and removes the clause 'product(A) :- call(A), call(A)'.

```
retract((product(X) :- 4)). Fails.
```

```
retract((legs(X, 4) :- animal(f(X)))).
                               Undefined.
```

```
retract((product(X) :- X, call(X))).
                               Undefined.
```

```
retract(X).                    instantiation_error
```

```
retract(4).                    type_error(callable, 4)
```

```
retract(atom(_)).              permission_error(access,
                                          static_procedure, atom/1).
```

80 set_input/1   *Stream selection and control*

Sets the current input stream.

▷ **How to use it:**   set_input(@stream_or_alias)

Example: set_input('user-input').

▷ **Description:** set_input(Stream_or_alias)

— If Stream_or_alias is a stream-term or alias of an open stream which is not
an output stream **then** sets the current input stream to Stream_or_alias
and succeeds with empty substitution.

▷ **Error cases**

Conditions	Error-term
o Stream_or_alias is a variable	instantiation_error
o Stream_or_alias is neither a variable nor a stream-term or alias	domain_error(stream_or_alias, Stream_or_alias)
o Stream_or_alias is not associated with an open stream	existence_error(stream, Stream_or_alias)
o Stream_or_alias is associated with an output stream	permission_error(input, stream, Stream_or_alias)

▷ **Examples**

Assume there is an open input stream with alias 'mickey' and the
current input stream is 'user_input'.

```
set_input('mickey').    Succeeds,
                        and the current input stream is now 'mickey'.

set_input(Mickey).      instantiation_error
```

81 set_output/1   *Stream selection and control*

Sets the current output stream.

▷ **How to use it:**   set_output(@stream_or_alias)

Example: set_output('user-output').

▷ **Description:** set_output(Stream_or_alias)

− If Stream_or_alias is a stream-term or alias of an open stream which is not an input stream **then** sets the current output stream to Stream_or_alias and succeeds with empty substitution.

▷ **Error cases**

Conditions	Error-term
○ Stream_or_alias is a variable	instantiation_error
○ Stream_or_alias is neither a variable nor a stream-term or alias	domain_error(stream_or_alias, Stream_or_alias)
○ Stream_or_alias is not associated with an open stream	existence_error(stream, Stream_or_alias)
○ Stream_or_alias is associated with an input stream	permission_error(output, stream, Stream_or_alias)

▷ **Examples**

Assume there is an open output stream with alias 'mickey' and the current output stream is 'user_output'.

set_output('mickey'). Succeeds,
                      and the current output stream is now 'mickey'.

set_output(Mickey).   instantiation_error

82 set_prolog_flag/2   *Flag updates*

Assigns a value to a flag.

▷ **How to use it:**   set_prolog_flag(+flag, @term)

Example: set_prolog_flag(unknown, fail).

▷ **Description:** set_prolog_flag(Flag, Value)

− **If** Flag is a valid changeable flag of the processor and Value is one of
  the autorized value for this flag **then** the current value of the flag Flag is
  updated to Value and succeeds with empty local substitution.

▷ **Error cases**

Conditions	Error-term
○ Flag or Value is a variable	instantiation_error
○ Flag is neither a variable nor an atom	type_error(atom, Flag)
○ Flag is an atom but an invalid flag for the processor	domain_error(prolog_flag, Flag)
○ Flag is an atom and a valid flag but Value is inappropriate for Flag	domain_error(flag_value, Flag + Value)
○ Flag is an atom and a valid flag and Value is appropriate, but Flag is not changeable	permission_error(modify, flag, Flag)

▷ **Examples**

```
set_prolog_flag(unknown, fail).
                        Succeeds,
        after updating the value of the flag 'unknown' to 'fail'.

set_prolog_flag(max_arity, 1000000000).
                        permission_error(modify, flag, max_arity)
```

83 set_stream_position/2   *Stream selection and control*

Assigns a given position to the position property of a given stream.

▷ **How to use it:**   set_stream_position(@stream_or_alias,
                                  @stream_position)

Example: set_stream_position(mickey, 1).

▷ **Description:** set_stream_position(Stream_or_alias, Position)

– If Stream_or_alias is a stream-term or alias of an open stream with property reposition(true) and Position is a stream position term **then** sets the current stream position of the stream to Position and succeeds with empty substitution.

NOTE — Position is an **implementation dependent** ground term. Therefore, usually, it will previously have been returned as a position/1 stream property of the stream.

▷ **Error cases**

Conditions	Error-term
○ Stream_or_alias is a variable	instantiation_error
○ Stream_or_alias is neither a variable nor a stream-term or alias	domain_error(stream_or_alias, Stream_or_alias)
○ Stream_or_alias is not associated with an open stream	existence_error(stream, Stream_or_alias)
○ Stream_or_alias has stream property reposition(false)	permission_error(reposition, stream, Stream_or_alias)
○ Position is a variable	instantiation_error
○ Position is neither a variable nor a stream position term	domain_error(stream_position, Position)

▷ **Examples**

```
Assume there is an input stream with alias 'mickey' which has
        properties:    reposition(true), position('end_of_file').
  set_stream_position(mickey, 1).  Succeeds after repositioning the
        stream 'mickey' and updating its position property with
        position(1).
        (The stream position term is implementation dependent)
```

84 setof/3

Assembles as a list the solutions of a goal for each different instantiation of the free variables in that goal. Each list is sorted (with duplicates removed) but the order in which each list is found is **undefined**.

▷ **How to use it:**   setof(@term, +body_term, ?list)

Example: setof(A, legs(A,N), B).

▷ **Description:** setof(Template, Sgoal, Slist)

– If the bagof-subgoal[23] G of Sgoal is a well-formed body-term different from a variable,
  let W be a witness of the free variables[23] of (Template ^ Sgoal), and
  let S be the list, solution of findall([W,Template], G, S),
  – If S is the empty list, **then** fails.
  – If S is a non-empty list, **then** let Lp be the list of pairs (L, ϕ) such that:
    - assuming S' is a sublist of (not already used) elements of S, formed by one element of S (the choice is **undefined**), say [w, t], and all the other elements of S, [w', t'], such that w and w' are variants. The elements in S' are ordered according to the total order defined by the relation *term-precedes* after elimination of duplicates[24]. And
    - ϕ is a unifier (3.2) of all terms w's in S' and W (it always exists), and L is the list formed with the terms tϕ such that the [w, t]'s are elements of S', in the same order, and Slistϕ and L are NSTO and unifiable.
    • If Lp is the empty list, **then** fails.
    • If Lp is a non-empty list, **then** succeeds with local substitution $\phi\sigma$ where σ is the unifier of Slistϕ and L and (L, ϕ) is an element of Lp not yet used.

NOTES:
1– According to the definition of findall/3, the transformed bagof-subgoal is executed.
2– setof/3 is re-executable as long as Lp is not empty, using not already chosen elements of the list Lp (**undefined** order).
3– setof/3 behaves like **bagof/3** except that the lists are sorted instead as being in solution order.

---

[23] See the Glossary.
[24] When two compared subterms are different variables this order is **implementation dependent**, but it must remain the same when ordering S'.

4– The order used for term ordering may not be the same (**implementation de-pendent**) for the lists produced for different solutions.

5– The number of elements of the list Lp, as the behaviour of setof/3, may be **undefined** if some tried pairs are STO.

6– If (Template ^ Sgoal) has no free variable and call(G) has at least one solution the predicate succeeds with one solution only.

7– The variables of Template and the non free variables of Sgoal remain uninstantiated after each success of setof(Template, Sgoal, Slist).

8– In most applications, the free variables are bound to ground terms after each success of the bagof-subgoal. In this case there is no need to consider the substitution ϕ in the definition, which becomes simpler.

▷ Error cases

Conditions	Error-term
○ The bagof-subgoal G of Sgoal is a variable	instantiation_error
○ The bagof-subgoal G of Sgoal is neither a variable nor a callable term nor a well-formed body-term	type_error(callable, G)
○ Slist is neither a variable nor a partial list nor a list	type_error(list, Slist)

▷ Examples

```
Assume the database contains the user-defined procedures:
                member/2, legs/2, insect/1, animal/1, spider/1
```

```
with the clauses:      legs(A, 6)        :- insect(A).
                       legs(A, 4)        :- animal(A).
                       legs(A, 8)        :- spider(A).
                       insect(bee)       :- true.
                       insect(ant)       :- true.
                       animal(horse)     :- true.
                       animal(cat)       :- true.
                       animal(dog)       :- true.
                       spider(tarantula) :- true.
                       member(X, [X | L]) :- true.
                       member(X, [Y | L]) :- member(X, L).
```

```
setof(A, legs(A,N), B).  Succeeds three times with substitutions:
                         { B <- [cat, dog, horse], N <- 4 }.
                         { B <- [tarantula],        N <- 8 };
                         { B <- [ant, bee],         N <- 6 };
   (undefined order, the free variable set is {N}, A remains unbound)
```

```
setof(N-L, bagof(A, legs(A,N), L), S).
                    Succeeds with substitution:
   {        S <- [4-[horse, cat, dog], 6-[bee, ant], 8-[tarantula]] }
   (the free variable set is empty, A remains unbound)
```

setof(X, (X=2; X=2), S). Succeeds once with substitution: {S <- [2]}
(the free variable set is empty, X remains unbound)

setof(X, (X=Y; X=Z), S). Succeeds once with substitution:
                                    { S <- [Y, Z] }, or { S <- [Z, Y] }
(implementation dependent)

setof(X, (Y^(X=1 ; Y=2) ; X=3), S).
                                Raises firstly a warning:
"the procedure '^'/2 is undefined."
(Assuming there is no definition for the procedure '^'/2, and
that the value associated with flag 'undefined_predicate'is
warning.), then   Succeeds with substitution: { S <- [3] }
(the free variable set is {Y})

setof(X, member(X,[V,U,f(U),f(V)]), L).
                                Succeeds with substitution:
                        { L <- [U,V,f(U),f(V)] } or { [V,U,f(V),f(U)]. }
(implementation dependent, the free variable set is {U,V})

setof(X, member(X,[V,U,f(U),f(V)]),[a,b,f(a),f(b)]).
                                Succeeds with substitution:
                            { U <- a, V <- b } or { U <- b, V <- a }
(implementation dependent, the free variable set is {U,V})

setof(X, (exists(U,V)^member(X,[V,U,f(U),f(V)])), [a,b,f(b),f(a)]).
                                Succeeds.   (empty free variable set)

setof(X, member(X,[V,U,f(U),f(V)]), [a,b,f(b),f(a)]).
                                Fails.

setof(f(X,Y), X = Y, [f(g(Z),Z)]).
                                Undefined.

setof(X, X^(true ; 4), L).
                                type_error(callable, (true ; 4))

85 stream_property/2 *Stream selection and control*

Enumerates all the pairs of open streams together with their properties.

▷ **How to use it:**   stream_property(?stream, ?stream_property)

Example: stream_property(S, file_name(F)).

▷ **Description:** stream_property(Stream, Stream_property)

- If Stream is a variable or a stream-term and Stream_property a variable
  or a valid stream property term, **then**
  let *SP* be the set of all pairs (S,P) such that S is the stream-term of
  a currently open stream which has property P and (S,P) and (Stream,
  Stream_property) are unifiable (3.2),
    - if *SP* is empty **then** fails.
    - if *SP* is not empty **then** if (Stream, Stream_property) and one not
      already chosen element (S,P) of *SP* (the choice is **implementation
      dependent**) are unifiable by substitution σ **then** succeeds with local
      substitution σ.

NOTE — stream_property/2 is re-executable as many times as there are elements
in *SP*.

▷ **Error cases**

Conditions	Error-term
○ Stream is neither a variable nor a stream-term	domain_error(stream, Stream)
○ Stream_property is neither a variable nor a valid stream property	domain_error(stream_property, Stream_property)

▷ Examples

```
stream_property(S, file_name(F)).
 Succeeds as many times as there are open streams with substitution:
          { S <- a stream-term,
               F <- the name of the file to which it is connected }; ...

stream_property(S, output).
 Succeeds as many times as there are open output streams
                                                with substitution:
          { S <- a stream-term }; ...

stream_property(S, property).
  domain_error(stream_property, property)
```

86 sub_atom/5   *Atomic term processing*

Enumeration of subatoms with their position and length.

▷ **How to use it:**   sub_atom(+atom, ?integer, ?integer,
                          ?integer, ?atom)

Example: sub_atom(anna, L1, 2, L2, A).

▷ **Description:** sub_atom(Atom, Before, Length, After, Sub_atom)

— If Atom is an atom, and Sub_atom is a variable or an atom, and Before,
Length and After are variables or non-negative integers **then**
let S be the list, ordered[25] according to the term ordering relation, of all
quadruples (11, 12, 13, A2) such that the name of Atom is the concatenation of the possibly empty character sequences A1, A2 and A3, whose
repective lengths are 11, 12, 13, and (11, 12, 13, A2) and (Before,
Length, After, Sub_atom) are unifiable (3.2) then
   — if S is empty **then** fails.
   — if S is not empty **then if** (Before, Length, After, Sub_atom) and the
   first not already chosen element (11, 12, 13, A2) of S are unifiable by
   the substitution σ **then** succeeds with local substitution σ.

NOTES:
1– sub_atom/5 is re-executable as many times as there are elements in S. The order
of the solutions follows the order of the list S (it is **implementation defined**
according to the char-code mapping 9.1.3).
2– The three lengths correspond respectively to the number of characters *before*
the sub-atom, the *length* of the sub-atom and the number of characters *after*
the sub-atom.

▷ **Error cases**

Conditions	Error-term
○ Atom is a variable	instantiation_error
○ Atom is neither a variable nor an atom	type_error(atom, Atom)
○ Before is neither a variable nor an integer	type_error(integer, Before)
○ Before is an integer that is less than zero	domain_error(not_less_than_zero, Before)

---

[25] The **implementation dependent** ordering on the variables is constant during
sorting.

o `Length` is neither a variable nor an integer	`type_error(integer, Length)`
o `Length` is an integer that is less than zero	`domain_error(not_less_than_zero, Length)`
o `After` is neither a variable nor an integer	`type_error(integer, Length)`
o `After` is an integer that is less than zero	`domain_error(not_less_than_zero, After)`
o `Sub_atom` is neither a variable nor an atom	`type_error(atom, Sub_atom)`

▷ Examples

```
sub_atom(anna, L1, 2, L2, A). Succeeds 3 times with substitutions:
                             { L1 <- 0, L2 <- 2, A <- 'an' };
                             { L1 <- 1, L2 <- 1, A <- 'nn' };
                             { L1 <- 2, L2 <- 0, A <- 'na' }.

sub_atom(abracadabra, 0, 5, X, S).
                         Succeeds with substitution:
                                 { X <- 6, S <- 'abrac' }.

sub_atom(abracadabra, B, 2, A, ab).
                         Succeeds twice with substitutions:
                                 { B <- 0,  A <- 9 };
                                 { B <- 7,  A <- 2 }.

sub_atom(abracadabra, X, 5, 0, S2).
                         Succeeds with substitution:
                                 { X <- 6, S2 <- 'dabra' }.

sub_atom('ab', B, L, A, Sa).    Succeeds 6 times with substitutions:
                         { B <- 0, L <- 0, A <- 2, Sa <- ''  };
                         { B <- 0, L <- 1, A <- 1, Sa <- a  };
                         { B <- 0, L <- 2, A <- 0, Sa <- ab };
                         { B <- 1, L <- 0, A <- 1, Sa <- ''  };
                         { B <- 1, L <- 1, A <- 0, Sa <- b  };
                         { B <- 2, L <- 0, A <- 0, Sa <- ''  }.

sub_atom('ab', B, L, A, 'ba'). Fails.

sub_atom('ab', B, 'a', A, 'ba').
                             type_error(integer, 'a')
```

87 (@>)/2 : term greater than   *Term comparison*

Tests whether the second argument term-precedes the first.

▷ **How to use it:**   @term @> @term

'@>'/2 is a predefined infix operator. Its priority is 700 and it is non-associative (**xfx**).

Example: foo(b) @> foo(a).

▷ **Description:** Term₁ @> Term₂

– **If** Term₂ *term_precedes* (2.1.2) Term₁ **then** succeeds with empty local substitution **else** fails.

▷ **Error cases**
None.

▷ **Examples**

foo(b) @> foo(a)	Succeeds.
'@>'(1, 1.0).	Succeeds.
north(a) @> foo(a, b)	Succeeds.
foo(b, Y) @> foo(a, X)).	Succeeds.
foo(X, a) @> foo(Y, b).	Succeeds or Fails. (implementation dependent)
north(a) @> south(a).	Fails.

88 (@>=)/2 : term greater than or equal   *Term comparison*

Tests whether the second argument is identical to or term-precedes the first.

▷ **How to use it:**   @term @>= @term

'@>='/2 is a predefined infix operator. Its priority is 700 and it is non-associative (**xfx**).

Example: foo(b) @>= foo(a).

▷ **Description:** Term$_1$ @>= Term$_2$

– **If** Term$_2$ is indentical to or *term_precedes* (2.1.2) Term$_1$ **then** succeeds with empty local substitution **else** fails.

▷ **Error cases**
   None.

▷ **Examples**

foo(b) @>= foo(a).	Succeeds.
X @>= X.	Succeeds.
'@>='(1, 1.0).	Succeeds.
north(a) @>= foo(a, b)	Succeeds.
foo(b, Y) @>= foo(a, X)).	Succeeds.
'@>='(foo(b, X), foo(a, Y)).	Succeeds.
north(a) @>= south(a).	Fails.
'@>='(short, shorter).	Fails.
foo(X, a) @>= foo(Y, b).	Succeeds or Fails. (Implementation dependent)

89 (==)/2 : term identical   *Term comparison*

Tests whether both arguments are identical.

▷ **How to use it:**   @term == @term

'=='/2 is a predefined infix operator. Its priority is 700 and it is non-associative (**xfx**).

Example: f(X,X) == f(X, X).

▷ **Description:** Term$_1$ == Term$_2$

– **If** Term$_1$ and Term$_2$ are identical **then** succeeds with empty local substitution **else** fails.

▷ **Error cases**
  None.

▷ **Examples**

```
f(X,X) == f(X,X).              Succeeds.

X = Y, X == Y.                 Succeeds once with substitution:
                                      { X <- Y } or { Y <- X }
                               (implementation dependent)

X = f(g(A,B),g(A,B)), X = f(U,V), U == V.
                               Succeeds with substitution:
                      { X <- f(g(A,B),g(A,B)), U <- g(A,B), V <- g(A,B) }

1.0e+1 == 10.0.                Succeeds.

     X ==  Y.                  Fails.

f(X,X) == f(X,Y).             Fails.

     1 == 1.0.                 Fails.
```

90 (@<)/2 : term less than   *Term comparison*

Tests whether the first argument term-precedes the second.

▷ How to use it: @term @< @term

'@<'/2 is a predefined infix operator. Its priority is 700 and it is non-associative (xfx).

Example: foo(a) @< foo(b).

▷ Description: Term₁ @< Term₂

$-$ If Term₁ *term_precedes* (2.1.2) Term₂ then succeeds with empty local substitution else fails.

▷ Error cases
None.

▷ Examples

foo(a) @< foo(b).	Succeeds.
1.0 @< 1.	Succeeds.
foo(a, X) @< foo(b, Y).	Succeeds.
foo(X, b) @< foo(Y, a).	Succeeds with empty substitution or fails. (implementation dependent)
foo(a, b) @< north(a).	Fails.

91 (@=<)/2 : term less than or equal   *Term comparison*

Tests whether the first argument is identical to or term-precedes the second.

▷ **How to use it:**   @term @=< @term

'@=<'/2 is a predefined infix operator. Its priority is 700 and it is non-associative (**xfx**).

Example: foo(a) @=< foo(b).

▷ **Description:** Term₁ @=< Term₂

– **If** Term₁ is indentical to or *term_precedes* (2.1.2) Term₂ **then** succeeds with empty local substitution **else** fails.

▷ **Error cases**
   None.

▷ **Examples**

foo(a) @=< foo(b).	Succeeds.
aardvark @=< zebra.	Succeeds.
short @=< short.	Succeeds.
short @=< shorter.	Succeeds.
foo(a, X) @=< foo(b, Y).	Succeeds.
'@=<'(X, X).	Succeeds.
'@=<'(X, Y).	Succeeds or Fails. (implementation dependent)
'@=<'(foo(X, b), foo(Y, a)).	Succeeds or Fails. (implementation dependent)

---

92 (\==)/2 : term not identical   *Term comparison*

Tests whether the arguments are different terms.

▷ **How to use it:**   @term \== @term

'\\==' /2 is a predefined infix operator. Its priority is 700 and it is non-associative (**xfx**).

Example: f(X,X) \== f(X, Y).

▷ **Description:** Term₁ \== Term₂

– **If** Term₁ and Term₂ are not identical **then** succeeds with empty local substitution **else** fails.

▷ **Error cases**
  None.

▷ **Examples**

```
f(X,X) \== f(X,Y).      Succeeds.

     X \==  Y.          Succeeds.

f(X,X) \== f(a, X)      Succeeds.

f(X,X) \== f(X,X).      Fails.

1.0e+1 \== 10.0.        Fails.
```

93 throw/1 : exception handling: error throwing *Logic and control*

Raises an error and throws a "ball" to be caught by some ancestor "catcher" (see catch/3).

▷ **How to use it:**   throw(+term)

Example: `catch(throw(exit(1)), exit(X), write(X))`.

▷ **Description:** throw(Ball)

– If `Ball` is not a variable, the execution model (see Section 4.3.3) reacts as follows:
  It seeks in the search tree for the closest ancestor node whose chosen predication has the form `catch(Goal, Catcher, Recovergoal)`, which is still executing its `Goal` argument[26] and such that a freshly renamed copy `Ball'` of `Ball` unifies with `Catcher` by substitution σ.
  – If there is no such ancestor then a "system-error" is raised (see below) and the behaviour is **implementation dependent**.
  – If there is such ancestor node whose goal label is `(catch(Goal, Catcher, Recovergoal), Cont)`[27] then
    (1) all the nodes between the current node and the ancestor are made deterministic (none of these nodes can thus be selected by backtracking) and
    (2) a second child is added to the ancestor node whose labels are the substitution σ and the goal `(call(Recovergoal), Cont)`σ,
    and backtracks (4.2.6). The execution will thus continue, with the new child as current node, at step (2.) of algorithm 4.2.5.

▷ **Error cases**

Conditions	Error-term
o `Ball` is a variable	`instantiation_error`
o A freshly renamed copy of `Ball` does not unify with the catcher argument of any ancestor node whose chosen predication is `catch/3`	`system_error`

---

[26] and not **Recovergoal**.
[27] If Cont is empty, then one assumes Cont = true.

▷ Examples

Assume the database contains the user-defined procedures:
                              p/0, q/0, r/1

with the clauses: p   :- true.   r(X) :- throw(X).
                           p   :- throw(b).

                           q   :- catch(p, B, write('hellop ')), r(c).


```
catch(throw(exit(1)), exit(X), write(X)).
                              Succeeds with substitution  { X <- 1 }
                              after outputting: 1

catch(q, C, write(helloq)).   Succeeds with substitution  { C <- c }
                              after outputting: helloq

catch(throw(true), X,X).      Succeeds with substitution
                                                      { X <- true }

catch(throw(fail), X, X).     Fails.

catch(throw(f(X,X)), f(X, g(X)), write(may_be)).
                              Undefined.

catch(throw(1), X, (fail;X)). type_error(callable, (fail;1))

catch(throw(fail), true, G).  system_error
```

94 true/0   *Logic and control*

Succeeds.

▷ **How to use it:**   true

Example: X =1, true, Y = 2.

▷ **Description:** true

— Succeeds with empty local substitution.

More precisely **true** is a basic goal used in the description of the search-tree visit and construction algorithm (see Section 4.2.5). If the current goal is (**true,G**), then the new current goal becomes G. If the current goal is **true**, then it corresponds to a success branch, and the execution continues with backtracking (Section 4.2.6).

▷ **Error cases**
None.

▷ **Examples**

```
X =1, true, Y = 2.      Succeeds with substitution { X <- 1, Y <- 2 }
                        (it behaves exactly like:    X =1, Y = 2.)

(X = Y -> fail; true). Is equivalent to: X \= Y.
```

---

95 (\=)/2 : (not Prolog) unifiable   *Term unification*

Tests whether two terms are not unifiable

▷ **How to use it:**   ?term \= ?term

'\\='/2 is a predefined infix operator. Its priority is 700 and it is non-associative (**xfx**).

Example: f(a,X) \= f(X,b).

▷ **Description:** Term₁ \= Term₂

- If Term₁ and Term₂ are *NSTO* (3.3.3) and not unifiable **then** succeeds with empty local substitution.
- If Term₁ and Term₂ are *NSTO* and unifiable **then** fails.
- If Term₁ and Term₂ are *STO* **then** the result is **undefined** (failure, success, loop or error are possible behaviours[28]).

▷ **Error cases**
  None.

▷ **Examples**

```
f(a,X) \= f(X,b).        Succeeds.

'\\='(1, 1.0).           Succeeds.

f(X, a) \= f(g(Y), Y).   Fails.

f(1, X) \=  f(2, a(X)).  Undefined.
            (STO case by possible equalisation of the second arguments,
                        a success in most existing processors).
```

---

[28] X = f(X), Y = f(Y), X \= Y may succeed, loop, fail or raise an error message. Succeeds if rational ("infinite") terms are allowed, loops if the unification does not terminate, fails on conforming processors with occurs-check test, raises an error message on strictly conforming processors (in a debugging mode for example).

96 (=)/2 : (Prolog) unify   *Term unification*

Explicit Prolog unification of two terms. Both arguments are made equal.

▷ **How to use it:**   ?term = ?term

'='/2 is a predefined infix operator. Its priority is 700 and it is non-associative (**xfx**).

Example: `f(X, a) = f(g(Y), Y).`

▷ **Description:** Term₁ = Term₂

— If Term₁ and Term₂ are $NSTO$ (3.3.3) and unifiable by substitution σ **then** succeeds with local substitution σ.
— If Term₁ and Term₂ are $NSTO$ and not unifiable **then** fails.
— If Term₁ and Term₂ are STO **then** the result is **undefined** (success, failure, loop or error are possible behaviours[29]).

▷ **Error cases**
None.

▷ **Examples**

```
f(X, a) = f(g(Y), Y).        Succeeds with substitution:
                                     { X <- g(a), Y <- a }

g(X) = f(a).                 Fails.

f(1, X) = f(2, a(X)).        Undefined.
(STO case by possible equalisation of the second arguments,
                a failure in most existing processors).
```

---

[29] `X = f(X)`, `Y = f(Y)`, `X = Y` may succeed, loop, fail or raise an error message. Succeeds if rational ("infinite") terms are allowed, loops if the unification does not terminate, fails on conforming processors with occurs-check test, raises an error message on strictly conforming processors (in a debugging mode for example).

97 unify_with_occurs_check/2 : unify   *Term unification*

(First order) logical unification of two terms. Both arguments are made identical.

▷ **How to use it:**   unify_with_occurs_check(?term, ?term)

Example: unify_with_occurs_check(f(a,X), f(X,a)).

▷ **Description:** unify_with_occurs_check(Term₁, Term₂)

– **If Term₁** and **Term₂** are unifiable (3.2) by the substitution σ **then** succeeds with local substitution σ.
– **If Term₁** and **Term₂** are not unifiable **then** fails.

▷ **Error cases**
   None.

▷ **Examples**

```
unify_with_occurs_check(f(a,X), f(X,a)). Succeeds with substitution:
                                                     { X <- a }

unify_with_occurs_check(X, g(X)).         Fails.

unify_with_occurs_check(f(X, Y, X, 1), f(a(X), a(Y), Y, 2)).
                                          Fails.

unify_with_occurs_check(f(1, X),f(2, a(X))).
                                          Fails.
```

---

98 (=..)/2 : univ   *Term creation and decomposition*

Term construction or decomposition.

In the case of success the second argument is the list whose head is the principal functor of the first argument and the tail the list of its arguments.

▷ **How to use it:**   +nonvar =.. ?list
                       -term =.. +list

'=..'/2 is a predefined infix operator. Its priority is 700 and it is non-associative (**xfx**).

Example: f(a,b) =.. [X | Y].

▷ **Description:** Term =.. List

- if Term is a compound term of the form $f(t_1, t_2, \ldots, t_n)$, $n > 0$ and List is a variable or an *acceptable list*[30], and List and $[f, t_1, t_2, \ldots, t_n]$ are NSTO (3.3.3) **then if** they are unifiable by substitution σ **then** succeeds with local substitution σ **else** fails.
- if Term is a compound term of the form $f(t_1, t_2, \ldots, t_n)$, $n > 0$ and List is a variable or an *acceptable list* and List and $[f, t_1, t_2, \ldots, t_n]$ are STO **then undefined.**
- if Term is atomic (an atom or a number) and List is is a variable or an *acceptable list* **then if** [Term] is unifiable with List by substitution σ **then** succeeds with local substitution σ **else** fails.
- if Term is a variable and List is a list of the form $[c]$ such that c is atomic **then** succeeds with local substitution { Term ← c }.
- if Term is a variable and List is a list of the form $[f, t_1, t_2, \ldots, t_n]$, $0 < n < maxarity$ such that f is an atom **then** succeeds with local substitution { Term ← $f(t_1, t_2, \ldots, t_n)$ }.

▷ **Error cases**

Conditions	Error-term
○ Term is a variable and List is not a list	instantiation_error

---

[30] An *acceptable list* is either an *empty list*, or a *singleton list* with a variable or a number as element, or a *nonempty list* whose head is a variable or an atom and its tail is a list of terms, or a *partial list*.

○ **Term** is a variable and **List** is a list whose head is a variable	`instantiation_error`
○ **Term** is a variable and **List** is the empty list	`domain_error(non_empty_list, List)`
○ **Term** is a variable and **List** is a list whose tail has a length greater than the **implementation defined** integer *maxarity*	`representation_error(max_arity)`
○ **List** is a list whose head **H** is neither an atom nor a variable, and whose tail is not the empty list	`type_error(atom, H)`
○ **List** is a list whose head **H** is a compound term, and whose tail is the empty list	`type_error(atomic, H)`
○ **List** is neither a variable nor a partial list nor a list	`type_error(list, List)`

▷ Examples

`f(a,b) =.. [X	Y].`	Succeeds with substitution: `{ X <- f, Y <- [a,b] }`
`f(a,b) =.. L.`	Succeeds with substitution: `{ L <- [f, a, b] }`
`T =.. [f, X, 1].`	Succeeds with substitution: `{ T <- f(X,1) }`
`foo(a, b) =.. [foo, b, a].`	Fails.
`f(X) =.. [f, u(X)].`	Undefined.
`X =.. [foo, a	Y].`	`instantiation_error`
`foo(a,b)  =.. [foo(X,Y)].`	`type_error(atomic, foo(X,Y))`

99 var/1   *Type testing*

Tests whether the argument is a variable.

▷ **How to use it:**   var(?term)

Example: var(X).

▷ **Description:** var(Term)

− **If** Term is a variable **then** succeeds with empty local substitution.
− **If** Term is not a variable (it is thus an atom, a number or a compound
term) **then** fails.

▷ **Error cases**
None.

▷ **Examples**

var(X).	Succeeds.
var(X), X = f(Y).	Succeeds with substitution { X <- f(Y) }
X = Y , var(X).	Succeeds with substitution { X <- Y } (or { Y <- X }, implementaion dependent)
X = f(Y) , var(X).	Fails.
var(a).	Fails.

100 write/1   *Term input/output*

Outputs a term to the current output stream in a form which is defined by
the option list [numbervars(true), quoted(false), ignore_ops(false)].

▷ **How to use it:**   write(?term)

Example: write(X = a).

▷ **Description:** write(Term)

– **If** the current output stream is not a binary stream,
   then outputs the term Term, freshly renamed, to the current output stream
   in a form which is defined by the write-options list [numbervars(true),
   quoted(false), ignore_ops(false)] (7.4.2), changes the stream position to take account of the characters which have been output, and succeeds
   with empty local substitution.

NOTE — It behaves like:
   current_output(S), write_term(S, Term, [numbervars(true)]).

▷ **Error cases**

Conditions	Error-term
○ The current output stream is associated with a binary stream OS	permission_error(output, binary_stream, OS)

▷ **Examples**

Assume the contents of the current output text stream are:
                                                        ... term.

write(X = a).   Succeeds with empty substitution, and
   the current output stream is left as: ... term._001=a
   (the part of the variable name '001' is implementation dependent)

write('$VAR'(51)).   Succeeds with empty substitution, and
   the current output stream is left as: ... term.Z1

101 write/2   *Term input/output*

Outputs a term to a text stream in a form which is defined by the write-option list [numbervars(true), quoted(false), ignore_ops(false)].

▷ **How to use it:**   write(@stream_or_alias, ?term)

Example: write(mickey, X = a).

▷ **Description:** write(Stream_or_alias, Term)

– If Stream_or_alias is the stream-term or alias of an open stream which is neither an input nor a binary stream,
then outputs the term Term, freshly renamed, in a form which is defined by the write-options list [numbervars(true), quoted(false), ignore_ops(false)] (7.4.2), changes the stream position to take account of the characters which have been output, and succeeds with empty local substitution.

NOTE — It behaves like:
    write_term(S, Term, [numbervars(true)]).

▷ **Error cases**

Conditions	Error-term
○ Stream_or_alias is a variable	instantiation_error
○ Stream_or_alias is neither a variable nor a stream-term or alias	domain_error(stream_or_alias, Stream_or_alias)
○ Stream_or_alias is not associated with an open stream	existence_error(stream, Stream_or_alias)
○ Stream_or_alias is associated with an input stream	permission_error(output, stream, Stream_or_alias)
○ Stream_or_alias is associated with a binary stream	permission_error(output, binary_stream, Stream_or_alias)

▷ Examples

Assume the contents of the open output text stream associated
with 'mickey' are: ... term.

write(mickey, X = a).   Succeeds with empty substitution, and
  the stream associated with 'mickey' is left as: ... term._001=a
  (the part of the variable name '001' is implementation dependent)

write(mickey, '$VAR'(51)).   Succeeds with empty substitution, and
  the stream associated with 'mickey' is left as: ... term.Z1

write(X, '$VAR'(51)).   instantiation_error

102 write_canonical/1   *Term input/output*

Outputs a term to the current output stream in a form which is defined by the option list [quoted(true), numbervars(false), ignore_ops(true)].

▷ **How to use it:**   write_canonical(?term)

Example: write_canonical(X = a).

▷ **Description:** write_canonical(Term)

– **If** the current output stream is not a binary stream,
   then outputs the term Term, freshly renamed, to the current output stream in a form which is defined by the write-options list [quoted(true), numbervars(false), ignore_ops(true)] (7.4.2), changes the stream position to take account of the characters which have been output, and succeeds with empty local substitution.

NOTE — It behaves like:
   current_output(S), write_term(S, Term, [quoted(true),
                                          ignore_ops(true)]).

▷ **Error cases**

Conditions	Error-term
○ The current output stream is associated with a binary stream OS	permission_error(output, binary_stream, OS)

▷ **Examples**

```
Assume the contents of the current output text stream are:
                                                    ... term.

write_canonical(X = a).        Succeeds with empty substitution,
    and the stream associated with mickey is left as:
                                        ... term.=(_001,a)
    (the part of the variable name '001' is implementation dependent)

write_canonical([1,2,3]).      Succeeds with empty substitution,
    and the current output stream is left as: ... term..(1,.(2,.(3,[])))
```

103 write_canonical/2   *Term input/output*

Outputs a term to a text stream in a form which is defined by the option list [quoted(true), numbervars(false), ignore_ops(true)].

▷ **How to use it:**   write_canonical(@stream_or_alias, ?term)

Example: write_canonical(mickey, X = a).

▷ **Description:** write_canonical(Stream_or_alias, Term)

– **if** Stream_or_alias is a stream-term or alias of an open stream which is neither an input nor a binary stream,
  then outputs the term Term, freshly renamed, in a form which is defined by the write-options list [quoted(true), numbervars(false), ignore_ops(true)] (7.4.2), changes the stream position to take account of the characters which have been output, and succeeds with empty local substitution.

NOTE — It behaves like:
    write_term(Stream_or_alias, Term, [quoted(true), ignore_ops(true)]).

▷ **Error cases**

Conditions	Error-term
○ Stream_or_alias is a variable	instantiation_error
○ Stream_or_alias is neither a variable nor a stream-term or alias	domain_error(stream_or_alias, Stream_or_alias)
○ Stream_or_alias is not associated with an open stream	existence_error(stream, Stream_or_alias)
○ Stream_or_alias is associated with an input stream	permission_error(output, stream, Stream_or_alias)
○ Stream_or_alias is associated with a binary stream	permission_error(output, binary_stream, Stream_or_alias)

▷ Examples

Assume the contents of the open output text stream associated
with 'mickey' are: ... term.

write_canonical(mickey, 'X = a'). Succeeds with empty substitution,
  and the stream associated with 'mickey' is left as:
                                          ... term.'X = a'

write_canonical(mickey, X = a).   Succeeds with empty substitution,
  and the stream associated with 'mickey' is left as:
                                          ... term.=(X,a)

write_canonical(mickey, [1,2,3]). Succeeds with empty substitution,
  and the stream associated with 'mickey' is left as:
                                    ... term..(1,.(2,.(3,[])))

write_canonical(mickey, '$VAR'(51)).
                            Succeeds with empty substitution
and the stream associated with 'mickey' is left as:
                                          ... term.$VAR(51)

write_canonical(X, '$VAR'(51)).   instantiation_error

104 write_term/2   *Term input/output*

Outputs a term to the current output stream in a form which is defined by the given write-options list.

▷ **How to use it:**   write_term(?term, +write_options_list)

Example: write_term(X = a , [ignore_ops(true)]).

▷ **Description:** write_term(Term, Options)

– **If** Options is a list of valid write-options[31], with no variable as element, **then** outputs the term Term, freshly renamed, to the current output stream in a form which is defined in Section 7.4.3, changes the stream position to take account of the characters which have been output, and succeeds with empty local substitution.

NOTES:

1– It behaves like:
current_output(S), write_term(S, Term, Options).
2– The default option values are **false**.

▷ **Error cases**

Conditions	Error-term
○ Options is a variable	instantiation_error
○ Options is neither a variable nor a list	type_error(list, Options)
○ Options is a list with an element E which is a variable	instantiation_error
○ An element E of the Options list is neither a variable nor a valid write-option	domain_error(write_option, E)
○ The current output stream is associated with a binary stream OS	permission_error(output, binary_stream, OS)

---

[31] See the Glossary.

▷ Examples

Assume the contents of the current output text stream are:
```
                                                 ... term.
```

```
write_term(X = a , [ignore_ops(true)]).
```
Succeeds with empty substitution, and
the current output stream is left as: ... term.=(_001,a)
(the part of the variable name '001' is implementation dependent)

```
write_term([1,2,3], []).  Succeeds with empty substitution, and
```
the current output stream is left as: ... term.[1,2,3]

```
write_term('$VAR'(51), [numbervars(false)]).
```
Succeeds with empty substitution, and
the current output stream is left as: ... term.$VAR(51)

```
write_term('$VAR'(51), [numbervars(true)]).
```
Succeeds with empty substitution, and
the current output stream is left as: ... term.Z1

```
write_term('$VAR'(51), X). instantiation_error
```

```
write_term(3, [quoted(no), numbervars(false)]).
```
                    domain_error(write_option, quoted(no))

105 write_term/3   *Term input/output*

Outputs a term to a text stream in a form which is defined by the given write-options list.

▷ **How to use it:**   write_term(@stream_or_alias, ?term,
                                      +write_options_list)

Example: write_term(mickey, X = a, [ignore_ops(true)]).

▷ **Description:** write_term(Stream_or_alias, Term, Options)

– If Stream_or_alias is a stream-term or alias associated to an open stream
  which is neither an input nor a binary stream, and Options is a list of
  valid write-options[32] (7.4.2), with no variable as element,
  then outputs the term Term, freshly renamed, in a form which is defined in
  Section 7.4.3, changes the stream position to take account of the characters
  which have been output, and succeeds with empty local substitution.

NOTE — The default options values are false.

▷ **Error cases**

Conditions	Error-term
o Options is a variable	instantiation_error
o Options is neither a variable nor a list	type_error(list, Options)
o Options is a list with an element E which is a variable	instantiation_error
o An element E of the Options list is neither a variable nor a valid write-option	domain_error(write_option, E)
o Stream_or_alias is a variable	instantiation_error
o Stream_or_alias is neither a variable nor a stream-term or alias	domain_error(stream_or_alias, Stream_or_alias)
o Stream_or_alias is not associated with an open stream	existence_error(stream, Stream_or_alias)
o Stream_or_alias is associated with an input stream	permission_error(output, stream, Stream_or_alias)

---

[32] See the Glossary.

○ Stream_or_alias is associated with a bi-   permission_error(output,
   nary stream   binary_stream,
                                              Stream_or_alias)

▷ Examples

```
Assume the contents of the open output text stream associated with
alias 'mickey' are:                                      ... term.

write_term(mickey, X = a, [ignore_ops(true)]).
                    Succeeds with empty substitution, and
   the stream associated with 'mickey' is left as:  ... term.=(_001,a)
   (the part of the variable name '001' is implementation dependent)

write_term(mickey, [1,2,3], [])
                    Succeeds with empty substitution, and
   the stream associated with 'mickey' is left as:    ... term.[1,2,3]

write_term(mickey, '$VAR'(51), [numbervars(false)]).
                    Succeeds with empty substitution, and
   the stream associated with 'mickey' is left as:   ... term.$VAR(51)

write_term(mickey, '$VAR'(51), [numbervars(true)]).
                    Succeeds with empty substitution, and
   the stream associated with 'mickey' is left as:          ... term.Z1

write_term(mickey, '$VAR'(51), X).
                    instantiation_error

write_term(mickey, 3, [quoted(no), numbervars(false)]).
                    domain_error(write_option, quoted(no))
```

106 writeq/1

Outputs a term to the current output stream in a form which is defined by the option list `[quoted(true), numbervars(true), ignore_ops(false)]`.

▷ **How to use it:**   `writeq(?term)`

Example: `writeq(X = a).`

▷ **Description:** `writeq(Term)`

- **if** the current output stream is not a binary stream,
  then outputs the term `Term`, freshly renamed, to the current output stream in a form which is defined by the write-options list `[quoted(true), numbervars(true), ignore_ops(false)]` (7.4.2), changes the stream position to take account of the characters which have been output, and succeeds with empty local substitution.

NOTE — It behaves like:
     `current_output(S), write_term(S, Term, [quoted(true),`
                                              `numbervars(true)]).`

▷ **Error cases**

Conditions	Error-term
○ The current output stream is associated with a binary stream OS	`permission_error(output, binary_stream, OS)`

▷ **Examples**

```
Assume the contents of the current output text stream are:
                                                        ... term.

writeq(X = a).      Succeeds with empty substitution, and
    the current output stream is left as:              ... term.X=a

writeq('$VAR'(51)).   Succeeds with empty substitution, and
    the current output stream is left as:              ... term.Z1
```

107 writeq/2   *Term input/output*

Outputs a term to a text stream in a form which is defined by the option list [quoted(true), numbervars(true), ignore_ops(false)].

▷ **How to use it:**   writeq(@stream_or_alias, ?term)

Example: writeq(mickey, X = a).

▷ **Description:** writeq(Stream_or_alias, Term)

– If Stream_or_alias is a stream-term or alias associated to an open stream which is neither an input nor a binary stream,
  then outputs the term Term, freshly renamed, in a form which is defined by the write-options list [quoted(true), numbervars(true), ignore_ops-(false)] (7.4.2), changes the stream position to take account of the characters which have been output, and succeeds with empty local substitution.

NOTE — It behaves like:
    write_term(S, Term, [quoted(true), numbervars(true)]).

▷ **Error cases**

Conditions	Error-term
o Stream_or_alias is a variable	instantiation_error
o Stream_or_alias is neither a variable nor a stream-term or alias	domain_error(stream_or_alias, Stream_or_alias)
o Stream_or_alias is not associated with an open stream	existence_error(stream, Stream_or_alias)
o Stream_or_alias is associated with an input stream	permission_error(output, stream, Stream_or_alias)
o Stream_or_alias is associated with a binary stream	permission_error(output, binary_stream, Stream_or_alias)

▷ Examples

Assume the contents of the open output text stream associated with
'mickey' are: ... term.

```
writeq(mickey, X = a).      Succeeds with empty substitution, and
   the stream associated with 'mickey' is left as:        ... term.X=a

writeq(mickey, '$VAR'(51)). Succeeds with empty substitution, and
   the stream associated with 'mickey' is left as:        ... term.Z1

writeq(X, '$VAR'(51)).      instantiation_error
```

6. Prolog Arithmetic

6.1 Arithmetic expressions

6.1.1 Arithmetic terms

Some terms represent arithmetic expressions when they are in the following positions:

– the right–hand argument of the built-in predicate is/2,
– both arguments of the *arithmetic comparison* built-in predicates
  (=:=)/2, (=\=)/2, (<)/2, (>)/2, (=<)/2, (>=)/2.

In that case they will be formed as a term (according to the rules defined in Section 2.1.1), using arithmetic functors and numbers only, otherwise the evaluation of the expression raises an exception (see below).

The *arithmetic functors* that are permitted in expressions are listed in Table 6.1. Some of them are predefined operators in **Standard Prolog** (see Table 9.2.2 in Chapter 9).

6.1.2 Numbers

Numbers are partioned into two subsets denoted I (*integers*) and F (*floating–point numbers*).

– An *integer* is a member of a set I defined as follows (see Section 9.5.1 for the translation of an integer token into an integer).

It depends on the value of the flag bounded:
  – **false:** $I = \mathcal{Z}$, the mathematical relative integers.
  – **true :** $I = \{x \in \mathcal{Z} \mid minint \leq x \leq maxint\}$, where *minint* and *maxint* denote the values of the flags min_integer and max_integer respectively[1].

---

[1] In **Standard Prolog** *minint* and *maxint* satisfy:
$maxint > 0$

and one of: $minint = -(maxint)$
$minint = -(maxint + 1)$.

Table 6.1. Predefined arithmetic functors:
functors that can be used in arithmetic expressions.

abs/1	absolute value
'+'/2	addition
atan/1	arc tangent
'/\\'/2	bitwise and
'\\'/2	bitwise complement
'<<'/2	bitwise left shift
'\\/'/2	bitwise or
'>>'/2	bitwise right shift
ceiling/1	smallest integer not smaller than
cos/1	cosine
exp/1	natural antilogarithm
'**'/2	exponentiation
float/1	conversion to float
float_fractional_part/1	float fractional part
float_integer_part/1	float integer part
'/'/2	floating–point division
'//'/2	integer division
floor/1	largest integer not greater than
log/1	natural logarithm (base e)
mod/2	modulo
'*'/2	multiplication
rem/2	integer remainder
round/1	integer nearest to
sign/1	sign of
'-'/1	sign reversal
sin/1	sine
sqrt/1	square root
'-'/2	subtraction
truncate/1	integer equal to the integer part of

There is also another parameter, specified by the flag
integer_rounding_function, which influences the definitions of the integer division ('//'/2) and the integer remainder ('rem'/2).

- A *floating–point number* is a member of a set F defined as follows (see Section 9.5.1 for the translation of a float token into a floating–point number).

  F is a finite subset of $\mathcal{R}$ (the reals) characterized by five parameters:

  $r \in \mathcal{Z}$ (the radix of F)
  $p \in \mathcal{Z}$ (the precision of F)
  $emin \in \mathcal{Z}$ (the smallest exponent of F)
  $emax \in \mathcal{Z}$ (the largest exponent of F)
  $denorm \in \{\text{true, false}\}$
                         (whether F contains denormalized values)

More details may be found in the standard [2] or in Annex A.5.2 of ISO/IEC 10967-1 – Language Independent Arithmetic (LIA) [1].

6.2 Expression evaluation

The evaluation of an arithmetic expression may cause exceptions. So the value of a ground expression whose evaluation does not raise an exception is first defined, then exceptions are described as "error cases".

6.2.1 Value of an expression

The value of a ground arithmetic expression is defined as follows.

- The result of the evaluation of a number is this number.
- The result of the evaluation of a compound term with principal functor F/N consists of evaluating the N arguments in an implementation dependent order and applying the operation corresponding to the arithmetic functor F/N to the N obtained values.

▷ **Error cases** If many errors may be raised during the evaluation of an expression, it is **implementation dependent** which one is raised.

Conditions	Error-term
○ A subexpression is a variable	`instantiation_error`
○ A subexpression is an atom A	`type_error(evaluable, A)`
○ A subexpression is a compound term whose principal functor F/N is not an arithmetic functor	`type_error(evaluable, F/N)`
○ A subexpression is a compound term whose principal functor is atan/1, cos/1, exp/1, log/1, sin/1 or sqrt/1, and whose argument is not a variable and is evaluated to a value V which is not a number	`type_error(number, V)`
○ A subexpression is a compound term whose principal functor is a bitwise operator such that none of its arguments is a variable but one of them is evaluated to a value V which is not an integer	`type_error(integer, V)`
○ The value of some operation is **int_overflow**	`evaluation_error(int_overflow)`
○ The value of some operation is **float_overflow**	`evaluation_error(float_overflow)`
○ The value of some operation is **underflow**	`evaluation_error(underflow)`
○ The value of some operation is **zero_divisor**	`evaluation_error(zero_divisor)`

○ The value of some operation is **unde-fined**

`evaluation_error(undefined)`

○ The flag bounded has value **false** and a system exception is raised because of exhaustion of resources

`system_error`

6.2.2 Arithmetic comparison operator definitions

The following table identifies the basic arithmetic operations corresponding to each arithmetic comparison built-in predicate (one operation depending on the types of the arguments, I or F):

Predicate indicator	Operation
`'=:='/2`	$eq_I,\ eq_F,\ eq_{FI},\ eq_{IF}$
`'=\\='/2`	$neq_I,\ neq_F,\ neq_{FI},\ neq_{IF}$
`'<'/2`	$lss_I,\ lss_F,\ lss_{FI},\ lss_{IF}$
`'=<'/2`	$leq_I,\ leq_F,\ leq_{FI},\ leq_{IF}$
`'>'/2`	$gtr_I,\ gtr_F,\ gtr_{FI},\ gtr_{IF}$
`'>='/2`	$geq_I,\ geq_F,\ geq_{FI},\ geq_{IF}$

See the profiles of the basic arithmetic operators in Section 6.2.4.

6.2.3 Arithmetic functors definitions

The following table identifies the basic arithmetic operations corresponding to each arithmetic functor not defined in Section 6.2.5 (one operation depending on the types of the arguments, I or F):

Arithmetic functor	Operations
`abs/1`	$abs_I,\ abs_F$
`'+'/2`	$add_I,\ add_F,\ add_{FI},\ add_{IF}$
`ceiling/1`	$ceiling_{F\to I}$
`float/1`	$float_{I\to F},\ float_{F\to F}$
`float_fractional_part/1`	$fractpart_F$
`float_integer_part/1`	$intpart_F$
`'/'/2`	$div_F,\ div_{II},\ div_{FI},\ div_{IF}$
`'//'/2`	$intdiv_I$
`floor/1`	$floor_{F\to I}$
`mod/2`	mod_I
`'*'/2`	$mul_I,\ mul_F,\ mul_{FI},\ mul_{IF}$
`rem/2`	rem_I
`round/1`	$round_{F\to I}$
`sign/1`	$sign_I,\ sign_F$
`'-'/1`	$neg_I,\ neg_F$
`'-'/2`	$sub_I,\ sub_F,\ sub_{FI},\ sub_{IF}$
`truncate/1`	$truncate_{F\to I}$

6.2.4 Profile of the basic arithmetic operations

The arithmetic system of **Standard Prolog** is based on the recent ISO standard for language independent arithmetic [1] in which all the basic arithmetic operations are specified. All details are provided in the standard [2]. Therefore we do not fully develop their definitions, but only give their profiles, which show the exceptional values raised by the basic operations (hence by the arithmetic comparison built-in predicates and the arithmetic functors not defined in the next section).

$abs_F : F \rightarrow F$
$abs_I : I \rightarrow I \cup \{\textbf{int\_overflow}\}$
$add_{FI} : F \times I \rightarrow F \cup \{\textbf{float\_overflow}, \textbf{underflow}\}$
$add_F : F \times F \rightarrow F \cup \{\textbf{float\_overflow}, \textbf{underflow}\}$
$add_{IF} : I \times F \rightarrow F \cup \{\textbf{float\_overflow}, \textbf{underflow}\}$
$add_I : I \times I \rightarrow I \cup \{\textbf{int\_overflow}\}$
$ceiling_{F \rightarrow I} : F \rightarrow I \cup \{\textbf{int\_overflow}\}$
$div_{FI} : F \times I \rightarrow F \cup \{\textbf{float\_overflow}, \textbf{underflow}, \textbf{zero\_divisor}\}$
$div_F : F \times F \rightarrow F \cup \{\textbf{float\_overflow}, \textbf{underflow}, \textbf{zero\_divisor}\}$
$div_{IF} : I \times F \rightarrow F \cup \{\textbf{float\_overflow}, \textbf{underflow}, \textbf{zero\_divisor}\}$
$div_{II} : I \times I \rightarrow F \cup \{\textbf{float\_overflow}, \textbf{underflow}, \textbf{zero\_divisor}\}$
$eq_{FI} : F \times I \rightarrow \{\textbf{true}, \textbf{false}\} \cup \{\textbf{float\_overflow}\}$
$eq_F : F \times F \rightarrow \{\textbf{true}, \textbf{false}\}$
$eq_{IF} : I \times F \rightarrow \{\textbf{true}, \textbf{false}\} \cup \{\textbf{float\_overflow}\}$
$eq_I : I \times I \rightarrow \{\textbf{true}, \textbf{false}\}$
$float_{F \rightarrow F} : F \rightarrow F$
$float_{I \rightarrow F} : I \rightarrow F \cup \{\textbf{float\_overflow}\}$
$floor_{F \rightarrow I} : F \rightarrow I \cup \{\textbf{int\_overflow}\}$
$fractpart_F : F \rightarrow F$
$geq_{FI}: F \times I \rightarrow \{\textbf{true}, \textbf{false}\} \cup \{\textbf{float\_overflow}\}$
$geq_F: F \times F \rightarrow \{\textbf{true}, \textbf{false}\}$
$geq_{IF}: I \times F \rightarrow \{\textbf{true}, \textbf{false}\} \cup \{\textbf{float\_overflow}\}$
$geq_I: I \times I \rightarrow \{\textbf{true}, \textbf{false}\}$
$gtr_{FI}: F \times I \rightarrow \{\textbf{true}, \textbf{false}\} \cup \{\textbf{float\_overflow}\}$
$gtr_F: F \times F \rightarrow \{\textbf{true}, \textbf{false}\}$
$gtr_{IF}: I \times F \rightarrow \{\textbf{true}, \textbf{false}\} \cup \{\textbf{float\_overflow}\}$
$gtr_I: I \times I \rightarrow \{\textbf{true}, \textbf{false}\}$
$intdiv_I : I \times I \rightarrow I \cup \{\textbf{int\_overflow}, \textbf{zero\_divisor}\}$
$intpart_F : F \rightarrow F$
$leq_{FI}: F \times I \rightarrow \{\textbf{true}, \textbf{false}\} \cup \{\textbf{float\_overflow}\}$
$leq_F: F \times F \rightarrow \{\textbf{true}, \textbf{false}\}$
$leq_{IF}: I \times F \rightarrow \{\textbf{true}, \textbf{false}\} \cup \{\textbf{float\_overflow}\}$
$leq_I: I \times I \rightarrow \{\textbf{true}, \textbf{false}\}$
$lss_{FI}: F \times I \rightarrow \{\textbf{true}, \textbf{false}\} \cup \{\textbf{float\_overflow}\}$
$lss_F: F \times F \rightarrow \{\textbf{true}, \textbf{false}\}$
$lss_{IF}: I \times F \rightarrow \{\textbf{true}, \textbf{false}\} \cup \{\textbf{float\_overflow}\}$
$lss_I: I \times I \rightarrow \{\textbf{true}, \textbf{false}\}$
$mod_I : I \times I \rightarrow I \cup \{\textbf{zero\_divisor}\}$
$mul_{FI} : F \times I \rightarrow F \cup \{\textbf{float\_overflow}, \textbf{underflow}\}$
$mul_F : F \times F \rightarrow F \cup \{\textbf{float\_overflow}, \textbf{underflow}\}$
$mul_{IF} : I \times F \rightarrow F \cup \{\textbf{float\_overflow}, \textbf{underflow}\}$
$mul_I : I \times I \rightarrow I \cup \{\textbf{int\_overflow}\}$
$neg_F : F \rightarrow F$

$neg_I : I \rightarrow I \cup \{\text{int\_overflow}\}$
$neq_{FI}: F \times I \rightarrow \{\text{true, false}\} \cup \{\text{float\_overflow}\}$
$neq_F: F \times F \rightarrow \{\text{true, false}\}$
$neq_{IF}: I \times F \rightarrow \{\text{true, false}\} \cup \{\text{float\_overflow}\}$
$neq_I: I \times I \rightarrow \{\text{true, false}\}$
$rem_I : I \times I \rightarrow I \cup \{\text{zero\_divisor}\}$
$round_{F \rightarrow I} : F \rightarrow I \cup \{\text{int\_overflow}\}$
$sign_F : F \rightarrow F$
$sign_I : I \rightarrow I$
$sub_{FI} : F \times I \rightarrow F \cup \{\text{float\_overflow, underflow}\}$
$sub_F : F \times F \rightarrow F \cup \{\text{float\_overflow, underflow}\}$
$sub_{IF} : I \times F \rightarrow F \cup \{\text{float\_overflow, underflow}\}$
$sub_I : I \times I \rightarrow I \cup \{\text{int\_overflow}\}$
$truncate_{F \rightarrow I} : F \rightarrow I \cup \{\text{int\_overflow}\}$

6.2.5 Arithmetic functors defined in Standard Prolog

atan/1 : $(I \cup F) \rightarrow F$
'/\\\\'/2 : $I \times I \rightarrow I$
'\\\\'/2 : $I \rightarrow I$
'<<'/2 : $I \times I \rightarrow I$
'\\\\/'/2 : $I \times I \rightarrow I$
'>>'/2 : $I \times I \rightarrow I$
cos/1 : $(I \cup F) \rightarrow F$
exp/1 : $(I \cup F) \rightarrow F \cup \{\text{float\_overflow, underflow}\}$
''/2** : $(I \cup F) \times (I \cup F) \rightarrow F \cup \{\text{float\_overflow, underflow, undefined}\}$
log/1 : $(I \cup F) \rightarrow F \cup \{\text{undefined}\}$
sin/1 : $(I \cup F) \rightarrow F$
sqrt/1 : $(I \cup F) \rightarrow F \cup \{\text{undefined}\}$

▷ **Description:** atan(Expr)

– **If** the evaluation of Expr, resulting in the value V, and the application of
the function atan/1 to its value are errorless **then** atan(Expr) has the
value of the principal value R of the arc tangent of V which satisfies
$-\pi/2 \leq R \leq \pi/2$

Example:

```
PI is atan(1.0) * 4.
    Succeeds with substitution { PI <- 3.14159 }
                                        (approximate value)
```

▷ **Description:** (Expr₁ /\ Expr₂)

– **If** the evaluation of $Expr_1$ and $Expr_2$, resulting in the respective values V1 and V2, and the application of the function '/\\'/2 to these values are errorless **then** (Expr₁ /\ Expr₂) has the value such that each bit is set iff each of the corresponding bits in V1 and V2 is set.
  The value is **implementation defined** if V1 or V2 is negative[2].

Example:

```
B is (17 * 256 + 125) /\ 255).
    Succeeds with substitution { B <- 125 }
```

▷ **Description:** \(Expr)

– **If** the evaluation of Expr, resulting in the value V, and the application of the function '\\'/1 to its value are errorless **then** \(Expr) has the value such that each bit is set iff the corresponding bit in V is not set.
  The value is **implementation defined**.

Examples:

```
B is \(10).
    Succeeds with substitution { B <-
                            implementation defined value }

B is \( \(10)).
    Succeeds with substitution { B <- 10 }
```

▷ **Description:** (Expr₁ << Expr₂)

– **If** the evaluation of $Expr_1$ and $Expr_2$, resulting in the respective values V1 and V2, and the application of the function '<<'/2 to these values are errorless **then** (Expr₁ << Expr₂) has the value of V1 left-shifted V2 bit positions, where the V2 least significant bit positions of the result are zero. The value is **implementation defined** if V2 is negative, or V2 is larger than the bit size of an integer.

---

[2] The value is **implementation defined** when an operand or value is negative because the representation of a negative integer is **implementation defined**.

Example:

```
B is '<<'(16, 2).
    Succeeds with substitution { B <- 64 }
```

▷ Description: (Expr₁ \/ Expr₂)

— **If** the evaluation of **Expr₁** and **Expr₂**, resulting in the respective values **V1** and **V2**, and the application of the function '\\/'/2 to these values are errorless **then** (Expr₁ \/ Expr₂) has the value such that each bit is set iff at least one of the corresponding bits in **V1** and **V2** is set.
The value is **implementation defined** if **V1** or **V2** is negative.

Example:

```
B is '\\/'(125, 255).
    Succeeds with substitution { B <- 255 }
```

▷ Description: (Expr₁ >> Expr₂)

— **If** the evaluation of **Expr₁** and **Expr₂**, resulting in the respective values **V1** and **V2**, and the application of the function '>>'/2 to these values are errorless **then** (Expr₁ >> Expr₂) has the value of **V1** right-shifted **V2** bit positions.
The value is **implementation defined** depending on whether the shift is logical (fill with zeros) or arithmetic (fill with a copy of the sign bit).
The value is **implementation defined** if **V2** is negative, or **V2** is larger than the bit size of an integer.

Example:

```
B is '>>'(16, 2).
    Succeeds with substitution { B <- 4 }
                (fill with zeros, implementation defined)
```

▷ Description: cos(Expr)

— **If** the evaluation of **Expr**, resulting in the value **V**, and the application of the function cos/1 to its value are errorless **then** cos(Expr) has the value of the cosine of **V** (measured in radians).

Example:

```
PI is atan(1.0) * 4, X is cos(PI / 2.0).
   Succeeds with substitution { PI <- 3.14159, X <- 0.0000 }
        (approximate values)
```

▷ Description: exp(Expr)

— If the evaluation of Expr, resulting in the value V, and the application of the function exp/1 to its value are errorless **then** exp(Expr) has the value of the exponential function of V.

Example:

```
E is exp(1.0).
   Succeeds with substitution { E <- 2.7818 }
                              (approximate value)
```

▷ Description: (Expr₁ ** Expr₂)

— If the evaluation of Expr₁ and Expr₂, resulting in the respective values V1 and V2, and the application of the function '**'/2 to these values are errorless **then** (Expr₁ ** Expr₂) has the value of V1 raised to the power of V2.
If V1 and V2 are both zero, the value is 1.0.

Example:

```
X is -5.0 ** 3 .
   Succeeds with substitution { X <- -125.0000 }
                              (approximate value)
```

▷ Description: log(Expr)

— If the evaluation of Expr, resulting in the value V, and the application of the function log/1 to its value are errorless **then** log(Expr) has the value of the natural logarithm of V.

Example:

```
One is log(2.7818).
   Succeeds with substitution { One <- 1.0000 }
                              (approximate value)
```

▷ **Description:** sin(Expr)

- If the evaluation of Expr, resulting in the value V, and the application of the function sin/1 to its value are errorless **then** sin(Expr) has the value of the sine of V (measured in radians).

Example:

```
PI is atan(1.0) * 4, X is sin(PI / 2.0).
    Succeeds with substitution { PI <- 3.14159, X <- 1.0000 }
                                            (approximate values)
```

▷ **Description:** sqrt(Expr)

- If the evaluation of Expr, resulting in the value V, and the application of the function sqrt/1 to its value are errorless **then** sqrt(Expr) has the value $\sqrt{(V)}$.

Example:

```
X is sqrt(1.21).
    Succeeds with substitution { X <- 1.1000 }
                                            (approximate value)
```

7. Prolog Environment: Sources and Sinks

This chapter describes the I/O system of **Standard Prolog** and how terms are input and output.

7.1 Overview

A *source/sink* is a fundamental notion. A *source* (resp. *sink*) is a physical object from which a processor inputs data (resp. to which a processor outputs results), for example a file, terminal, interprocess communication channel, or other **implementation defined** possibility permitted by the processor. Each source/sink is associated with a finite or potentially infinite sequence of bytes or characters. It always has a beginning, but only has an end if it is finite. A source/sink is specified as an **implementation defined** ground term (a *source/sink-term*) in a call of open/4.

A program can output results to a sink or input Prolog data from a source.

Streams provide a logical view of the source/sinks.

Any stream may be associated with an *alias* which is an atom given by the user which may be used to refer to that stream or a *stream-term* (an **implementation dependent** non atomic ground term). The association is created when a stream is opened, and automatically ends when the stream is closed. A particular alias will refer to at most one stream at any one time, but a stream may be associated with more than one alias. All subsequent references to the source/sink are made by referring to the stream-term associated with a stream or its alias.

Here is a simple example:

```
test :- open('/usr/editor/myfile.txt', write, MyStream,
                            [type(text), alias(mickey)]),
        write_term(mickey, 'Hello, world', [quoted(true)]),
        close(MyStream, [force(true)]).
```

Each I/O operation will name a stream and can give an option list.

Two streams are predefined and open during the execution of every goal, referring to the keyboard and the screen respectively: the standard input stream has the alias user_input and the standard output stream has the alias user_output. They are the *current input* and *current output streams*. But current input and output can be redirected using the built-in predicates set_input/1 and set_output/1.

When the current input (resp. output) stream is closed, the standard input (output) stream becomes the current input stream.

The standard input and output streams cannot be closed.

Output to a stream need not be sent to the sink connected to that stream immediately. When it is necessary to be certain that output has been delivered, this can be done by executing the built-in predicate flush_output/1. A stream is always flushed when it is closed. All further details are provided in the definitions of the I/O built-in predicates.

The *stream position* of a stream is represented by an **implementation dependent** ground term (a *stream position term*) which uniquely identifies an absolute position of the source/sink to which the stream is connected during the time that the stream is open and defines where in the source/sink the next input or output will take place. It is **implementation defined** whether or not the stream position of a particular source/sink can be arbitrarily changed during execution of a Prolog goal. If it can, then:

1. At any time, the stream can be repositioned by calling
   set_stream_position/2.
2. Two positions are represented by **implementation defined** terms which correspond to *end-of-stream* and *past-end-of-stream* (see the stream properties in Section 7.3.4).

When an output stream is repositioned, further output will overwrite the existing content of the sink.

When an input stream is repositioned, the content of the stream is unaltered, and can be re-input.

7.2 Streams in Standard Prolog

Streams in **Standard Prolog** are text streams or binary streams. It is **implementation defined** whether record-based streams, non-record-based streams, or both are supported.

7.2.1 Text streams

A *text stream* is a sequence of characters where each character is a member of the extended character set (**ECS**, 9.1.1). A text stream is also regarded as a sequence of lines where each line is a possibly empty sequence of characters followed by an **implementation dependent** new-line character.

A processor may add or remove space characters at the ends of lines in order to conform to the conventions for representing text streams in the operating system. Any such alterations to the stream are **implementation defined**.

It is **implementation defined** whether the last line in a text stream is followed by a new-line character. If so, closing a stream which is a sink will cause a new-line character to be output if the stream does not already end with one.

The effect of outputting a symbolic control character (9.5.1) to a text stream is **implementation defined**.

When a stream is connected to a record-based stream, each record is regarded as a line during Prolog execution.

7.2.2 Binary streams

A *binary stream* is a sequence of bytes.

If bytes are output to a sink via a binary stream, and then input from that sink via a binary stream, then the bytes input are identical to those output, except that an **implementation defined** number of zero-valued bytes may be appended to the end of the data input.

7.3 Properties of the streams

Streams are created with the built-in predicate open/4 by providing an I/O mode and an option list. They are closed with the built-in predicate close/2 and another option list. During their life-time they have *current stream properties* which may be consulted using the built-in predicate stream_property/2.

7.3.1 I/O modes

An I/O mode is an atom which defines the I/O operations that may be performed on a source/sink. The following I/O modes are specified in **Standard Prolog**:

read — The source/sink is a source. If it is a file, it will already exist and input starts at the beginning of that source.

write — The source/sink is a sink. If the sink already exists then it is emptied (the initial content is lost), and output starts at the beginning of that sink, else an empty sink is created.

append — The source/sink is a sink. If the sink already exists then output starts at the end of that sink, else an empty sink is created.

7.3.2 Options at stream creation

The stream-options supported at stream creation in **Standard Prolog** are:

type(T) — Specifies whether the stream is a text stream or a binary stream.
T will be:

  text — the stream is a text stream, or
  binary — the stream is a binary stream.
  DEFAULT: text

reposition(*bool*) — *bool* will be:

  true — it is possible to reposition the stream.
  false — it is **implementation defined** whether or not it is possible
    to reposition the stream.
  DEFAULT: false
  It depends on the particular source/sink whether or not repositioning is
  possible, for example, it is impossible when the source/sink is a terminal.

alias(A) — A will be an atom (used as an alias to denote the stream).
  DEFAULT: only the standard streams have default aliases: user_input
  and user_output

eof_action(*action*) — The effect of attempting to input from a stream
  whose stream position is past-end-of-stream will be specified by the value
  of the atom *action*:

  error — A permission-error exception is raised signifying that no more
    input exists in this stream (see read_term/3).
  eof_code — The result of input is as if the stream position is end-of-
    stream.
  reset — The stream position is reset so that it is not past-end-of-stream,
    and another attempt is made to input from it. This is likely to be use-
    ful when inputting from a source such as a terminal. There may also
    be an **implementation dependent** operation to reset the source
    to which the stream is attached.
  DEFAULT: **implementation defined**

If the stream-option list contains contradictory stream-options, the rightmost
option is the one which applies.

7.3.3 Options at stream closure

A close-option modifies the behaviour of close/2 if an error condition is satisfied while trying to close a stream. Its purpose is to allow an error handling
routine to do its best to reclaim resources.

  The stream-option supported at stream closure in **Standard Prolog** is:

force(*bool*) — *bool* will be:

false — If an error condition is satisfied, the stream is not closed.

true — If a resource error condition or system error condition is satisfied, there is no error; instead the stream is closed and the goal succeeds. This option closes the stream but data and results may be lost, and the stream may be left in an inconsistent state.

DEFAULT: **false**

If the close-option list contains contradictory stream-options, the rightmost option is the one which applies.

7.3.4 Current stream properties

The stream properties supported in **Standard Prolog** are:

file_name(F) — When the stream is connected to a source/sink which is a file, F is an **implementation defined** term which identifies the file which is the source/sink for the stream.

mode(M) — M is the I/O mode (7.3.1) which was specified when the source/sink was opened.

input — This stream is connected to a source.

output — This stream is connected to a sink.

alias(A) — A is one of the aliases (an atom) associated with the stream (there may be several aliases).

position(P) —

 – If the stream has property **reposition(true)**, P is the current stream position of the stream (an **implementation dependent** ground term). The terms P denoting stream positions end-of-stream and past-end-of-stream are **implementation defined**.

 – If the stream has property **reposition(false)**, it is **implementation defined** what should be P.

end_of_stream(E) — E is:

 at — the stream position is end-of-stream.

 past — the stream position is past-end-of-stream.

 not — the stream position is neither end-of-stream nor past-end-of-stream.

eof_action(A) — A has the value which was specified when the source/sink was opened (7.3.2).

reposition(*bool*) — *bool* has the value which was specified when the source/sink was opened (7.3.2).

type(T) — T has the value which was specified when the source/sink was opened (7.3.2).

Table 7.1 defines the properties of the standard streams.

Table 7.1. Properties of the standard streams

standard input	standard output
mode(read)	mode(append)
input	output
alias(user_input)	alias(user_output)
eof_action(reset)	eof_action(reset)
reposition(false)	reposition(false)
type(text)	type(text)

7.4 Inputting and outputting terms

Terms are input from sources and output on sinks using respectively the built-in predicates **write_term/3** and **read_term/3** and their derived built-in predicates. They all use read-options or write-options.

7.4.1 Read-options list

A read-options list is a list of *read-options* which affect the built-in predicate **read_term/3** and similar ones. The read-options supported in **Standard Prolog** are:

variables($Vars$) — After inputting a term, $Vars$ is a list of the variables in the term resulting from inputting, in left-to-right traversal order.

variable_names(VN_list) — After inputting a term, VN_list is a list of elements where each element is a term **A** = **V** such that
V is a variable of the term resulting from inputting, corresponding to a non anonymous variable in the original term, and
A is an atom whose name is the characters of **V** in the original term.

singletons(VN_list) — After inputting a term, VN_list is a list of elements where each element is a term **A** = **V** such that
V is a non anonymous variable which occurs only once in the term resulting from inputting, and
A is an atom whose name is the characters of **V** in the original term.

7.4.2 Write-options list

A write-options list is a list of write-options which affects the built-in predicate write_term/3 and similar ones. The write-options supported in **Standard Prolog** are:

quoted(*bool*) — *bool* will be:
> true — each atom and functor is quoted if this would be necessary for the term to be input by read_term/3.
> false — each atom and functor is written as specified by its syntax.
> DEFAULT: false

ignore_ops(*bool*) — *bool* will be:
> true — Each compound term is output in functional notation. Neither operator notation nor list notation is used when this write-option is in force (see 7.4.3, case 5).
> false — Compound terms are output using operator notation or list notation (see 7.4.3, case 5[1], second and third items).
> DEFAULT: false

numbervars(*bool*) — *bool* will be:
> true — a term of the form '$VAR'(N), where N is an integer, is output as a variable name consisting of a capital letter possibly followed by an integer. The capital letter is the (i+1)th letter of the alphabet and the integer is j, where
>
> > i = N mod 26
> > j = N // 26
>
> The integer j is omitted if it is zero. For example,
>
> > '$VAR'(0) is written as A
> > '$VAR'(1) is written as B
> > . . .
> > '$VAR'(25) is written as Z
> > '$VAR'(26) is written as A1
> > '$VAR'(27) is written as B1
> > . . .
>
> false — Variables are output with normal syntax as described in the next Section 7.4.3, case 1.
> DEFAULT: false

If the write-options list contains contradictory write-options, the rightmost write-option is the one which applies.

---

[1] The standard omits to specify a particular way to output curly bracketed terms. Therefore a functional notation should be assumed.

7.4.3 Writing a term

When a term `Term` is output using `write_term/3` and similar built-in predicates, the action which is taken in **Standard Prolog** is defined by the rules below:

1. If `Term` is a VARIABLE, a character sequence representing that variable is output. The sequence begins with _ (underscore) and the remaining characters are **implementation dependent**. The same character sequence is used for each occurrence of a particular variable in `Term`. A different character sequence is used for each distinct variable in `Term`.
   If `Term` has the form `'$VAR'(N)` for some positive integer `N`, and there is an effective write-option `numbervars(true)`, a variable name as defined in Section 7.4.2 is output,

2. If `Term` is an INTEGER with value N_1, a character sequence representing N_1 is output. The first character is - if the value of N_1 is negative. The other characters are a sequence of decimal digit characters. The first decimal digit is 0 if the value of `Term` is zero.

3. If `Term` is a FLOAT with value F_1, a character sequence representing F_1 is output. The first character is - if the value of F_1 is negative. The other characters are an **implementation dependent** sequence of characters which conform to the syntax for floating-point numbers.
   If there is an effective write-option `quoted(true)`, then the characters output are such that if they form a number with value F_2 in a term input by `read_term/3`, then
   $$F_1 = F_2$$
   A processor may output the floating point value 1.5 as 1.5 or 1.5E+00 or 0.15e1.

4. If `Term` is an ATOM then if there is an effective write-option `quoted(true)` and the sequence of characters forming the atom could not be input as a valid atom without quoting, then `Term` is output as a quoted token, else `Term` is output as the sequence of characters forming the name of the atom.

5. If `Term` is a COMPOUND TERM then
   - if `Term` has a principal functor, different from `'.'/2`, which is not an operator defined in the current operator table, or if there is an effective write-option `ignore_ops(true)`, then the term is output in *functional notation*, that is:
   a) The atom of the principal functor is output.
   b) ((open char) is output.
   c) Each argument of the term is output.
   d) , (comma char) is output between each successive pair of arguments.

e)) (close char) is output.

- if **Term** is a list-term or a list and there is an effective write-option
  `ignore_ops(false)`, then **Term** is output using list notation, as shown
  in Section 2.2.2.

- If **Term** has a principal functor which is an operator different from
  '.'/2, and there is an effective write-option `ignore_ops(false)`, then
  the term is output in *operator notation*, that is:

a) The atom of the principal functor is output in front of its argument
   (prefix operator), between its arguments (infix operator), or after
   its argument (postfix operator). In all cases, a space is output to
   separate an operator from its argument(s) if any ambiguity could
   otherwise arise.

b) Each argument of the term is output. When an argument is itself
   to be output in operator notation, it is preceded by ((open) and
   followed by) (close) if the principal functor is an operator whose
   priority is so high that the term could not be re-input correctly with
   same set of current operators, or if the argument is an atom which
   is a current operator.

- if **Term** is a list-term or a list and there is an effective write-option
  `ignore_ops(false)`, but '.'/2 is declared as operator, then **undefined** (two of the previous cases may apply).

8. Prolog Flags and Directives

In **Standard Prolog** *Flags* are reserved atoms with an associated predefined value, which define some parameters of a processor. Some of them are fixed with a given processor; their value is **implementation defined** and cannot be updated. Some others may be modified by the user and are said *changeable*.

Directives are predefined built-in predicates. They are used in Prolog text only as queries to be immediately executed when loading it. They are aimed at initialising changeable flags, or at updating the predefined operator table or the character conversion table. They are also used to influence the preparation of Prolog texts or term inputting during program execution. Such directives are needed in particular because there is no "consulting" built-in predicate in **Standard Prolog**.

8.1 Unchangeable flags

They concern the integer arithmetic and the maximum arity of a predicate or functor. Their default value is **implementation defined**. Their current associated value may be obtained in a program by using the built-in predicate current_prolog_flag/2.

Flag: bounded

POSSIBLE VALUES: true, false

– It is used in the definition of I (the integers, Section 6.1.2).

Flag: max_arity

POSSIBLE VALUE: The default value only (denoted *maxarity* or **unbounded**).

– *maxarity* is a positive integer which is the maximum arity allowed for any compound term.
– The value is **unbounded** when the processor has no limit for the number of arguments for a compound term.

Flag: integer_rounding_function

POSSIBLE VALUES: down, toward_zero

– It is used in the definition of I (the integers, Section 6.1.2).

Flag: max_integer

POSSIBLE VALUE: The default value only (denoted $maxint$).

– It is used in the definition of I (the integers, Section 6.1.2).

Flag: min_integer

POSSIBLE VALUE: The default value only (denoted $minint$).

– It is used in the definition of I (the integers, Section 6.1.2).

8.2 Changeable flags

Their current associated value may be updated during the preparation of a Prolog text by the directive set_prolog_flag/2, or in a program by using the built-in predicate set_prolog_flag/2. Current flags and values may be obtained in a program by using current_prolog_flag/2.

Flag: char_conversion

POSSIBLE VALUES: on, off
DEFAULT: on

– If the value is on, unquoted characters in Prolog texts being prepared for execution or when inputting terms are converted according to the current character conversion table (9.1.2).
– If the value is off, unquoted characters in Prolog texts and term inputting are not converted.

Flag: debug

POSSIBLE VALUES: on, off
DEFAULT: off

– If the value is off, procedures have the meaning defined in **Standard Prolog**.
– If the value is on, the effect of executing any predication is **implementation defined**.

Flag: double_quotes

POSSIBLE VALUES: chars, codes, atom
DEFAULT: **implementation defined**.

– This flag determines the subterm corresponding to a double quoted list token appearing in a Prolog text or in a term input by read_term/3 (9.5.1).
  – If the value is chars, a double quoted list token is input as a list of one char atoms.
  – If the value is codes, a double quoted list token is input as a list of character codes.
  – If the value is atom, a double quoted list token is input as an atom.

Flag: unknown

POSSIBLE VALUES: error, warning, fail
DEFAULT: error

– It defines the effect of attempting to execute a procedure which does not exist (see Section 4.3.2 in Chapter 4).

8.3 Directives for initialising flags and tables

They have the same procedure name and actions as the corresponding built-in predicate, but they act on the Prolog text in which they occur. Their arguments will satisfy the same constraints as those required for an errorless execution of the corresponding built-in predicate, otherwise their behaviour is **undefined**.
It is **implementation defined** whether or not a directive affects the values associated with flags in other Prolog texts or during execution.

set_prolog_flag/2

A directive set_prolog_flag(Flag, Value) enables the value associated with a Prolog flag to be altered in subsequent Prolog text preparation or term inputting.

op/3

A directive op(Priority, Op_specifier, Operator) enables the operator table (defined in Section 9.2) to be altered in subsequent Prolog text preparation or term inputting. Its initial state is defined by the predefined operator Table 9.2.2.

`char_conversion/2`

A directive `char_conversion(In_char, Out_char)` enables the character conversion table, to be altered in subsequent Prolog text preparation or term inputting. The table is defined in Section 9.1.2.

8.4 Directives for preparation of Prolog texts and goals

They act on the Prolog text in which they occur. They should not be redefined and the procedures indicated in the arguments of the directives will not be a built-in predicate. The effect in that case is **undefined**.

`discontiguous/1`

A directive `discontiguous(PI)` where PI is a predicate indicator, a list of predicate indicators or a predicate indicator sequence, specifies that each user-defined procedure indicated by PI may be defined by clauses which are not in consecutive order in that Prolog text.

More than one directive `discontiguous(PI)` may specify the clauses of the user-defined procedure P to be discontiguous. The first directive `discontiguous(PI)` indicating procedure P will precede all clauses for the procedure P (otherwise the effect of the directive is **undefined**).

`dynamic/1`

A directive `dynamic(PI)`, where PI is a predicate indicator, a list of predicate indicators or a predicate indicator sequence, specifies that each user-defined procedure indicated by PI is dynamic.

More than one directive `dynamic(PI)` may specify a user-defined procedure P to be dynamic in a Prolog text. If P is defined to be a dynamic procedure in one Prolog text, then a directive `dynamic(PI)` indicating P will occur in every Prolog text which contains clauses for P. The first directive `dynamic(PI)` that specifies a user-defined procedure P to be dynamic will precede all clauses for P (otherwise the effect of the directive is **undefined**).

NOTE — The standard suggests public/1 as a directive to declare public static predefined user procedures.

`ensure_loaded/1`

A directive `ensure_loaded(P_text)` specifies that the Prolog text being prepared for execution will include the Prolog text denoted by P_text where

P_text is an **implementation defined** ground term designating a Prolog text unit.

When multiple directives ensure_loaded(P_text) exist for the same Prolog text, that Prolog text is included only once in the Prolog text prepared for execution. The position where it is included is **implementation defined**.

include/1

If F is an **implementation defined** ground term designating a Prolog text unit, then Prolog text $P1$ which contains a directive include(F) is identical to a Prolog text $P2$ obtained by replacing the directive include(F) in $P1$ by the Prolog text denoted by F.

initialization/1

A directive initialization(T) includes a term T' resulting from the transformation of the well-formed term T in a set of goals which will be executed immediately after Prolog texts have been prepared for execution. The order in which any such goals will be executed is **implementation defined**.

The meaning of the directive is **undefined** if the term T is not a well-formed body-term.

multifile/1

A directive multifile(PI) where PI is a predicate indicator, a list of predicate indicators or a predicate indicator sequence, specifies that the clauses for each user-defined procedure indicated by PI may have clauses in more than one Prolog text.

More than one directive multifile(PI) may specify a user-defined procedure P to be multifile. Each Prolog text that contains clauses for the user-defined procedure P will contain a directive multifile(PI) indicating the procedure P. The first directive multifile(PI) indicating procedure P will precede all clauses for the procedure P (otherwise the effect of the directive is **undefined**).

9. Prolog Syntax

Programmers write *Prolog texts* or input terms from sources. This chapter describes the syntax of Prolog texts in **Standard Prolog** and the syntax of terms as they will be represented in sources or as they may be output on sinks.

A Prolog text is a sequence of directives and clauses in an order which is specified by directives. Directives and clauses are represented by terms. Furthermore several I/O built-in predicates input and output terms. Such terms are also called read-terms.

Read-terms are formed with functors and some of the functors are unary or binary predefined operators which may be written in a prefix, infix or postfix notation with or without parentheses. The syntax explains how to write expressions with operators. Its originality lies in the possibility to update dynamically the set of operators.

9.1 Character sets and character conversion table

The elementary unit of any text is the character. In the definition of **Standard Prolog** different character sets are used. These are described in the next section.

9.1.1 The Prolog character set and other character sets

Figure 9.1 illustrates the different character sets and their relationships. They are:

- The *Processor character set* (**PCS**) which denotes all possible characters and may include in particular national characters and characters which require several bytes to be represented.
- The *Extended character set* (**ECS**), the set of characters allowed in text streams, which is an **implementation defined** subset of **PCS**. It is partitioned into graphic, alphanumeric, solo, layout and meta characters.
- The set of the *one-char atoms*. It is the subset of the atoms whose name is represented by a single character. It has a nonempty intersection with

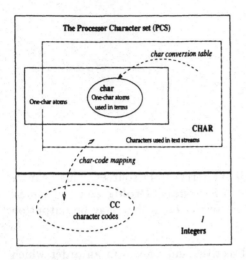

The Processor Character set (PCS)

char conversion table

char
One-char atoms
used in terms

One-char atoms

CHAR

Characters used in text streams

char-code mapping

CC
character codes

I

Integers

Fig. 9.1. The character sets and the character codes set in **Standard Prolog**.

ECS. Both sets are uncomparable. For example it may happen that the one-char atom '•' is not in **ECS**, when the character ∞ is in **ECS** but not a one-char atom.

- The *Prolog character set* (**char**). It is the set of the characters used to represent read-terms in the syntax of **Standard Prolog** (as described in Section 9.5). It is a common subset of the one-char atoms and the **ECS**. The other characters in **ECS** are considered as an extension of the Prolog character set. The Prolog character set is, like the **ECS**, partitioned into graphic, alphanumeric, solo, layout and meta characters.

The charaters which are in **ECS** but not in **char** are **implementation defined**.

9.1.2 The character conversion table

The characters of the Prolog character set (**char**) are the basic units used in the syntax of Prolog texts and terms. Therefore characters in the extended character set (**ECS**) which are not in the Prolog character set must be "converted" in order to be parsed and understood by a processor. The *character conversion table* associates one single character in **char** to each character in **ECS**.

This character conversion table may or may not be used by the I/O predicates. It is empty by default (no conversion, i.e. each character is "converted" to itself).

The character conversion table is accessed by the built-in predicate current_char_conversion/2 and updated before inputting terms from streams during execution with char_conversion/2.

It may be initialised during the preparation of a Prolog text, using directives char_conversion/2 (8.2). It is **implementation defined** whether or not the character conversion table is affected during execution by the directives executed during the preparation of a Prolog text.

9.1.3 Character code

To each character in **ECS** there corresponds a unique integer and reciprocally, by the *char-code mapping*. This integer is called *character code*[1]. The subset of the integers corresponding to a character code is denoted **CC** (see Figure 9.1) and is called the *set of character codes*[2]

The *char-code mapping* is **implementation defined**, but it satisfies several constraints[3].

– The character code of an unquoted character (non-quote-char 9.5.1) is subject to the following restrictions:
  – The character codes of each **capital letter char** from A to Z is monotonically increasing.
  – The character codes of each **small letter char** from a to z is monotonically increasing.
  – The character codes of each **decimal digit char** from 0 to 9 is monotonically increasing and contiguous.
– The character code of a quoted character (9.5.1) which is not a **control**, **octal** or **hexadecimal escape sequence** is the character code of the unquoted character that the quoted character denotes.
– The character code of a quoted character which is an **octal** (**hexadecimal**) **escape sequence** is the value of the octal (hexadecimal) characters interpreted as an octal (hexadecimal) integer.

The char-code mapping is accessed by the built-in predicate **char_code/2**.

9.2 Expression and operator table

In **Standard Prolog** terms are normally written as explained in Section 2.1.1: in functional notation. In this case the structure of the term is completely specified without any ambiguity. It is also possible to simplify the presentation of some terms writing them as unbracketed expressions. Thus expressions are written using functors in *operator notation*.

---

[1] This integer is also called *collating sequence integer* in the standard by reference to the term ordering that it serves to define.

[2] A character code may correspond to more than one byte in a stream. Thus, inputting a single character may consume several bytes from an input stream, and writing a single character may output several bytes to an output stream.

[3] These requirements on the char-code mapping are satisfied by both ASCII (11.3) and EBCDIC.

9.2.1 The operator table

The *operator table* defines which atoms will be regarded as operators when a sequence of tokens is parsed as a read-term by the built-in predicate read_term/3, or a term is output by the built-in predicate write_term/3 or similar built-in predicates, or a Prolog text is prepared for execution.

Each operator is characterised by three parameters: **name** (an atom), **specifier** (one of the atoms: xf, yf, xfx, xfy, yfx, fx, fy), and **priority** (an integer between 1 and 1200).

The specifier of an operator (defined in Table 9.1) is a mnemonic that defines the arity, the class (prefix, infix or postfix) and the associativity (left-, right- or non-associative) of the operator.

Table 9.1. Specifiers for operators

Specifier	Class	Associativity
fx	prefix	non-associative
fy	prefix	right-associative
xfx	infix	non-associative
xfy	infix	right-associative
yfx	infix	left-associative
xf	postfix	non-associative
yf	postfix	left-associative

The arity is equal to the number of x and y in the specifier, and x (y) defines which operand may be unbracketed and how implicit associativity works. The *implicit associativity* is particularly useful for writing subexpressions with the same operator without parenthesis. For example the expression (1+2+3+4) is the term '+'('+'('+'(1, 2),3),4))) if the specifier of '+' is yfx.

The *priority of an operator* is defined below (9.2.3).

9.2.2 The predefined operator table

In **Standard Prolog** the initial state of the operator table is fixed. It may be updated using the directive or built-in predicate op/3. The initial state (the predefined operators) is given in Table 9.2.2[4].

---

[4] Two operators ((-->)/2 and (?-)/1) are in the table, but their meaning is **undefined** in **Standard Prolog**. In many processors they are used in DCG rules for the first and as initial goal constructor for the second.

Table 9.2. The predefined operator table.

Priority	Specifier	Operator(s)
1200	xfx	`:- -->`
1200	fx	`:- ?-`
1100	xfy	`;`
1050	xfy	`->`
1000	xfy	`' , '`
900	fy	`\+`
700	xfx	`= \=`
700	xfx	`== \== @< @=< @> @>=`
700	xfx	`=..`
700	xfx	`is =:= =\= < =< > >=`
500	yfx	`+ - /\ \/`
400	yfx	`* / // rem mod << >>`
200	xfx	`**`
200	xfy	`^`
200	fy	`- \`

9.2.3 Parsing an expression

Parsing is influenced by the priorities.

The *priority of a term* is normally 0, when it is written in functional, list or curly notation, or if it is a bracketed expression or an atomic term. But if the term is written as an unbracketed expression in operator notation, its priority is the priority of its principal functor.

"Unbracketing" rule:

If an unbracketed expression has priority p, one of its operands may be written without parenthesis if its priority is less than p. If the position of the operand corresponds to 'y' in the specifier of the operator of the expression then the priority of the operand may also be equal[5].

If an expression is written without parenthesis and formed according to the rule above, it is parsed as a term in which the operands are subterms, according to the specified associativity, with decreasing priorities. For example the expression (1 * 2 + 3 * 4) is the term '+'('*'(1, 2), '*'(3, 4)) as the priority of '*' is less than the priority of '+', according to Table 9.2.2, and (1 + 2 * 3 + 4) is the term '+'('+'(1, '*'(2, 3)),4).

If the rule above is violated, it is a syntax error. For example the expression (X = Y = Z) cannot be parsed, since = has specifier xfx and no subexpression can be built with a priority less than the priority of =. Hence, expected operands must be bracketed, like, for example, ((X = Y) = Z) which can be parsed because the bracketed subexpression has priority 0.

---

[5] Hence the principal functor of the operand may be the same operator and the subexpression may be unbracketed.

Notice however that some expressions still remain ambiguous. For example assume there are two operators with the same priority and denoted `xfy` and `yfx` with the same corresponding specifier. Thus the expression 1 `xfy` 2 `yfx` 3 may be parsed as the term `xfy(1, yfx(2, 3))` or `yfx(xfy(1, 2), 3)`.

Therefore in **Standard Prolog** there is one additional rule to (arbitrarily) disambiguate such cases (the only possible cases are expressions of the form 1 `xfy` 2 `yfx` 3 and `fy` 1 `yf`, where both operators have same priority): the expression is parsed considering the first operator to have higher priority. So these expressions are parsed like 1 `xfy` (2 `yfx` 3) and `fy` (1 `yf`) respectively.

9.2.4 Valid operator table

There are still some problematic situations. If two operators have the same class and name (and different priorities), some expressions may be ambiguous.

An operator table is a *valid operator table* if it fulfills the following conditions:

- There are no two operators with the same class and name.
- There are no two operators with the same name, one infix and the other postfix[6].

Updating the operator table, using the built-in predicate `op/3`, must preserve the validity of the table.

9.3 Presentation of the syntax

The syntax of **Standard Prolog** is presented using definite clause grammar style (DCG).

A DCG is a grammar[7] specifying terminal strings by rewriting rules, with additional restrictions specified by built-in predicates and some procedures specified in Section 9.5.2.

DCG rules have the form:

Nonterminal   --> Sequence of *nonterminals, terminals*
                                 and *procedure calls*

nonterminals are predications, *terminals* are sequences of characters quoted by " (double quote character) or by ' (single quote character) and *procedure calls* are Prolog goals between braces. '|' holds for alternative.

---

[6] This restriction, as the (arbitrary) disambiguation rule above, contribute to limiting the lookahead during parsing and improve parsing efficiency.

[7] It is basically a context free grammar in which the nonterminals may have arguments. A DCG is also a Prolog program (assuming a classical transformation).

A rule deriving the empty string has the form:

Nonterminal --> ε

Syntactic rules define the syntax of a term (also called the *concrete syntax*). Each nonterminal has at least one argument which defines the corresponding term. In the case of several arguments, the term corresponds to the first one.

There are goals between braces. They represent the conditions which must be satisfied to apply the rule.

The syntax presented here is ambiguous: the same expression may sometimes lead to different terms. The rules defined in Section 9.2.3 above must be applied to remove the ambiguities. The DCG rules may be read as a **Standard Prolog** program[8].

9.4 Syntax of Prolog text

A Prolog text is a sequence of directive-terms and clause-terms. All are read-terms. As specified below, a read-term has an "end" delimiter (a dot). A dot which is an end delimiter must be followed by a layout text if there may be any confusion with subsequent term[9]

9.4.1 Syntax of directive

The characters of a *directive-term* in Prolog text will satisfy the same constraints as those required to input a read-term during a successful execution of the built-in predicate **read_term/3**. The principal functor will be (:-)/1, and its argument will be a directive (one of the predications described in Sections 8.3 and 8.4).

9.4.2 Syntax of clause

The characters of a *clause-term* in Prolog text will satisfy the same constraints as those required to execute successfully the built-in predicate **asserta/1**. The principal functor will be (:-)/2, its first argument will be a callable term (an atom or a compound term) and the second a well-formed body-term (2.2.3), or, if the principal functor is not (:-)/2, a callable term.

---

[8] The executable version of the syntax (in the file referred to in Annex 11.2) includes these (transformed) DCG rules with small modifications to take into account the disambiguation rules.

[9] A dot may also by used as a graphic character (11.3). Therefore in the sequence **f(1)./*** the point is parsed as part of the atom **./*** and not as the end delimiter of the compound term **f(1)**.

9.5 Syntax of read-term

9.5.1 Term definition

read_term(T)   --> term(T, 1200), end

The nonterminal term has two arguments. The first one is the corresponding term, the second is an integer which is the precedence context of the term.
The *precedence context* is an integer between 0 and 1200 which represents the
highest priority that the term may have.

So parsing "starts" with the highest possible priority (e.g. any term is
acceptable).

A read-term may have two kinds of variables (9.5.1): named and anonymous variables. All variables in the resulting term are freshly renamed with
an **implementation dependent** name. However the information, whether
they were anonymous or not, is kept in the syntax, as their original name as
well, in the case of named variables (this information is used in the built-in
predicate **read_term/3** and similar built-in predicates)[10].

The titles of the next subsections correspond to the first subterm parsed
by scanning a sequence of characters from left to right.

Number term.

term(T, P)   --> float_number(F), rest_term(F, T, 0, P)
                                    | integer(I), rest_term(I, T, 0, P)
                                    | name('-'), float_number(F),
                                        rest_term(MF, T, 0, P), { MF is -F }
                                    | name('-'), integer(I),
                                        rest_term(MI, T, 0, P), { MI is -I }

The nonterminal rest_term has 4 arguments: the first one is the subterm
already parsed, the second the complete term, the third the priority of the
subterm and the last one the precedence context of the term currently anal-
ysed (its maximal priority).

Variable term.

term(T, P)   --> variable(V), rest_term(V, T, 0, P)

Atom term.

term(T, P)   --> atom(A), { notoperator(A) },
                                        rest_term(A, T, 0, P)

term(Op, P)   --> atom(Op), { current_op(_,_,Op) }

---

[10] This information is used by the built-in predicates **read_term/3** and similar, but
in order to keep the syntax presentation simple, this information is not explicitly
coded here.

atom(A)   --> name(A)

atom('[ ]')   --> open_list, close_list

atom('{}')   --> open_curly, close_curly

Compound term in functional notation.

term(T, P)   --> atom(F), open_compound_term,
                                          term(Arg, 999),
                                          arg_list(L), { Term =.. [F, Arg | L] },
                                          rest_term(Term, T, 0, P)

arg_list([T | L])   --> comma, term(T, 999), arg_list(L)

arg_list([ ])   --> close

Compound term in list notation.

term(T, P)   --> open_list, term(Arg, 999), items(List),
                                          rest_term('.'(Arg, List), T, 0, P)

items('.'(H, List))   --> comma, term(H, 999), items(List)

items(Tail)   --> head_tail_separator, term(Tail, 999), close_list

items('[ ]')   --> close_list

Compound term in curly notation.

term(T, P)   --> open_curly, term(Term, 1200), close_curly,
                                          rest_term('{}'(Term), T, 0, P)

Bracketed term.

term(T, P)   --> open, term(Term, 1200), close,
                                          rest_term(Term, T, 0, P)

term(T, P)   --> open_compound_term, term(Term, 1200), close,
                                          rest_term(Term, T, 0, P)

Double quoted string term.

term(T, P)   --> double_quoted_list(DQL),
                                          rest_term(DQL, T, 0, P)

Back quoted string term.

term(T, P)	-->	back_quoted_string(BQS), rest_term(BQS, T, 0, P)

Back quoted strings are defined syntactically in **Standard Prolog**, but the corresponding term is **undefined**.

back_quoted_string(QL)	-->	layout_text_sequence, back_quoted_string_token(QL)
	|	back_quoted_string_token(QL)

Compound term in operator notation.

term(T, P)	-->	atom(Op), term(Arg, ArgPrec), { prefix_operator(OpPrec, Op, ArgPrec), P >= OpPrec, Term =.. [Op, Arg], } rest_term(Term, T, OpPrec, P)

rest_term(Term, T, LeftPrec, P)	-->	atom(Op), { infix_operator(OpP, Op, LAP, RAP), P >= OpP, LeftPrec =< LAP,}, term(Arg2, RAP), { NewTerm =.. [Op, Term, Arg2] }, rest_term(NewTerm, T, OpP, P)

rest_term(Term, T, LeftPrec, P)	-->	atom(Op), { postfix_operator(OpPrec, Op, LAP), P >= OpPrec, LeftPrec =< LAP, NewTerm =.. [Op, Term] }, rest_term(NewTerm, T, OpPrec, P)

rest_term(Term, T, LeftPrec, P)	-->	comma, { P >= 1000, LeftPrec < 1000 }, term(RightTerm, 1000), rest_term(','(Term, RightTerm), T, 1000, P)

rest_term(Term, Term, _, _)	-->	ε

Name and delimiter.

name(A)	-->	layout_text_sequence, name_token(X), { atom_chars(A, X) }
	|	name_token(X), { atom_chars(A, X) }

variable(var(V))	-->	layout_text_sequence, variable_token(X), { atom_chars(V, X) }
	|	variable_token(X), { atom_chars(V, X) }

integer(N)	-->	layout_text_sequence, integer_token(N)
	|	integer_token(N)

```
float_number(R)                  -->   layout_text_sequence,
                                       float_number_token(X),
                                       { number_chars(R, X) }
                                 |     float_number_token(X),
                                       { number_chars(R, X) }

double_quoted_list(QL)           -->   layout_text_sequence,
                                       double_quoted_list_token(QL)
                                 |     double_quoted_list_token(QL)

open                             -->   layout_text_sequence, " (" | " ("

open_compound_term               -->   " ("

close                            -->   layout_text_sequence, " )" | " )"

open_list                        -->   layout_text_sequence, " [" | " ["

close_list                       -->   layout_text_sequence, " ]" | " ]"

open_curly                       -->   layout_text_sequence, " {" | " {"

close_curly                      -->   layout_text_sequence, " }" | " }"

head_tail_separator              -->   layout_text_sequence, " |" | " |"

comma                            -->   layout_text_sequence, " ," | " ,"

end                              -->   layout_text_sequence, " ." | " ."
```

Layout text.

layout_text_sequence	-->	layout_text, layout_text_sequence
	|	layout_text
layout_text	-->	comment
	|	layout_char(_)
comment	-->	single_line_comment
	|	bracketed_comment
single_line_comment	-->	"%", comment_text, new_line_char(_)
bracketed_comment	-->	comment_open, comment_text,
		comment_close
comment_open	-->	"/*"
comment_close	-->	"*/"
comment_text	-->	char(_), comment_text
	|	ε

Name token.

name_token(A)	-->	letter_digit_token(A)
	|	graphic_token(A)
	|	quoted_token(A)
	|	semicolon_token(A)
	|	cut_token(A)
letter_digit_token([S | A])	-->	small_letter_char(S),
		alpha_num_seq_char(A)
alpha_num_seq_char([A | L])	-->	alpha_numeric_char(A),
		alpha_num_seq_char(L)
alpha_num_seq_char([ ])	-->	ε
graphic_token([C | L])	-->	graphic_token_char(C), graphic_token(L)
graphic_token([C])	-->	graphic_token_char(C)

graphic_token_char('\')	-->	"\"
graphic_token_char(C)	-->	graphic_char(C)
quoted_token(Qs)	-->	"'", single_quoted_item_seq(Qs), "'"
single_quoted_item_seq([C | S])	-->	single_quoted_character(C), single_quoted_item_seq(S)
single_quoted_item_seq(S)	-->	continuation_escape_sequence, single_quoted_item_seq(S)
single_quoted_item_seq([ ])	-->	ε
continuation_escape_sequence	-->	"\", new_line_char(_)
semicolon_token([';'])	-->	";"
cut_token(['!'])	-->	"!"

Quoted character.

single_quoted_character(C)	-->	non_quote_char(C)
single_quoted_character(SC)	-->	"C"

Where C is '' or " or '
and SC is respectively ' or " or '
The single quote character (') is
duplicated in a single quoted sequence

double_quoted_character(C)	-->	non_quote_char(C)
double_quoted_character(DC)	-->	"C"

Where C is ' or "" or '
and DC is respectively ' or " or '
The double quote character (") is
duplicated in a double quoted sequence

back_quoted_character(C)	-->	non_quote_char(C)

back_quoted_character(*BC*)   --> *"C"*
                                         Where *C* is ' or " or ' '
                                         and *BC* is respectively ' or " or '
                                         The back quote character (') is
                                         duplicated in a back quoted sequence

non_quote_char(C)   --> graphic_char(C)
                                      | alpha_numeric_char(C)
                                      | solo_char(C)
                                      | space_char(C)
                                      | meta_escape_sequence(C)
                                      | control_escape_sequence(C)
                                      | octal_escape_sequence(C)
                                      | hexadecimal_escape_sequence(C)

meta_escape_sequence(C)   --> "\", meta_char(C)

control_escape_sequence(C)   --> "\", symbolic_control_char(C)

symbolic_control_char(*C*)   --> *"CHAR"*
                                         Where *CHAR* is one of
                                         the following characters:
                                         a (alert), b (backspace), r (carriage return),
                                         f (form feed), t (horizontal tabulation),
                                         n (new line) and v (vertical tabulation)
                                         and *C* is a non printable character
                                         from the list (respectively):
                                         BEL, BS, CR, NP, HT, NL and VT
                                         (see for example the ASCII Table 11.4).

octal_escape_sequence(C)   --> "\", octal_digit_seq_char(Octal), "\",
                                         { compute_char(Octal, 8, C) }

octal_digit_seq_char([D | L])   --> octal_digit_char(D), octal_digit_seq_char(L)

hexadecimal_escape_sequence(C)   --> "\x", hexadecimal_digit_seq_char(Hexa), "\"
                                         { compute_char(Hexa, 16, C) }

hexadecimal_digit_seq_char([D | L]) --> hexadecimal_digit_char(D),
                                         hexadecimal_digit_seq_char(L)

Variable token.

variable_token(V)   --> anonymous_variable(V) | named_variable(V)

anonymous_variable(['_'])   --> "_"   underscore

named_variable(['_', A | S])   --> "_", alpha_numeric_char(A),
                                                alpha_num_seq_char(S)

named_variable([C | S])   --> capital_letter_char(C), alpha_num_seq_char(S)

Integer token.

integer_token(N)   --> integer_constant(Chars),
                                                { number_chars(N, Chars) }

integer_token(N)   --> character_code_constant(N)
                                             | binary_constant(N)
                                             | octal_constant(N)
                                             | hexadecimal_constant(N)

integer_constant([C | N])   --> decimal_digit_char(C), integer_constant(N)

integer_constant([C])   --> decimal_digit_char(C)

character_code_constant(Char)   --> "0'", single_quoted_character(Char)

binary_constant(Decimal)   --> "0b", binary_digit_seq_char(BinDigits),
                                                { compute_integer(BinDigits, 2, Decimal) }

binary_digit_seq_char([C | L])   --> binary_digit_char(C), binary_digit_seq_char(L)

binary_digit_seq_char([C])   --> binary_digit_char(C)

octal_constant(Dec)   --> "0o", octal_digit_seq_char(OcDigits),
                                                { compute_integer(OcDigits, 8, Dec) }

hexadecimal_constant(Dec)   --> "0x", hexadecimal_digit_seq_char(HexaDigits),
                                                { compute_integer(HexaDigits, 16, Dec) }

Floating point number token.

float_number_token(R)	-->	integer_constant(N), fraction(F), exponent(E), { concat(N, F, E, R) }
float_number_token(R)	-->	integer_constant(N), fraction(F), { concat(N, F, R) }
fraction(['.' | N])	-->	".", integer_constant(N)
exponent(E)	-->	exponent_char(C), sign(S), integer_constant(N), { concat([C | S], N, E) }
sign(S)	-->	"-" | "+" | ε **Where** S is ['-'], ['+'] or [ ]
exponent_char(C)	-->	"e" | "E" **Where** C is 'e' or 'E'

Double quoted list token.

double_quoted_list_token(T)	-->	'"', double_quoted_item_seq(QL), '"', { translate_double_quotes(QL, T) }
double_quoted_item_seq([C | S])	-->	double_quoted_character(C), double_quoted_item_seq(S)
double_quoted_item_seq(S)	-->	continuation_escape_sequence, double_quoted_item_seq(S)
double_quoted_item_seq([ ])	-->	ε

Back quoted strings.

back_quoted_string_token(*undefined_back_quoted_string_term*)	-->	'`', back_quoted_item_seq(QL), '`'
back_quoted_item_seq([C | S])	-->	back_quoted_character(C), back_quoted_item_seq(S)
back_quoted_item_seq(S)	-->	continuation_escape_sequence, back_quoted_item_seq(S)
back_quoted_item_seq([ ])	-->	ε

9.5.2 Procedures used in the DCG

The meaning of the non standard procedures used in the description of the syntax (in braces) is given here[11].

prefix_operator($Prec, Op, RightArgPrec$) — : **iff** Op is a unary prefix operator (specifier is **fx** or **fy**) with precedence $Prec$ and $RightArgPrec$ is an integer corresponding to a possible precedence of its operand. If Op has specifier **fy** then $RightArgPrec \leq Prec$ else (specifier **fx**) $RightArgPrec < Prec$.

postfix_operator($Prec, Op, LeftArgPrec$) — : **iff** Op is a unary postfix operator (specifier is **xf** or **yf**) with precedence $Prec$ and $LeftArgPrec$ is an integer corresponding to a possible precedence of its operand. If Op has specifier **yf** then $LeftArgPrec \leq Prec$ else (specifier **xf**) $LeftArgPrec < Prec$.

infix_operator($Prec, Op, LeftArgPrec, RightArgPrec$) — : **iff** Op is a binary infix operator (specifier in {**xfx**, **xfy**, **yfx**}) with precedence $Prec$ and $LeftArgPrec$ and $RightArgPrec$ are integers corresponding to possible precedences of the operands. If Op is right associative (specifier **xfy**) then $LeftArgPrec < Prec$ and $RightArgPrec \leq Prec$, else if Op is left associative (specifier **yfx**) then $LeftArgPrec \leq Prec$ and $RightArgPrec < Prec$, else (specifier {**xfx**) $LeftArgPrec < Prec$ and $RightArgPrec < Prec$.

compute_integer($Digits, Base, Decimal$) — : **if** $Digits$ is a list of digits in base $Base$ **then** $Decimal$ is the decimal representation of the sequence of digits in $Digits$.

compute_char($Code, Base, Char$) — : **if** $Code$ is a list of digits in base $Base$ representing a character code **then** $Char$ is the character whose code is represented by the sequence of digits in $Code$.

translate_double_quotes(QL, T) — : **if** QL is a list of characters **then** T is the corresponding term according to the value of the flag **double_quotes**:

chars — T is the list of one-char atoms corresponding to the characters in QL.

codes — T is the list of character codes of the characters in QL.

atom — T is the atom whose name is the sequence of characters in QL.

---

[11] The definition of the procedures is non deterministic, in the sense that the same text may by parsed in different manners resulting in the same term. The executable version of the syntax (in the file referred to in Annex 11.2) is deterministic.

concat$(L_1, L_2, ..., L_n, L)$ — : **if** $L_1, L_2, ..., L_n$ are lists **then** L is their concatenation (in this order).

notoperator(A) — : **if** A is an atom **then** A is not an operator in the current operator table.

9.6 Syntax errors

There is a syntax error when a sequence of characters which are being input as a read-term do not conform to the syntax. The error-term has the form **syntax_error**(*imp_dep_atom*) where *imp_dep_atom* denotes an **implementation dependent** atom (see **read_term/3**).

10. Writing Portable Programs

The purpose of this chapter is to introduce some methodology to help write portable programs easily.

In **Standard Prolog** many features are undefined or incompletely specified. Therefore it is difficult to guarantee the portability of a program even on standard conforming processors.

In this respect it suffers the same limitations as any standardized language and the same methodology applies. We focus here on some very specific features of **Standard Prolog**, namely the unification and the logical database update view.

The unification is partly undefined and its portability is related to complex properties (NSTO/STO). We show here how simple rules may be applied to write portable programs.

The logical database update view is implemented now on most commercial Prolog processors. Therefore most Prolog programmers are now familiar with it. Although this view induces some "logical" flavour to a feature which is obviously "non logical", programmers may still feel uncomfortable when using it, due to its complexity (interferences with the control in the execution model). Therefore we provide here some simple rules which are safe in the sense that the behaviour of programs is clear without deep understanding of the database update view. Furthermore they make clauses updating independent from other views and thus increase the portability of programs.

10.1 Unification

10.1.1 A first solution

According to the definition of unification in **Standard Prolog**, portable programs must be NSTO.

Here are two very simple rules characterising NSTO programs:

Rule 1: *If in a program and goals only atoms, numbers and variables are used in the arguments of the predications (no compound term), the program is NSTO.*

Rule 2: *If in a program all the heads of the clauses have no duplicated variable, the program is NSTO with any goal.*

The first rule corresponds to *Datalog* programs, a language for querying deductive database. The second is more general (there is no limitation to the functors used) but also more difficult to satisfy in practice.

In fact most of the clauses of a database will fulfill this condition. Unfortunately in most cases some clauses will not satisfy the condition and this will be sufficient to inhibit the portability. This is true in particular as soon as equality is used [1].

One may try to find more general rules. For example, a variable occurs twice in the head of a clause, but if during execution of a goal every call to the corresponding predication is such that one of the variables is instantiated by a ground term, then the execution of this goal is NSTO. Such conditions and more complex ones may be found in [5]. Although some of the conditions are automatizable and may be verified by compilers, programmers cannot use them easily and moreover many interesting programs will remain STO.

Another approach must be found.

10.1.2 Introduction of unification with occurs-check

The second rule above gives us a way to identify the "risky" places where an "occur-check problem" may arise: they correspond to clauses with duplicated variables in the head. Therefore in these clauses and only for these ones, a small transformation may be performed and unify_with_occurs_check/2 introduced.

We illustrate this using a simple example.

Let us specify palindromes. By definition a *palindrome* is a list which is the reverse of itself. For example, [a,n,n,a] is a palindrom.

The (recursive) direct definition results from the following observations: an empty list is a palindrom, as is a list with one element. If a list has more than two elements, it is a palindrom if the first and last elements are identical and the sublist obtained by removing the first and the last elements is a palindrom. This is written formally in the following axioms, using difference lists.

$L_1 - L_2$ denotes a list formed by the elements of L_1 from which the last elements L_2 have been removed. For example $[a, n, n, a, b, e, l] - [b, e, l]$ denotes the list $[a, n, n, a]$ and $[a, n, n, a] - []$ or $[a, n, n, a|X] - X$ denote the list $[a, n, n, a]$ too. The most general empty list $[]$ is denoted $L - L$.

Here is the program:

---

[1] It is the case of using "Prolog unify" (=/2), but also of equality defined with the single fact equal(X, X).

```
palindrome(L- L).
palindrome([A|L]- L).
palindrome([A|L]- M) :- palindrome(L- [A|M]).
```

Notice that with goals like `palindrom(1-m)`. where 1 is a list and m any term the program terminates and analyses or generates palindroms (i.e. `palindrom(1-m)` succeeds if and only if 1-m denotes a list which is a palindrom), otherwise fails. If 1 is a variable or a partial list the program does not terminate, although it has some interesting behaviour.

However the two first clauses correspond to "risky" situations. If the goal is a ground term it is easy to observe that, according to the Prolog computation rule and because all the variables of the body (third clause) occur in the head too, the execution is NSTO with this goal. But if one uses variables in the goal, this program may be STO, for example with the goal `palindrom([a|X]-X)`. On the other hand, one would like to be able to use such goal or goal like `palindrom([X,Y|Z]-Z)` soundly (i.e. it should succeed once only, unifying X and Y together).

If one does not know in advance all the possible goals, it may be useful to write this program in such a way that it is standard conforming for any goal. This is possible using the following transformation:

When some variable has more than one occurrence in the head of a clause, rename the occurrences in such a way that the head has no duplicated variables and add the corresponding equalities as first predications in the body of the clause (hence the meaning is not modified). But instead of using equality ('='/2), use unify_with_occurs_check/2.

Here is the result with our example:

```
palindrom(L- M) :- unify_with_occurs_check(L, M).
palindrom([A|L]- M) :- unify_with_occurs_check(L, M).
palindrom([A|L]- M) :- palindrom(L- [A|M]).
```

This transformation is general and may be used on every program.

10.1.3 What to do with the built-in predicates

Most of the built-in predicates in **Standard Prolog** do not need occurs-checks. But the following ones may do:

arg/3, bagof/3, clause/2, copy_term/2, findall/3, read_term/2, read_term/3, retract/1, \=/2, setof/3, =/2 and =../2.

With the built-in predicates, the transformation can be applied if one suspects a possibility of positive occurs-check. One way to perform it simply is to put a different new variable at the place of one of the risky argument (for example with copy_term/2 it is the second argument) and execute unify_with_occurs_check/2 with this variable and the corresponding original term as arguments.

For example, instead of writing
    findall(X, p(X), [f(U, g(U))]) ...
one may prefer to write
    findall(X, p(X), S), unify_with_occurs_check(S, [f(U, g(U))])
to have a unique behaviour if the procedure p/1 has a fact like
    p(f(Y, Y)).

10.2 The database update view

Standard Prolog contains four built-in predicates which may modify the
database: abolish/1, asserta/1, assertz/1, retract/1. In **Standard
Prolog** the so called *logical database update view* is used. First we give a
comprehensive introduction to this view, then we deduce some recomenda-
tions.

10.2.1 The database update view in the execution model
for a subset of Standard Prolog

Let us assume first that there is no built-in predicate except those for clause
creation and destruction and let us consider a node of the search-tree where
no built-in predicate is executed.

As the search-tree is constructed the database may be modified. In order
to understand better what happens, let us attach to each node an additional
label corresponding to the *current database* used to build the children of this
node. Assume first that all the *current clauses* (the clauses of the current
database) are used to build these children. Each child (say $1, 2, \ldots, n$) is now
labelled by a new database (say $NewP_1, NewP_2, \ldots, NewP_n$). This situation
is depicted in Figure 10.1 (the c_i's correspond to the clauses chosen to build
the child). The first child has the label P, like the parent node, because its
children will be built with the same database. But the other children may
have different databases (denoted $NewPi$), because during the construction
of the sub-search-trees of the other children some modification of the database
may have taken place.

If there is no modification of the database during the development of the
sub search-trees, like in definite Prolog, all the $NewP_i$'s and P are the same
and all the children are visited and expanded using the same database.

Now consider a child i different from the first ($i > 1$) and assume that
the clause to which it corresponds has been removed during the construction
of an older sibling (i.e. $NewP_i$ no longer contains the clause c_i). Is it normal
to choose and to try to execute it or not?

Assume now that the youngest child n has been reached and executed,
and the current database, say $NewP$ obtained after the "fail" visit of n,
contains new clauses appended to the clauses of P. Should these new clauses

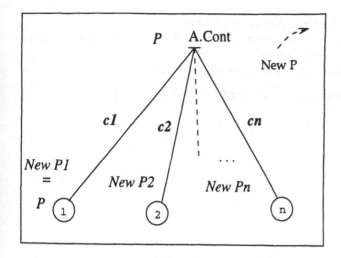

Fig. 10.1. The logical database update view.

be considered to create dynamically new children or not? Notice that such a situation occurs with **assertz/1** only. With **asserta/1** no young child can be created (although subsequent uses will consider the modified database)[2].

10.2.2 The logical database update view

The database update view depends on the way the previous questions are answered. The standard adopts the following view: the retracted clauses are selected but not the appended ones. It is called the **logical view**. In other words, the children are fixed at the first visit of the parent node and remain unchanged whatever the modifications of the database may be.

10.2.3 The database update view in Standard Prolog

The *(logical) database update view* in **Standard Prolog** is the generalisation of this principle to all re-executable built-in predicates too.

Namely, the number of children is fixed at the first visit (when the children are built) and not modified by the visit-construction of the sub-search-trees.

10.2.4 A simple view

Although the logical view has been adopted, some programmers are used to the so-called "immediate view". There is a "minimal" way of thinking about the views, in a such manner that does not depend on the view (it is of course undecidable whether a given database satisfies the requirements of the logical view). Here are some possible rules:

---

[2] In fact one may consider that new children are added in that case to the left of the first node. Because the Prolog computation rule visits the search-tree in a left to right manner, these new (oldest) children will not be visited.

1. `asserta/1` may be used without restriction.
2. Never use `retract/1` or `assertz/1` on a predicate which is active except to retract already used clauses.
3. Never use `abolish/1` on a predicate which is active.

These restrictions comply with a prudent use of database updates.

11. Annexes

11.1 Compliance

Here is an (adapted) extract of the standard explaining the requirements a
standard conforming processor which uses extensions will satisfy.

11.1.1 Prolog processor

A *conforming Prolog processor* will:

1. Correctly prepare for execution Prolog text which conforms to:
   a) the specification of Prolog texts in **Standard Prolog**, and
   b) the **implementation defined** and **implementation specific** features of the Prolog processor,
2. Correctly execute Prolog goals which have been prepared for execution and which conform to:
   a) the specification of Prolog goals in **Standard Prolog**, and
   b) the **implementation defined** and **implementation specific** features of the Prolog processor,
3. Reject any Prolog text or read-term whose syntax fails to conform to:
   a) the specification of Prolog text or read-term in **Standard Prolog**, and
   b) the **implementation defined** and **implementation specific** features of the Prolog processor,
4. Specify all permitted variations in the manner described in **Standard Prolog**, and
5. Offer a strictly conforming mode which will reject the use of an **implementation specific** feature in Prolog text or while executing a goal.

11.1.2 Prolog text

Conforming Prolog text will use only the constructs specified in **Standard Prolog**, and the **implementation defined** and **implementation specific** features supported by the processor.

Strictly conforming Prolog text will use only the constructs specified in **Standard Prolog**, and the **implementation defined** features supported by the processor.

11.1.3 Prolog goal

A *conforming Prolog goal* is one whose execution is defined by the constructs specified in **Standard Prolog**, and the **implementation defined** and **implementation specific** features supported by the processor.

A *strictly conforming Prolog goal* is one whose execution is defined by the constructs specified in **Standard Prolog**, and the **implementation defined** features supported by the processor.

11.1.4 Documentation

A *conforming Prolog processor* will be accompanied by documentation that completes the definition of every **implementation defined** and **implementation specific** feature specified in **Standard Prolog**.

11.1.5 Extensions

A processor may support, as an **implementation specific** feature, any construct that is implicitly or explicitly undefined in **Standard Prolog**.

Syntax. A processor may support one or more additional characters in **ECS** (9.1.1) and additional syntax rules as an **implementation specific** feature if and only if:

1. any sequence of tokens that conforms to the syntax of Prolog text and read-terms defined in Chapter 9 will correspond to the term defined there,
2. any sequence of tokens that conforms to the syntax of a term defined in Section 9.5 will have the abstract syntax defined in that clause,
3. any sequence of characters that conforms to the syntax of Prolog tokens defined in Section 9.5.1 will be parsed to those Prolog tokens.

Back quoted "strings" could be defined as an extension.

Predefined operator table. A processor may support one or more additional predefined operators (Table 9.2.2) as an **implementation specific** feature.

Character conversion table. A processor may support some other initial value in Table (9.1.2), as an **implementation specific** feature.

Objects. A processor may support one or more additional objects, called *type* in this section only[1], as an **implementation specific** feature if and only if, for every additional type T supported by a processor:

1. No term with type T will also have a type T' where T and T' are different.
2. For every two terms t and t' with types T and T' respectively, t *term_precedes* t' (2.1.2) will depend only on T and T' unless $T = T'$.
3. The processor will define in its accompanying documentation terms corresponding to additional types and well-formed clauses, bodies and goals[2].
4. The processor will define in its accompanying documentation, the token syntax and the corresponding term of every term of type T.
5. The processor will define in its accompanying documentation, the effect of evaluating as an expression a term of type T (6.2).
6. The processor will define in its accompanying documentation, the effect of writing a term of type T (7.4.3).

Flags. A processor may support one or more additional flags as an **implementation specific** feature.

Directives. A processor may support one or more additional directive indicators (8) as an **implementation specific** feature.

Built-in Predicates. A processor may support one or more additional built-in predicates and/or side effects as an **implementation specific** feature.

When a processor supports additional built-in predicates as an **implementation specific** feature, it may also support as an **implementation specific** feature one or more additional forms of error-term.

Arithmetic functors. A processor may support one or more additional arithmetic functors (6.1.1) as an **implementation specific** feature.

Sources and sinks. A processor may support additional I/O modes (7.3.1), such as a mode for both inputting and outputting, as **implementation specific** features.

A processor may support one or more additional open- and close-options (7.3.2, 7.3.3) as an **implementation specific** feature.

A processor may support one or more additional stream properties (7.3.4) as an **implementation specific** feature.

A processor may support one or more additional read- or write-options (7.4.1, 7.4.2) as an **implementation specific** feature.

---

[1] "Type" denotes here subsets of basic objects like variables, atoms, numbers, etc., used to build terms. Additional types could be "string" or "complex number". This notion of "type" should not be confused with the other notion used to describe the templates (5.2.2). We do not use this notion of "type" in the description of **Standard Prolog** to denote categories of objects, in order to avoid any confusion. **Standard Prolog** is indeed a typeless language.

[2] It is denoted in the standard as "the effect of converting a term of type T to a clause and vice versa".

11.2 The ftp package

The ftp package contains an executable specification of **Standard Prolog**[3] written in **Standard Prolog** and examples.

11.2.1 The package

All the needed files and directories are in a single directory called SdProlog. This directory contains the following files:

read.me — An abstract on this annex.

manual.txt — A full manual (in ASCII text form).

exe-spec.pl l-pred.pl syntax.pl interf.pl ex-test.pl util.pl — The code of the executable specification which is a Prolog text.

make — A Prolog text which may be consulted to load the executable specification.

examples — A directory containing sample programs written in **Standard Prolog**. They are self documented and may be run on any standard conforming processor. These programs may not be runnable with the executable specification due to lack of resources[4].

bips-ex — A directory containing as many files as there are built-in predicates. Each file consists of the collection of examples listed in this book, the examples used in the standard together with some other examples.

The file corresponding to a built-in predicate has the same name, except for some cases where another mnemonic name is used (e.g. arith-eq instead of (=:=)/2, or not-prov instead of (\+)/1).

11.2.2 How to run the executable specification

The executable specification is a specific implementation of **Standard Prolog**. So, all concepts which are **implementation defined, implementation dependent** or **undefined** have received some interpretation. For example there may be an explicit warning when the unification is undefined.

---

[3] It includes an implementation of the formal specification published in the informative annex of the standard [2].

[4] The executable specification is close to the formal specification published in the standard and therefore is not efficient at all. It serves only to test small programs and goals.

The executable specification must be run on a standard conforming processor. However the way it has been designed makes it runnable on most existing Prolog processors.

To run the executable specification on a Prolog processor, load the file make. In most existing Prolog processors this is achieved by executing the goal:

```
?- consult(make).
```

A short help can be obtained thus by executing the goal help_me.

The following goals can then be executed.

run_subs(prog) — where prog is an atom whose name is the path-name of a Prolog text file whose contents is a program to be tested. Only very small programs can be run without resource error[5]. Goals can then be entered and tested with the program denoted in the argument. The outcome of each goal is an answer substitution.

run_forest(prog) — Same as run_subs(prog) but the outcome is a full search-tree.

run_subs — Same as run_subs/1 but without program.

run_forest — Same as run_forest/1 but without program.

run_bip(examplesBipFile) — where examplesBipFile is an atom whose name is the path-name of a file with examples to be tested. The examples must be written in a form described in Section 11.2.3. An "expected result" is indicated and the execution compares the results given by the executable specification and the expected result. The result of the comparison is given.

The complete documentation is in the file manual.txt.

11.2.3 Examples of uses

We show here how to use the executable specification to test examples in **Standard Prolog**.

Testing programs. Assume that add is a file whose contents are:

```
plus(0,A,A).
plus(s(A),B,s(C)) :- plus(A,B,C).
```

---

[5] The executable specification is close to the formal specification published in the standard and therefore is not efficient at all. It serves only to test small programs and goals.

Then one executes:
run_subs(add).
[add] goal ?- plus(A,B,s(0)).
([add] goal ?- is the executable specification prompt which is now displayed.)

The goal is displayed again followed by all the answer substitutions obtained by running the executable specification with this goal and the given environment:

```
plus(A,B,s(0))
            A <-- 0
            B <-- s(0)
    success ---------
            A <-- s(0)
            B <-- 0
    success ---------

            end -----
```

[add] goal ?- plus(0,0,s(0)).

```
    plus(0,0,s(0))
            failure  -----
```

search tree form.

Testing built-in predicates. To test a sample of examples for a given built-in predicate, a file must be firstly prepared (say bip_examples) whose contents are the examples to be tested written in the format described above, and the following goal:
run_bip(bip_examples).

The format of the examples is the following: a list whose elements are (in this order):

1. A goal,

2. (optional) A program, entered as a list of clauses or by its file name. Example:

    [(plus(0,A,A) :- true), (plus(s(A),B,s(C)) :- plus(A,B,C))]
    or
      program(add)
    where 'add' is the file containing the definition of the predicate 'plus'.

3. An expected answer:
    − A list of answer substitutions in the order in which they are expected. The operator substitution is: <--. Example:

```
[[Var₁ <-- Term₁₁, ..., Varₙ <-- Term₁ₙ],

 [Var₁ <-- term₂₁, ..., Varₙ <-- Term₂ₙ], ...]
```

or
- **success** if a success with an empty answer substitution is expected,
  or
- **failure** if a finitely failed search tree is expected (a finite search-tree with no success branch),
  or
- *error-term* which is a term identifing the expected error. Examples: `instantiation_error`, `type_error(atom, 1)`, `permission_error(modify, static_procedure, foo/2)`, ...,
  or
- `impl_dep` or `impl_defined` or `undefined` if the expected behaviour is implementation dependent or defined or undefined.

Examples:

```
[ (X=1; X=2),[ [X <-- 1], [X <-- 2] ] ].

[ 1 =:= 1.0, success ].

[ 2 < 1, failure ].

[ functor(T, F, 3), instantiation_error ].

[ f(X,1) = f(a(X),2), undefined ].

[ f(X,1) @< f(Y,2), impl_dep ].
```

The execution of `run_bip/1` compares, for each element of the sample file, the expected result with the executable specification computed result for the goal, and displays (1) the expected result (as in the file), and (2) the results obtained with the executable specification if there is a discrepancy, or the message `INTENDED RESULT` otherwise.

Example: assume there is a sample file 'functor' with examples as follows: (Note that some erroneous expected answers are given just to illustrate the behaviour of the 'run_bip' predicate.)

```
[functor(foo(a,b,c),foo,3),         % The goal.
                   success].        % The expected behaviour.

[functor(foo(a,b,c),X,Y),
```

```
          [[X <-- foo, Y <-- 2]]].              % Should instantiate Y by 3.

[functor(foo(a),foo,2), success].              % Should fail.

[functor(foo(a),fo,1), failure].

[functor(X,1.1,0), [[X <-- 1.1]]].

[functor([_|_],'.',2), failure].               % Should succeed.

[functor(X, foo, a), failure].                 % type_error(integer,a)
                                               % expected instead.

[(current_prolog_flag(max_arity,A),
  X is A + 1,                                  % complex goal.
  functor(T, foo, X)),
  representation_error(max_arity)].
```

The test will give:

```
| ?- run_bip('functor').

----------------------------------------------
Goal      : functor(foo(a,b,c),foo,3)
Intended result   :
          success

Specif result :        INTENDED RESULT
================================================
Goal      : functor(foo(a,b,c),A,B)
Intended result   :
          A <-- foo
          B <-- 2

Specif result :
     The substitution found is :
          A <-- foo
          B <-- 3
     success ---------
================================================
Goal  : functor(foo(a),foo,2)
Intended result   :
          success

Specif result :        Must fail
================================================
Goal  : functor(foo(a),fo,1)
Intended result   :
          failure

Specif result :        INTENDED RESULT
================================================
Goal  : functor(A,1.1,0)
```

```
Intended result   :
          A <-- 1.1

Specif result :        INTENDED RESULT
===============================================
Goal   : functor([A|B],.,2)
Intended result   :
          failure

Specif result :        Must succeed
===============================================
Goal   : functor(A,foo,a)
Intended result   :
          failure

Specif result :   system_error_action: type_error(integer,a)
    Goal in error : type_error(integer,a)
===============================================
Goal   : current_prolog_flag(max_arity,A),B is A+1,functor(C,foo,B)
Intended result   :
          representation_error(max_arity)

Specif result :
          system_error_action: representation_error(max_arity)
                    INTENDED RESULT
-----------------------------------------------
```

11.3 Elements of lexical analysis

This annex defines the syntax (in DCG form) of the *Prolog character set* (defined in 9.1.1) used in the syntax of term (9.5).

Prolog character set.

char(C)	-->	graphic_char(C)
	|	alpha_numeric_char(C)
	|	solo_char(C)
	|	layout_char(C)
	|	meta_char(C)

Graphics characters.

graphic_char(*GC*)   -->   "*GC*"

Where GC is one of these characters:
'#', '$', '&', '*', '+', '-', '.', '/', ':',
'<', '=', '>', '?', '@', '^', '~'

Alphanumeric characters.

alpha_numeric_char(C)	-->	alpha_char(C)
	|	decimal_digit_char(C)

alpha_char('_')   -->   "_"   underscore

alpha_char(C)   -->   letter_char(C)

letter_char(C)	-->	capital_letter_char(C)
	|	small_letter_char(C)

small_letter_char(*Lower*)   -->   "*Lower*"

Where *Lower* is one of alphabetical lower case characters (characters from **a** to **z**)

capital_letter_char(*Upper*)   -->   "*Upper*"

Where *Upper* is one of alphabetical upper case characters (characters from **A** to **Z**)

decimal_digit_char(*DD*)   -->   "*DD*"

Where *DD* is one of digits between 0 and 9

binary_digit_char(*BD*)   -->   "*BD*"

Where *BD* is one of the two digits 0 or 1

octal_digit_char(*OD*)   -->   "*OD*"

Where *OD* is one of digits between 0 and 7

hexadecimal_digit_char(*XD*)   -->   "*XD*"

Where *XD* is one of digits between 0 and 9 and letters between **A** or **a** and **F** or **f**

Solo characters.

solo_char(C)   --> $"C"$
                                                Where C is one of these characters:
                                                '!', '(', ')', ',', ';', '[', ']', '{', '}', '|', '&'

Layout characters.

layout_char(C)   --> space_char(C)
                                             | horizontal_tab_char(C)
                                             | new_line_char(C)

space_char(' ')   --> " "

new_line_char(C)   --> $"C"$
                                                Where C is implementation dependent
                                                New Line character (in ASCII this
                                                character is **NL** of decimal code 10)

horizontal_tab_char(C)   --> $"C"$
                                                Where C is implementation dependent
                                                Horizontal Tabulation character (in ASCII
                                                this character is **HT** of decimal code 9)

Meta characters.

meta_char(C)   --> $"C"$
                                                Where C is one of these characters:
                                                '\', ';', '"', ' ̔'

11.4 ASCII table

Table 11.4 represents for each character in **char**, as defined in 9.1.1, its ASCII code in octal, hexadecimal and decimal notation. It also gives the codes of characters represented by a symbolic control character which are quoted characters (defined by symbolic_control_char nonterminal in 9.5.1).

Oct	Hex	Dec	Chr	Oct	Hex	Dec	Chr	Oct	Hex	Dec	Chr	Oct	Hex	Dec	Chr
000	00	0	NUL	001	01	1	SOH	002	02	2	STX	003	03	3	ETX
004	04	4	EOT	005	05	5	ENQ	006	06	6	ACK	007	07	7	BEL
010	08	8	BS	011	09	9	HT	012	0A	10	NL	013	0B	11	VT
014	0C	12	NP	015	0D	13	CR	016	0E	14	SO	017	0F	15	SI
020	10	16	DLE	021	11	17	DC1	022	12	18	DC2	023	13	19	DC3
024	14	20	DC4	025	15	21	NAK	026	16	22	SYN	027	17	23	ETB
030	18	24	CAN	031	19	25	EM	032	1A	26	SUB	033	1B	27	ESC
034	1C	28	FS	035	1D	29	GS	036	1E	30	RS	037	1F	31	US
040	20	32	SP	041	21	33	!	042	22	34	"	043	23	35	#
044	24	36	$	045	25	37	%	046	26	38	&	047	27	39	'
050	28	40	(	051	29	41	)	052	2A	42	*	053	2B	43	+
054	2C	44	,	055	2D	45	-	056	2E	46	.	057	2F	47	/
060	30	48	0	061	31	49	1	062	32	50	2	063	33	51	3
064	34	52	4	065	35	53	5	066	36	54	6	067	37	55	7
070	38	56	8	071	39	57	9	072	3A	58	:	073	3B	59	;
074	3C	60	<	075	3D	61	=	076	3E	62	>	077	3F	63	?
100	40	64	@	101	41	65	A	102	42	66	B	103	43	67	C
104	44	68	D	105	45	69	E	106	46	70	F	107	47	71	G
110	48	72	H	111	49	73	I	112	4A	74	J	113	4B	75	K
114	4C	76	L	115	4D	77	M	116	4E	78	N	117	4F	79	O
120	50	80	P	121	51	81	Q	122	52	82	R	123	53	83	S
124	54	84	T	125	55	85	U	126	56	86	V	127	57	87	W
130	58	88	X	131	59	89	Y	132	5A	90	Z	133	5B	91	[
134	5C	92	\	135	5D	93	]	136	5E	94	^	137	5F	95	_
140	60	96	`	141	61	97	a	142	62	98	b	143	63	99	c
144	64	100	d	145	65	101	e	146	66	102	f	147	67	103	g
150	68	104	h	151	69	105	i	152	6A	106	j	153	6B	107	k
154	6C	108	l	155	6D	109	m	156	6E	110	n	157	6F	111	o
160	70	112	p	161	71	113	q	162	72	114	r	163	73	115	s
164	74	116	t	165	75	117	u	166	76	118	v	167	77	119	w
170	78	120	x	171	79	121	y	172	7A	122	z	173	7B	123	{
174	7C	124			175	7D	125	}	176	7E	126	~	177	7F	127	DEL

11.5 Glossary of auxiliary concepts

This glossary contains the definitions of some concepts used in the description of **Standard Prolog** but defined nowhere else. Some of them have been used by the standardizers to describe **Standard Prolog** and are used in this book with a slightly different meaning which is explained here. Words in itallic are defined in this glossary.

Anonymous variable	An anonymous variable is a variable represented in a Prolog text or in a read-term by _ (underscore character). It denotes a fresh variable (i.e. one which differs from all other variables) for which the user does not want to provide a name.
Bagof-goal	A term whose principal functor is not *caret* or a compound term whose principal functor is *caret*, the first argument a term and the second argument a bagof-goal. With a bagof-goal two notions are associated: the *free variables* and the *bagof-subgoal*.
Bagof-subgoal	The bagof-subgoal of a *bagof-goal* is the *greatest* *subterm* whose principal functor is not *caret* and which is the second argument of a *caret* functor. Example: X ^ Y ^ f(X,Y,Z ^ X), the bagof-subgoal is f(X,Y,Z ^ X).
Byte	A byte is an integer in the range $[0..255]$.
Caret	A predefined operator denoted ^ of arity 2. Its precedence is 200 and it is right associative (**xfy**). So, if the operator has not been redefined, X ^ Y ^ Z ^ t is the term ^(X, ^(Y, ^(Z, t))).

Constant	A constant is either an atom, an integer or a floating-point number.

End-of-stream	When all of a stream S has been input (for example by get_byte/2 or read_term/3) S has a stream position end-of-stream. It thus has the property end_of_stream(at).

Free variables (bagof-goal)	The free variables of a *bagof-goal* are the variables of the *bagof-subgoal* which do not occur in any first argument of a *caret* operator for which the *bagof-subgoal* is a *subterm* of its second argument. Example: X ^ Y ^ f(X,Y,Z ^ X), the set of the free variables is {Z}.

Partial list	A partial list is a list-term whose tail is a variable. So a partial list of N elements and tail X is written [a1, a2, ..., aN| X] and is the term .(a1, .(a2, ..., .(aN, X) ...)). There is no empty partial list.

Past-end-of-stream	If one tries to input, more data from a stream which has the property end_of_stream(at) (*end-of-stream*), the stream has a stream position past-end-of-stream and property end_of_stream(past).

Predicate indicator pattern	A predicate indicator pattern is a predicate indicator or a compound term whose principal functor is '/'/2 and the arguments are either a variable, or an atom for the first, or a positive integer for the second. For example: '/'(reverse,X).

Predicate indicator sequence A predicate indicator sequence is a compound term ',' (PI_1, PI_n) where PI_1 is a predicate indicator, and PI_n is a predicate indicator or a *predicate indicator sequence*. A predicate indicator sequence ',' (P1/A1, ',' (P2/A2, P3/A3)) is normally written as P1/A1, P2/A2, P3/A3. There is no term corresponding to an empty predicate indicator sequence.

Sequence of terms A sequence of terms is a compound term ',' (T_1, T_n) where T_1 is a term, and T_n is a term or a *sequence of terms*. A sequence of terms ',' (T1, ',' (T2, T3)) is normally written as T1, T2, T3. There is no term corresponding to an empty sequence of terms.

Subexpression A subexpression of an expression is this expression or, if the expression is a compound term, a *subexpression* of one of its arguments.

Subterm A subterm of a term is this term or, if the term is a compound term, a *subterm* of one of its arguments.

Top level process, goal A process whereby a Prolog processor repeatedly inputs from the standard input and executes queries. Each query is called *top level goal* (this concept is undefined in the standard). The answer substitutions of a top level goal may be displayed on the standard output in a manner which is **implementation defined**.

Valid read-option

A valid read-option is a term whose principal functor is the same as the one used in the read-option terms supported in **Standard Prolog** (or in some extension) as described in Section 7.4.1 (an element of { variables, variable_name, singletons}) and whose arguments are variables or have the same form as the one expected in their description (e.g. the option singletons must have one variable as argument, or a list whose elements are variables or terms A = V where A and V are variables or atoms).

Valid write-option

A valid write-option is a term whose principal functor is the same as the one used in the write-option terms supported in **Standard Prolog** or in some extension as described in Section 7.4.2 and whose arguments (if any) are variables or atoms denoting one of the allowed values.

Valid stream property

A valid stream property is a term whose principal functor is the same as the one used in the stream property terms supported in **Standard Prolog** or in some extension as described in Sections 7.3.2, 7.3.3 or 7.3.4 and whose arguments (if any) are variables or atoms denoting one of the allowed values.

Witness

A witness of a term $term_1$ is another term $term_2$ in which every variable of $term_1$ occurs exactly once. If $term_1$ has no variable, its witness is an atom.

Thematic classification of the built-in predicates

The order in each category corresponds to the alphabetical order used in Chapter 5 (predicate indicator and arity, or speakable name). Except for the first and last categories, the category name used in the standard has been retained.

All solutions

'bagof'/3
'findall'/3
'setof'/3

Arithmetic comparison

'=:='/2 (arithmetic equal)
'=\\='/2 (arithmetic not equal)
'>'/2 (arithmetic greater than)
'>='/2 (arithmetic greater than or equal)
'<'/2 (arithmetic less than)
'=<'/2 (arithmetic less than or equal)

Arithmetic evaluation

'is'/2 (evaluate expression)

Atomic term processing

'atom_chars'/2
'atom_codes'/2
'atom_concat'/3
'atom_length'/2
'char_code'/2
'number_chars'/2
'number_codes'/2
'sub_atom'/5

Byte input/output

'get_byte'/1
'get_byte'/2
'peek_byte'/1
'peek_byte'/2
'put_byte'/1
'put_byte'/2

Character input/output

'get_char'/1
'get_char'/2
'get_code'/1
'get_code'/2
'peek_char'/1
'peek_char'/2
'peek_code'/1
'peek_code'/2
'put_char'/1
'put_char'/2
'put_code'/1
'put_code'/2
'nl'/0
'nl'/1

Clause retrieval and information

'clause'/2
'current_predicate'/1

Clause creation and destruction

```
'abolish'/1
'asserta'/1
'assertz'/1
'retract'/1
```

Flag updates

```
'current_prolog_flag'/2
'set_prolog_flag'/
```

Logic and control

```
'call'/1
'catch'/3
','/2 (conjunction)
'!'/0 (cut)
';'/2 (disjunction)
'fail'/0
'halt'/0
'halt'/1
'->'/2 (if-then)
';'/2 (if-then-else)
'\\+'/1 (not provable)
'once'/1
'repeat'/0
'throw'/1
'true'/0
```

Stream selection and control

```
'at_end_of_stream'/0
'at_end_of_stream'/1
'close'/1
'close'/2
'current_input'/1
'current_output'/1
'flush_output'/0
'flush_output'/1
'open'/3
'open'/4
'set_input'/1
'set_output'/1
'set_stream_position'/2
'stream_property'/2
```

Term comparison

```
'@>'/2 (term greater than)
'@>='/2 (term greater than or equal)
'=='/2 (term identical)
'@<'/2 (term less than)
'@=<'/2 (term less than or equal)
'\\=='/2 (term not identical)
```

Term creation and decomposition

```
'arg'/3
'copy_term'/2
'functor'/3
'=..'/2 (univ)
```

Term unification

```
'\\='/2 (not Prolog unifiable)
'='/2 (Prolog unify)
'unify_with_occurs_check'/2 (unify)
```

Type testing

```
'atom'/1
'atomic'/1
'compound'/1
'float'/1
'integer'/1
'nonvar'/1
'number'/1
'var'/1
```

Term input/output

```
'char_conversion'/2
'current_char_conversion'/2
'current_op'/3
'op'3/
'read'/1
'read'/2
'read_term'/2
'read_term'/3
'write'/1
'write'/2
'write_canonical'/1
'write_canonical'/2
'write_term'/2
'write_term'/3
'writeq'/1
'writeq'/2
```

Bibliography

1. ISO/IEC 10967-1, Information Technology — Programming languages — Language independent arithmetic — Part 1: Integer and Floating Point Arithmetic, ISO, 1994.
2. ISO/IEC 13211-1, Information Technology — Programming Languages — Prolog — Part 1: General Core, 1995.
3. W.F. Clocksin and C.S. Mellish, Programming in PROLOG, Springer-Verlag, 297p, 4th ed. 1994.
4. Alain Colmerauer and Philippe Roussel, The birth of Prolog, PrologIA, 31p, 1992.
5. Pierre Deransart and Jan Małuszyński, A Grammatical View of Logic Programming, (One chapter is devoted to NSTO property and tests) The MIT Press, 1993.
6. Richard A. O'Keefe, The Craft of Prolog, The MIT Press, Series in Logic Programming, 1990.
7. Leon Sterling and Ehud Shapiro, The Art of PROLOG : Advanced Programming Techniques The MIT Press, Series in Logic Programming, 4th ed. 1995.

Index

Printing: Mercedesdruck, Berlin
Binding: Buchbinderei Lüderitz & Bauer, Berlin